The Intimate Bond

Also by Brian Fagan

The Intimate Bond

HOW ANIMALS SHAPED HUMAN HISTORY

Brian Fagan

BLOOMSBURY PRESS

NEW YORK · LONDON · OXFORD · NEW DELHI · SYDNEY

Bloomsbury Press
An imprint of Bloomsbury Publishing Plc

1385 Broadway	50 Bedford Square
New York	London
NY 10018	WC1B 3DP
USA	UK

www.bloomsbury.com

BLOOMSBURY and the Diana logo are trademarks of Bloomsbury Publishing Plc

First published 2015
This paperback edition published 2016

© Brian Fagan, 2015

ISBN: HB: 978-1-62040-572-7
PB: 978-1-62040-573-4
ePub: 978-1-62040-574-1

Library of Congress Cataloging-in-Publication Data is available.

2 4 6 8 10 9 7 5 3

Typeset by Newgen Knowledge Works (P) Ltd., Chennai, India
Printed and bound by CPI Group (UK) Ltd, Croydon, CR0 4YY

To find out more about our authors and books visit www.bloomsbury.com.
Here you will find extracts, author interviews, details of forthcoming events
and the option to sign up for our newsletters.

Bloomsbury books may be purchased for business or promotional use.
For information on bulk purchases please contact Macmillan Corporate and
Premium Sales Department at specialmarkets@macmillan.com.

To

Our beasts, numerous and ever changing as they are.

This history is for them.

"Some people talk to animals. Not many listen though. That's the problem."

A. A. Milne, *Winnie-the-Pooh*

Contents

Preface

THIS IS A BOOK about respect, partnership, love, and cruelty, about the complex and ever-dynamic relationship between animals and humans that defined and changed history. We are, of course, ourselves animals, but with a difference. We're *Homo sapiens*, the wise people, with unique cognitive abilities that set us apart from all other beasts. Fluent speech, our penchant for forethought and reasoning, and our complex emotional reactions distinguish us from other living things—a boundless chasm that can never be fully bridged. We are also social animals with a strong psychological impulse to bond with other animals. Our affection for the beasts around us, whether pets or working animals, sometimes leads us to attribute human emotions and feelings to them. Many children's books revolve around the doings of such creatures as cats, dogs, and elephants, like the immortal family of Babar and Celeste, whose adventures have entertained generations of the young in many lands.

The endless debate over the humanity of animals is, however, irrelevant to these pages. We're concerned here with a purely historical inquiry—the ways in which our relationships with animals have altered over time. Most histories dwell on individuals, on monarchs and rulers, on nobles and generals, but also on common folk and such issues as gender relations and social inequality. This book attempts something different. I describe how animals and our relationship with them, transformed history.

WE HUMANS HAVE LIVED in intimate association with animals of all kinds, large and small, mammals and invertebrates, predators and harmless antelope, for more than two and a half million years. Our remotest forebears were predators in a world of predators—both hunter and hunted. Over tens of thousands of years, they developed an awesome knowledge of the habits of creatures of all kinds. Survival depended on it, but they may have lacked the urge to bond psychologically with animals, to link them symbolically to their lives. Ultimately, the humans were mere predators.

Everything changed when *Homo sapiens*, with its unique cognitive abilities, appeared on the historical stage. Superior hunting abilities; new, more sophisticated weaponry; but above all a reasoning intelligence transformed our relationship with prey. Quite when this happened remains uncertain, but it was at least seventy thousand years ago, when the number of humans on earth was still infinitesimal. This was a yet ill-defined moment when we became fully social animals with a strong impulse to bond, not only with one another, but also with other living things. Our urge to make a connection with fellow creatures is so powerful that it takes a lot to override it.

Relationships are intangible, ties of verbal and nonverbal communication expressed by gesture or speech, by caresses or subtle twitches of finger or eyebrow. They are the essence of history, in their way more important than the most spectacular buildings or artistic masterpieces. We can discern them only through an opaque mirror into the past, through documents and artistic renderings, through artifacts and animal bones. Herein lies one of the great limitations of archaeology, which deals, for the most part, with the material remains of human behavior. Nevertheless, we can trace the broad outlines of the changing animal-human relationship from a scatter of fascinating clues, which survive from at least twenty millennia in the past.

The story in these pages begins with the Ice Age's European artists of twenty thousand years ago, who painted and engraved their prey on the walls of caves and rock shelters, such as France's Lascaux Cave and the Cave of Altamira in northern Spain. They defined their world in terms of powerful ritual partners: animals. The hunters treated beasts with respect, as individuals, as creatures with personalities, as living beings in both a material and ritual partnership with people. We can imagine living creatures such as bears, reindeer, or ravens acting like human beings in ritual narratives, deeply involved in the creation and definition of the human cosmos. This close kinship and partnership between humans and animals survives to this day among Australian Aborigines and some Arctic subsistence hunters.

Eight animals are major players in our story, the first being the dog (followed by the goat, sheep, pig, cattle, donkey, horse, and camel). More than fifteen thousand years ago, relationships of familiarity and respect led to cooperation and companionship between people and wolves, the ancestors of the first animals to become members of human families. Whether just a companion—a pet, if you will—or a working dog, the canine changed, albeit subtly, the relationship between humans and beasts. An enduring partnership, a close interdependence, came into being.

Then came the revolution, the eventful millennia when people domesticated farm animals, starting about twelve thousand years ago. Goats, sheep, pigs, and, soon afterward, cattle—the taming of these now-commonplace farm animals may have been almost a subconscious act, which involved no fear on either side. There were advantages on both sides in these history-changing partnerships. What were now farm animals, bred in captivity, acquired better grazing and foraging carefully orchestrated by deliberate herding, and security from predators. Humans acquired predictable meat supplies, milk, and a whole range of valuable by-products—everything from hides and fur to horn and sinew for thongs. Perhaps most important of all, these four farm animals caused people to create permanent settlements, to anchor themselves to field and grazing grounds and well-defined territories that passed from one generation to the next.

The relationship between herders and the herded was a close one in the early days, when herds were small and individual animals were still important. One's animals were far more than just food; they were part of the tapestry of daily life, of one's status in society. For subsistence farmers, working animals were social instruments as well as companions, friends about whom one had no illusions. They became crucial links between generations, between the living and revered ancestors, intimate symbols of sustenance and interconnections between people.

Agriculture and animal domestication were not revolutionary human inventions, but the consequences of them changed history, especially with the appearance of cities and civilizations. Cattle soon became far more than sources of meat, horns, and hides. They became wealth on the hoof, the stuff of gifts and ritual feasting. They were symbols of virility and kingship for Egyptian pharaohs and other rulers, such as the Minoan lords of Crete thirty-five hundred years ago. They also became pack animals for the first time. Soon after 3000 BCE, we find oxen hauling solid-wheeled carts and working plows in Mesopotamian fields. Cattle now served as transportation, as day-to-day laborers on tracks and in the field. At the same time, they were symbols of power and wealth and also sacrificial beasts offered to the gods.

Out in the countryside, subsistence farmers and herders still maintained small herds, even knew individual animals by name, as they were to do right into modern times. It was in close-packed, rapidly growing cities and their hinterlands that the relationship between animals and humans underwent a profound change. Such were the demands for meat and other animal products for urban markets that the scale of stock raising expanded dramatically. Cattle and sheep farms raised hundreds of beasts. Working animals gradually became impersonal commodities, raised and sold by the household head for profit. This is not to say that many people did not still enjoy close relationships with their beasts, but the sheer magnitude of the need for food triggered by population growth militated against an intimate bond.

By 2500 BCE, animals were playing a new, but inconspicuous, role in a slowly globalizing world, in what one might call a pack animal revolution. I argue that one of the most important animals in history was our sixth beast, the humble donkey, and later, the mule, a hybrid of ass and horse. Donkeys were the first of the caravan animals, which transformed overland travel in arid lands long before camels, at a time when most previous long-distance communication was by water. They were catalysts for the growth of the Egyptian state, linked broad areas of Southwest Asia for many centuries, provisioned armies, and carried rulers long before horses pulled chariots. The prolific donkey carried loads and people and was exploited and worked hard, sometimes even to death, in a relationship that treated pack animals as a form of mass transit rather than as individual beasts.

Intimate relationships between animals and people, like those between humans, are ultimately between individuals. In a way it was the sheer number of donkeys that caused most of them to be mere load carriers. Individual farmers, even great lords and priests, may have cherished their carefully groomed mounts, but most were like automobiles—just used. History tells us that the bonds between horses, our seventh animal, and people were much closer, not because equines could serve as pack animals, haul carts, and pull plows, which they did, but because of the unique bond between horse and rider. Successful horsemanship requires a sensitive understanding between rider and steed that needs constant reinforcement, especially when herding animals or training chariot teams. The horse and rider became such a formidable pair that these animals were prized possessions, symbols of prestige and kingship. Mongol armies swept across Eurasia and changed history, their deeds epitomized by the campaigns of Genghis Khan. It was no coincidence that cavalry became potent shock troops on the battlefield. Their effectiveness depended on a close relationship between soldier and steed.

Our eighth animal, the camel, was another history changer, not only because of its unique qualities in arid environments, but because of a relationship with people, who invented saddles that turned camels into such effective pack animals that they are said to have banished the wheeled cart from the eastern Mediterranean for centuries, as well as conquering the Sahara. Those who rode and drove camels developed an almost mystical rapport with their charges, guiding their load carriers to water across seemingly trackless landscapes.

Caravans of pack animals have been one of the great threads of history for the past five thousand years. They carried commodities and people, rare objects, and diplomatic expeditions, and supported armies. Above all, they fostered interconnectedness between widely separated peoples and states—fostering trade or political interactions and awareness of distant lands and peoples, of cultural diversity. With goods and foodstuffs, ideas passed from Asia to the Mediterranean and from

Africa to the north. We shouldn't ignore the power of the pack animals that provisioned Roman armies and carried two-thirds of Europe's gold from West Africa in the fifteenth century CE. Thousands of people spent their entire lives on the move; great caravan crossroads such as medieval Cairo, Damascus, and Samarkand were nodes of interconnection. These storied trading points were made possible only by thousands of pack animals and the men and women who drove and understood them. With such a scale of interconnection, it was inevitable that animals became tools—I call them pickup trucks.

It's hard for us to imagine living in a world where oars, sails, human hands, and, above all, animals powered daily life. In this now largely vanished, animal-driven universe, millions of subsistence farmers still lived on intimate terms with their animals. For instance, many medieval farmers shared their houses with their stock, knew each animal individually, and valued it as a contributor to their daily lives. Theirs was a genuine partnership with their beasts, such as had sustained human life and determined the course of history for thousands of years. However, with the steady growth in urban populations and, eventually, with the Industrial Revolution, the intimate ties between human and beast evaporated into an intensified dichotomy between respect and pride of ownership and the animal as commodity.

The centuries leading up to the Industrial Revolution were when humans truly took control, going far beyond the primitive breeding practices of Roman and medieval farmers. By the eighteenth century, controlled breeding of farming animals such as cattle and pigs transformed human relationships with animals to one where people admired their breeding handiwork. The sedulous care with which proud owners cherished racehorses and prize livestock was widespread among the aristocracy by the early nineteenth century. Once again, however, the inexorable forces of expanding cities and urban population growth created insatiable demands for meat. Industrial-scale stock raising accelerated with a rising obsession with flesh per slaughtered beast, with calculated meat yields. Food needs aside, many people do not realize that the Industrial Revolution and its growing cities depended heavily on working animals for everything from grain milling to hauling loads, for mining coal and moving canal barges. Hard work meant long hours and harsh treatment, so much so that cruelty to working animals became an emerging issue in Victorian times, coinciding with the growing popularity of domestic pets in middle-class households.

Animals for food, beasts for vivisection—these were emerging issues during the nineteenth century and into the twentieth. It is only in recent years, however, that a growing and aggressive concern over animal rights has extended into feedlots and laboratories. Today, there's a movement toward a broader view of the personhood of animals, which sets aside the power that people have to oppress and mistreat the domesticated animals that have helped shape our history. At present, most of them are our servants, to be eaten and otherwise exploited. Will we continue on this indefensible course, or is change afoot? History provides the background but, alas, no ready solutions.

Author's Note

PLACE NAMES ARE SPELLED according to the most common usage. Archaeological sites and historic places are spelled as they appear most commonly in the sources I used to write this book. Some obscure locations are omitted from the maps for clarity, as are familiar geographical labels including the Alps and the Caucasus Mountains; interested readers should consult the specialist literature. The terms *Middle East*, *Near East*, and *Southwest Asia* are used interchangeably, as all three are in common use. *Levant* refers to the eastern Mediterranean coastal region.

The references and notes tend to emphasize sources with extensive bibliographies, to allow the reader to enter the more specialized literature if desired.

All radiocarbon dates have been calibrated, and the CE/BCE convention is used.

Every reasonable effort has been made to contact copyright holders for the illustrations. Anyone with questions should contact the author.

These maps show most locations referred to in the text. Some places, mainly archaeological sites, are omitted for clarity, but their general locations are clear from the narrative. North America is not included, as the few references to people and sites there give geographical information that is sufficient.

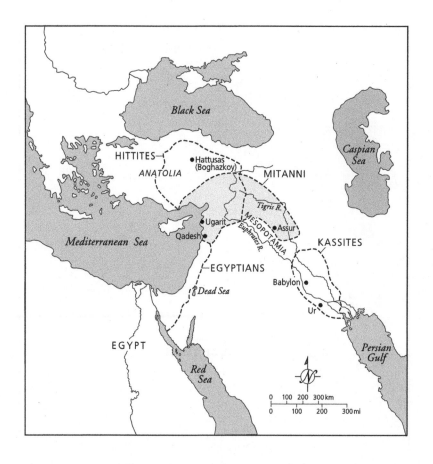

Black Sea

HITTITES
ANATOLIA
● Hattusas
(Boghazkoy)
MITANNI

Tigris R.

MESOPOTAMIA
● Ugarit
Qadesh ●
Euphrates R.
● Assur

KASSITES

Caspian
Sea

Mediterranean Sea

EGYPTIANS

Babylon ●

Dead Sea

Ur ●

EGYPT

Red
Sea

Persian
Gulf

N

0   100 200 300 km
0   100   200   300 mi

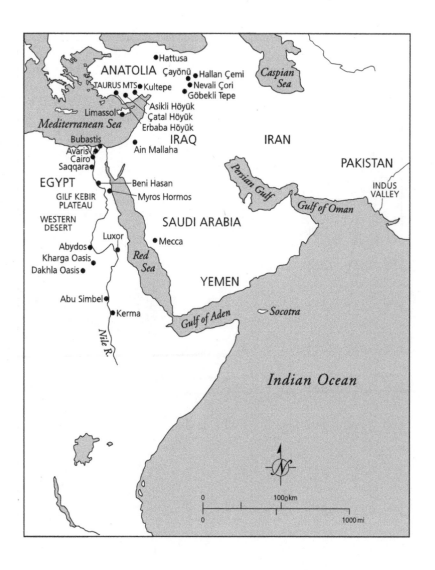

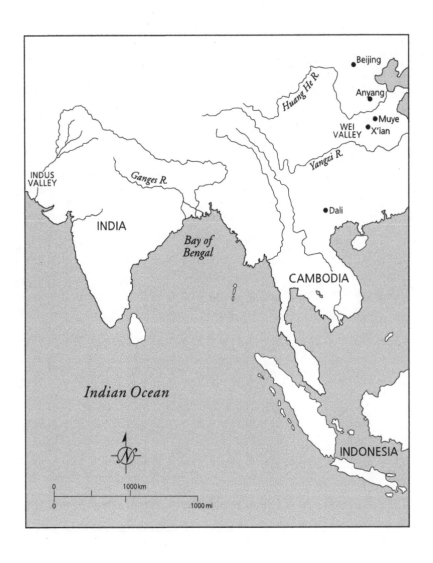

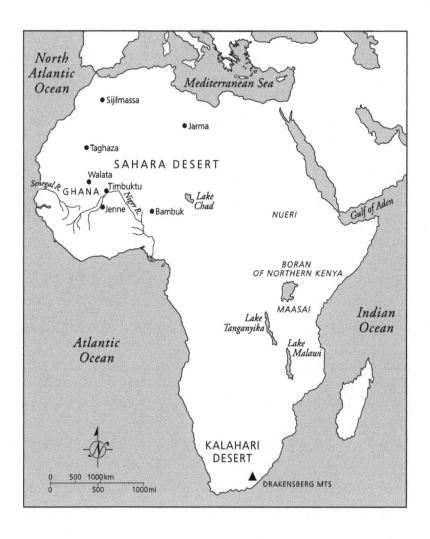

North
Atlantic
Ocean

Mediterranean Sea

• Sijilmassa

• Jarma

•Taghaza

SAHARA DESERT

Senegal R. GHANA
Walata
•
Timbuktu
•
Niger R.
•Jenne • Bambuk

Lake
Chad

NUERI

Gulf of Aden

BORAN
OF NORTHERN KENYA

MAASAI

Lake
Tanganyika

Indian
Ocean

Atlantic
Ocean

Lake
Malawi

0   500 1000 km
0   500   1000 mi

KALAHARI
DESERT

DRAKENSBERG MTS

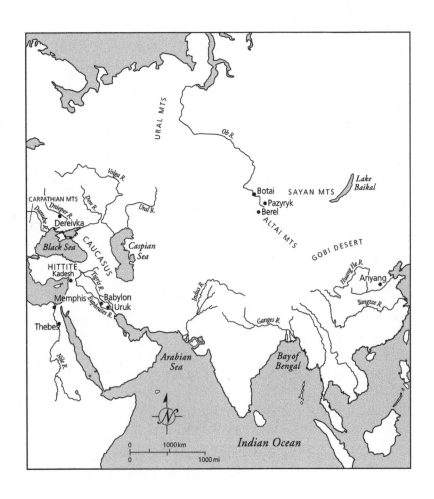

URAL MTS

Ob R.

Volga R.

Ural R.

Don R.

CARPATHIAN MTS

Dnieper R.

Danube R.

Dereivka

Black Sea

CAUCASUS

Caspian
Sea

HITTITE

Kadesh

Tigris R.

Memphis

Euphrates R.

Babylon

Uruk

Thebes

Nile R.

Indus R.

Arabian
Sea

Ganges R.

Bay of
Bengal

Botai

Pazyryk

Berel

SAYAN MTS

Lake
Baikal

ALTAI MTS

GOBI DESERT

Huang He R.

Anyang

Yangtze R.

N

0   1000 km
0   1000 mi

Indian Ocean

Hunters and the Hunted

Chronological Table

BCE

25,000	Cro-Magnons and other late Ice Age people hunt wild horses in Europe and Eurasia.
c.15,000?	Dogs are domesticated in Europe and Eurasia, perhaps elsewhere also. Post-Ice Age global warming begins.
11,000	Larger, sedentary settlements in Southwest Asia, based on hunting and foraging, emerge.
c.10,000	Domestication of goats, pigs, and sheep begins at several locations in Southwest Asia. Pigs may have been first.
9,000 or earlier	Cattle are domesticated in several places in Southwest Asia.
7,000	Cattle are domesticated in North Africa.
6,000	Cattle and small stock spread into temperate Europe.
4,500 (estimate)	Donkeys are domesticated in North Africa and Southwest Asia.
4,000 (estimate)	Horses are tamed in southern Eurasia at several locations.
3,600	Botai culture emerges in southern Eurasia. Horses are almost certainly ridden by then.
3,000	Carts are in use in Mesopotamia and southern Eurasia—hauled by cattle. Horses come into use in Mesopotamia.
2,000	The horse-drawn chariot and the spoked wheel are invented.

First millennium
BCE

Nomad cultures, including Scythians, are found
on the Eurasian Steppe.

Assyrian donkey caravans found in Anatolia and
along the Nile.

Greek accounts refer to the "barbarian" Scythians.

The camel is domesticated.

The Roman Empire expands. Cattle, small stock,
and mules are used as commodities; horses are a
sign of aristocratic distinction and prestige.

First millennium
CE

First camel safaris cross the Sahara Desert.

Llamas are domesticated and in use as pack animal in the Andes.

1750s   Robert Bakewell and others experiment with farm
animal breeding. Rise of racehorse breeding is seen.

Early nineteenth
century

The heyday of military cavalry takes place—
Napoleonic, Indian, and Crimean Wars are fought.

First public outcries about animal cruelty are heard.

Pit ponies are in widespread use.

The heyday of urban pack animals takes place.

The rise of middle class pet keeping is seen.

1851   The first formal London dog show is held.

1871   The first London cat show is held.

1887/1911 Animal cruelty legislation passes in Parliament.

1899–1918 Last widespread use of animals in warfare takes
place—the Boer War and World War I.

CHAPTER 1

Partnership

Pech Merle Cave, southwestern France, Late Ice Age, 24,600 years ago. Fat lamps flicker in the darkness. Dark shadows ebb and flow across the rugged cave wall, deep below the bright realm aboveground. The hunters huddle against the dank rock, gaze upward at the two black spotted horses opposite them. The beasts face in opposite directions. The natural shape of the rock emphasizes the head of the right-hand animal as the soft, irregularly pulsating light gives an impression of movement. A shaman chants softly as he invokes the power of the horses that reside behind the wall. He thrusts with an ocher-tipped stick and imprints red dots on the two beasts, symbolic wounds from an imaginary hunt. The chanting rises to a crescendo. At least three people, perhaps both men and women, step forward, plant their hands on the rock by the horses, and blow black soot onto the wall. The supernatural power of the animals courses through their hands to validate their hunts. The hand imprints are still there after nearly twenty-five thousand years.[1]

This was a common practice, and occurs at other Ice Age sites. At Gargas Cave, in the Pyrenees, generations of visitors—men, women, and children, even infants—left their hand impressions on the walls, some close to cracks filled with bone slivers. More than two hundred hand impressions survive in one chamber alone. Red iron oxide or black manganese powder outlined the participants' hands, giving the impression that their hands had melted into the rock, into the supernatural realm.

Pech Merle lies in a landscape of deep valleys and floodplains, where herds of wild horses grazed at the height of the last Ice Age. For generations, the hunters have lived alongside their harems and the stallions, walking close to the beasts in open sight, without a care on either side.

Figure 1.1 *The horses of Pech Merle. Centre de Préhistoire du Pech Merle, Cabrerets, France.*

They know many of the beasts by sight, may even have given some of them names. At every season, young men lurk quietly in the shadows, watching the animals as they feed or scrape with their hooves for dried grass under winter snow. They've watched their changing appearances in winter and summer, observed the movements of the local herds, seen matings and battles between competing stallions. Observing animals has taught the hunters much about poisonous plants and nature's pharmacopeia. They know the horses as well as their fellow band members, and they always treat the animals with respect, on account of their spiritual power. It is almost as if they were in love with their prey. And when they stalk them and move in for a kill, they butcher the dead animal with care and treat it with deference as a partner in the hunt.

A SPECULATIVE INTERPRETATION, TO be sure, but judging from anthropological sources, it's almost certainly speculation with more than a grain of truth. There's not a hunting society on earth that does not treat its prey with respect. The Australian Aborigines have bewilderingly elaborate oral traditions surrounding animals of all kinds, real and mythic, which form an integral part of "the Dreaming," their cosmic vision of the landscape and human existence. The Cree hunters of Canada's northern forest believe that everyone has a spirit, as does everything in the world, be it an animal, a plant, rocks, even tents and their doorways.[2] In addition to these individual spirits, some more important than others, some categories of beings, especially animals, also have spiritual identities, which are said to be master of them—say, caribou or moose. The same applies to humans. Some individuals have special powers, such as that of elders, who have acquired a lifetime of experience with animals and their environment. They sometimes have powers of divination, knowledge and spiritual power that lead to success in the hunt. There can be little doubt that the symbolism behind the Ice Age paintings in French and Spanish caves reflects a powerful link between people and the animals they hunted. And such ties were not ones of domination. (It's worth noting that the word *animal* has roots in the Latin word *anima*, or "soul.")

Balance, Involvement, and Respect

THE ROUTINE OF LATE Ice Age life, year in, year out, revolved around not mass killings, but individual hunts. Taking a solitary deer, trapping arctic ptarmigan, snaring hares, or stalking a wild horse—all were part and parcel of a life lived close to a remarkable, and often formidable, bestiary. The hunters dwelled among animals, saw them every day of their lives, and were on terms of easy familiarity with them. They lived alongside their prey in a form of close intimacy that it is hard for us to understand. These creatures were not mere animals to be slaughtered with a repeater rifle or a crossbow. Rather, they were living individuals with their own habits and distinctive characteristics, often in small herds that were nearby for months on end. But how does this compare with our modern-day attitudes toward wild animals? Western society's view of nature was expressed in the Book of Genesis more than four thousand years ago: "And God said unto them, 'be fruitful and multiply, and fill the earth, and subdue it and have dominion over the fish of the sea and over the birds of the heavens and over every living thing that moves on the earth.'" [3]

Genesis leaves us in no doubt that we humans are in control of the earth and the animals that dwell upon it. Nature is something different. Humankind stands outside the realm of the environment, its beasts and plants, and controls their destiny. This is a fundamental assumption of modern conservation, with its talk of pristine wilderness where human access is carefully restricted. As the anthropologist Tim Ingold memorably remarks, it's "like putting a 'do not touch' notice in front of a museum exhibit: we can observe, but only from a distance."[4] We foster a profound sense of detachment from the wilderness, a "do not interfere" syndrome, which is totally incompatible with the traditional, hunting way of life known to us both from cave paintings and from studies of surviving hunting peoples such as the Australians. Such societies' dealings with animals were dynamic, intimate, and respectful.

We know from studies of surviving hunters and gatherers in many parts of the world over the past century or more that the natural environment is not something passive that has food there for the taking. It's alive, saturated with a wide diversity of powers. If people are to survive, they have to maintain associations with these powers, be they animal, vegetable, or mineral—just as they have to sustain ties with other humans. This means that they have to treat the landscape, and its animals and plants, with consideration. What's involved is something very different. Successful hunting depends on the personal ties that the hunter builds with animal powers, carefully constructed through previous hunts. The meat obtained from a kill is a return on a long-term investment in following the proper procedures for hunting the prey. Many hunting societies, both from ancient and modern times, appear to have practiced a conscious form of conservation by managing their resources.

For traditional hunters, the same powers that animate the environment are those that are responsible for the extinction or survival of *humans*. As another anthropologist, Richard Nelson, wrote of the Koyukon hunters of Alaska, "the proper role of humankind is to serve a dominant nature."[5] The well-being of humanity depends on acts of propitiation and respect. So the Koyukon yield to the forces of their environment: they never confront it. We may talk of two separate worlds, those of humans and nature, but the reality for the Koyukon and other hunters was that there was one world, of which humans formed a very small part.

Dancing with Eland

ANTHROPOLOGICAL RESEARCH IN THE Arctic and sub-Arctic, in tropical Africa and Australia, chronicles a closely maintained balance between hunters and the powers in all kinds of natural environment, and with prey. Everywhere, hunters engaged in a deep and meaningful involvement of their entire beings with animals. A successful hunt that ended in a kill was thought of as proof of friendly relations between the hunter and his quarry, which willingly allowed itself to be killed. A kill was not an act of violent subjugation, but a successful attempt to draw the creature into a familiar realm of social being, part of a process of coexistence and mutual interchange. We can be certain that such close links developed tens of thousands of years ago as part of human strategies for survival.

The San hunter-gatherers of southern Africa lived in landscapes teeming with animals of all sizes—great antelope herds, migrating wildebeest, zebra, and many smaller prey. Then there were the predators such as lions, leopards, hyenas, and other formidable beasts like the buffalo, the elephant, and the rhinoceros. Every creature, however large or small, was an integral part of the San world. Each had a place in the cosmic and supernatural order; each had its own distinctive identity and personality in the vibrant living and supernatural worlds of which the hunters were a part. The San were members of this tapestry of animal life and took their part in it, enjoying a close familiarity with the creatures they hunted and ate. They treated all beasts, large and small, with consideration, even if some of them had reputations as killers or tricksters. One trod carefully in the predator-rich landscapes of the past, where one survived by careful observation, the carefully hoarded knowledge and experience passed by word of mouth from one generation to the next, and by meticulous communication with the supernatural forces of the world around one.

To the San, one of the most important prey was the eland, the largest and fattest of all antelope. San artists painted hundreds of eland on rock shelter walls, often with human figures cavorting around them, mainly in the Drakensberg Mountains in eastern South Africa.[6] Until recently, San in the Kalahari Desert in Botswana still danced next to the carcass of a freshly killed eland. As they activated their potency, the medicine men (shamans) trembled, then sweated and bled from their noses. A dying eland trembles, sweating profusely, with melted fat gushing like blood from its wide-open mouth. Perhaps the San compared the human trance with the trauma of an eland in its death throes. In a San Bull Dance, miming and sounds make the beast appear real before the eyes of the participants. As the shaman dances, he hallucinates and "sees" the eland standing beyond the glow of the fire.

In time, the dancers become one with the eland, and the transfiguration is complete: They have become the eland. Thus, the animal and the human become interchangeable. San artists mixed fresh eland blood with ocher, making their paintings storehouses of potency long after their composition. In some rock shelters, imprints of human hands covered with paint cover the walls. By placing their hands on the rock or the painting, people acquired the potency of the eland, which flowed into their bodies. It was as if the great antelope dwelled behind the rock, at least in spirit, sharing its potency with its hunters in a form of spiritual closeness. The same may have been true of Ice Age hunters thousands of years earlier. The close pairing of hunter and hunted, of people and animals, transcends millennia.

Not only the San, but all subsistence hunters who depended on game, found themselves enmeshed in close dealings with animals. So the hunter had to behave toward his prey in much the same way as he would toward people. He was cautious, for he could never predict exactly how the prey would act. For this reason, detailed knowledge of an animal, its habits and diet, appearance and behavior, was of fundamental importance. Hunters spent large amounts of time observing animals, getting to know them in the same way as one gets to know a friend and his or her moods and idiosyncrasies. One worked to control one's associations with one's prey over a long period, using one's own experience and that of others—as well as a huge body of myth, lore, and storytelling that defined animals and their personalities.

Animals and humans inhabited the same world, engaging with one another not only in body or mind, but as whole beings. Humans and animals were equals, not in roles of dominance and subjugation— which was what happened when people began domesticating animals of all kinds. The realm that divided the social world of humans and the rest of nature was permeable and easily crossed. To write a narrative history of animal-human relations among hunters is to write a history of human concern with animals, the notion that we attend to them, are with them; something very different from the disengaged way in which we have made sharp distinctions between animals and society, nature and humans. What we need to examine today is the quality of our relations with animals, something that hunters of the past understood (and, indeed, surviving hunters of the present understand) very clearly.

Tales from Distant Time

THE COMMUNICATION BETWEEN HUNTERS and animals goes back into deep time. Countless stories from the remote past, unimaginable numbers of years ago, passed, and still pass, from one generation of hunters and foragers to the next. In northern lands, much of the storytelling unfolded during the long hours of winter darkness, as people lay in their warm beds. The Koyukon tell stories of "Distant Time" that begin before the present order of existence came into being. This was a time when animals were human, had human forms, and lived in a human society, speaking human language. At some point in Distant Time, some people died and were transformed into the animals and plants that inhabit the landscape today. Richard Nelson calls this a "dreamlike metamorphosis" that left some human qualities and personality traits in local animals. In Koyukon society, just as in innumerable other traditional societies around the world, such stories, often of great length, are the equivalent of the creation story in Genesis. The tales explain the origins of the sun, moon, and constellations; account for prominent landmarks; and often feature a central figure, the Raven.

The Raven features prominently in creation tales in many Native American societies. To the Koyukon, he was a contradiction: "omnipotent clown, benevolent mischief-maker, buffoon, and deity."[7] Raven manipulated the environment, caused rivers to flow only one way to make them more of a challenge for paddlers. He created animals, devised mortality for people, caused difficulties for them. As one Koyukon remarked to Richard Nelson, "It's just like talking to God, that's why we talk to the raven. He created the world."[8] Animals were close to people, although they were different: they had no souls, which are different from an animal's spirit. But they are close to humans in that they display a range of emotions, communicate among themselves, and understand what humans say and do. The interaction between animal and human is intensely close, which means that the spirits are easily offended by peoples' disrespectful behavior.

It follows, then, in Koyukon belief, society that there is proper conduct toward nature, as powerful spirits will readily punish irreverent or insulting behavior, and waste. Killing animals does not offend, but living and dead animals must be treated with respect as a source of human life. If the hunter shows disrespectful behavior, he will have no luck. The Koyukon avoid pointing at animals, and speak carefully, not boastfully, about them. They must kill without causing suffering, and they avoid losing wounded prey. Strict rules surround the treatment of killed beasts. There are rules for butchering animals properly, and for the appropriate care of meat. Taboos surround meat consumption, and inedible animal parts are respectfully buried or burned.

The Koyukon consider the environment both natural and supernatural, to the point that it's a second society in which the people live. As they hunt and walk through the forest, hunters know that spirits surround them. Each animal is far more than just a beast sighted. It is a personality, known from stories in the Distant Time. As Nelson puts it, "It is a figure in the community of beings."[9] Everything in the Koyukon world that treats of animals dwells at least partially in the realm of the supernatural. In both the Kuyukon and the San, on the other side of the world, each band's shamans used their powers to control the spirits of nature, for curing, and, as spirit helpers, to communicate with the protective spirits of caribou and other prey, attracting animals and creating abundance.

The Whim of Supernatural Power

IN WARMER ENVIRONMENTS, LIKE those of Africa and Australia, hunting societies, both ancient and historical, relied heavily on plant foods of all kinds, with hunting being more of a sporadic activity, even in the game-rich landscapes of sub-Saharan Africa. Storage of fresh meat is a problem without the natural refrigeration of subzero temperatures. Contrast this with northern latitudes, where the hunter has always relied almost entirely on game meat or fish for survival.[10] Winter storage is vital; the hunter must kill many more animals for food and for other purposes, because plant foods and vegetation usable for clothing or shelter are in very short supply most of the year.

Migratory species such as caribou and reindeer have been favored prey for thousands of years in the north during and since the Late Ice Age. They still are today, for basic hunting practices have changed little, even if the weaponry is radically different. Both migrate in large herds, the routes and strategic river crossing points relatively predictable. One might assume that the hunters followed the marching herds and harvested whatever beasts they needed. This conventional assumption is completely wrong, for reindeer move much faster than humans, unencumbered as they are by children and personal possessions. Much caribou or reindeer hunting involved, and still involves, ambushing and trapping them at strategic locations, especially in late summer and early fall, when the beasts are in prime condition. Far more is at stake than merely meat, for the hunter requires an equal amount of fat, making fat-bearing animals in prime condition a favored target, especially bucks in the fall, who may carry up to 20 percent of their weight in fat ahead of rutting season. Many northern hunting groups today would kill beasts for their fat, then abandon the carcasses to rot, except for the tongue and the marrow from lower leg bones, prized delicacies. Much of the year, does and fawns are preferred, while unborn fawns are much enjoyed—much to the consternation of today's conservationists. The same practices were probably followed in ancient times.

Then there are the hides, which serve all kinds of uses—fawn skins for underwear, buckskins for boots, for example. This is apart from the hides used for thongs, tents, bags, kayaks, and other purposes. Back in 1771, the naturalist Samuel Hearne estimated that every Chipewyan individual near Hudson's Bay consumed more than twenty caribou hides a year for domestic purposes alone.[11] Again, there was huge wastage of meat, which was left to rot in the warm temperatures of late summer. These abandoned carcasses were a boon for scavengers such as ravens and wolves, both of whom followed reindeer herds throughout much of the year. The wastage was enormous, but not enough alone to cause the extinction of reindeer or caribou herds. Wastage was, however, inevitable, when opportunism, careful observation, and only partial consumption of the prey worked well enough to ensure survival. Success depended on weighing the many factors such as temperature, snow depth, and snow hardness, so that changing migration routes could be fathomed ahead of time. The alternative was starvation.

In small hunting groups, the leaders were individuals with more than average strength, endurance, and hunting expertise, and who had the ability to gauge communal opinion and translate it into action. As a leader accumulated meat and other goods from his hunting skills, he redistributed his "wealth" to others in the band. There was no such thing as individual wealth, in the sense that there is with domesticated animals, where each owner seeks more beasts for him or herself. Leadership was ephemeral, and passed from one hunter to another in societies where the prey's reproduction lay in the hands of supernatural forces.[12] Power over the supernatural, often in the hands of a specialist shaman, was all-important in societies where herds ensured the survival of humans. Contrast this with societies with domesticated animals, where people were or are responsible for perpetuating their herds.

To many hunters, the animals made themselves available at the whim of a supernatural power, a spiritual master who decided which animals would be provided for human consumption and then regenerated. This is why hunters treated killed animals with respect—to avoid offending the spirits. To northern peoples, the reindeer and caribou were immortal, unconquerable. In a real sense, to ancient and living hunters, such as the San and the northern hunter, killing game is an act of renewal. As the flesh and hides are respectfully consumed or used, the soul of the dead beast is released to its spiritual master.

Following the Honeyguide

THERE ARE NUMEROUS EXAMPLES of close interactions between wild animals and humans, which are certainly not domestication. They are loosely formed alliances of benefit to both sides, often inconspicuous and perpetuated for generations, such as that between the Boran cattle herders of northern Kenya and the honeyguide bird (see sidebar "Honeyguides and Humans"). The honeyguide locates bees' nests; the Boran open them. Such is the interdependency between the Boran and the honeyguide that the people consider killing one an act of murder.

Honeyguides and Humans

The greater honeyguide, *Indicator indicator*, loves beeswax and other components of the honeycomb.[13] It is one of the few birds that can digest wax, but it has a problem. While it can locate nests, it's unable to open them, located as they are in narrow crevices, tree hollows, and termite mounds. Also, the restricted entrances are protected by aggressive bees, whose stings can penetrate honeyguide feathers, with fatal results. The birds devour wax in times when insects are rare, at the end of the dry season—a moment when the Boran, too, are short of food and milk and turn to honey. The Boran also consider the bee a superb pharmacist, its honey a treatment for a wide range of human diseases, among them malaria and pneumonia, this quite apart from its nutritional value, especially when mixed with fresh cattle blood or milk. But humans have a problem, too. They can break open nests and remove the honey, but they have trouble locating them. For hundreds, probably thousands, of years, therefore, honeyguides and humans have worked together to obtain honey.

Figure 1.2 *The Greater Honeyguide,* Indicator indicator. © *Morphart/ Fotolia.*

When hunting for nests, a man blows air into his clasped fists, shells, or hollowed-out nuts. The penetrating whistle sound can be heard over distances of several kilometers. Sometimes the hunter lights a smoky fire, knocks against wood, or shouts to attract the birds. By the same token, the honeyguides seek out human partners. They fly close to the hunter, perch on conspicuous bushes or trees and make a *tirr-tirr* call. As the man approaches, the bird increases the tempo of the call and flies toward the bee colony. The honeyguide flies from one perch to another, in a more or less straight line, until it reaches the nest, then falls silent as the hunter begins his final search. Everyone who collects honey leaves some of the comb for the birds. No one knows how this unique closeness developed, but the guiding season coincides with the time when both birds and humans are short of their normal staple diets, and they rely on one another to find food in this unique form of symbiosis. The partnerships is also a function of mobility—constant movements of cattle herders, the migratory habits of the bees, and the broad range of the honeyguide. The avian guides save the hunters huge amounts of time and increase their success rate significantly.

In legend and folklore, animals were active players in the drama of creation and in the endless unfolding of daily life. These stories, like the experience of the hunt, passed by word of mouth, through tale, chant, ceremony, and dance, and hard experience from one generation to the next, a priceless archive of knowledge about animals when people lived in close intimacy with their prey. All this changed as animals reshaped human society.

Wolves and People

CHAPTER 2

Curious Neighbors and Wolf-dogs

Central Europe, a summer night eighteen thousand years ago. The Cro-Magnon hunters and their families eat by the light of the flames around a campfire. They throw discarded reindeer bones into the intense darkness without, perhaps an open space or the slope below a natural rocky overhang. As the flames leap higher, the band sees flickers from the wolf eyes that observe them from nearby. Everyone knows the beasts are there, waiting patiently until the people settle down for the night. Sometime later, the families wrap themselves in reindeer hides and drift into deep sleep. Quietly, the hungry wolves grab the discarded bones and carry them away, but the families are unafraid. They have no fear that the wolves will consider them prey, for the pack has stayed close to the band and lived off its discards for generations. Even children know individual animals by sight. Both humans and beasts behave unthreateningly, predictably, both social animals who rely on one another in inconspicuous ways.

AT SOME POINT, AFTER centuries of juxtaposition in bitterly cold landscapes, and also in warmer climates, in all manner of places, some wolves joined humans and evolved into dogs. Quite why they did so, and when, is a matter of ongoing debate, but we know that it happened long before we became farmers, settled in permanent villages, and herded farm animals, probably well before fifteen thousand years ago.

All the experts agree that the Eurasian gray wolf (*Canis lupus*) was the ultimate ancestor of domestic dogs. Genetics tell the tale.[1] The mitochondrial DNA of dogs, inherited through females, differs at the most by a mere 2 percent from that of wolves, whereas that of their closest wild relative, the coyote, shows a 4 percent difference (see sidebar "Dogs, Wolves, and DNA"). It may well be more complicated than that, for interfertility between canids is commonplace, which would make for a more diverse ancestry.[2]

Fifteen millennia in the past, the world was in the final grip of the Ice Age. Enormous ice sheets mantled Scandinavia and much of North America; global sea levels were about ninety-one meters (three hundred feet) lower than today. A vast expanse of open, treeless steppe extended from the Atlantic deep into Siberia; an intensely frigid, windy land bridge linked Northeast Asia and Alaska. Nine-month winters were the norm, Europe and Eurasia home to a remarkable bestiary of cold-adapted mammals, among them aurochs (the primordial ox), bison, reindeer, and wild horses. Predators large and small abounded, among them the gray wolf and human beings, both of whom preyed on animals of all kinds. The humans were adept, ingenious hunters, popularly known as Cro-Magnons, named after a rock shelter in southwestern France where they first came to light in 1868.[3] They first settled in small numbers throughout Europe about forty-three thousand years ago. For tens of thousands of years, wolves and people shared a challenging environment, not necessarily competing, but each closely observing the other, often at surprisingly close quarters. This juxtaposition led to profound changes in the relationship between them.

Big Bad Wolves?

WOLVES RECEIVE CONSISTENTLY BAD press, which goes back a long way, probably because they killed cattle and sheep. They are ravening, fierce killers. They decimate sheep in their pens, attack children, and haunt dark forests on the margins of small villages. The fictional Big Bad Wolf is an enduring stereotype, with deep roots in medieval folklore. In Norse mythology, Skoll the wolf swallows the sun when the world perishes in

Ragnarök, a cataclysm of violent battle and natural disasters. Big Bad Wolf has become a menacing antagonist, a generic cautionary tale, even featured in Disney movies and on *Sesame Street* (where he repented of his sins and took up a hobby: blowing bubbles).[4] In fact, we now know that many individual wolves are timid and even friendly, as well as being intensely curious.

Bad press went hand in hand with wholesale slaughter. Fifteen thousand years ago we lived alongside wolves in what must have been a state of cautious but easy familiarity. In some places, they must have been as commonplace a sight as people walking dogs on city streets today. Once we became farmers, however, we turned on our predator neighbors, to protect our stock when the wolf's traditional wild prey became scarce. As herds and flocks proliferated and people settled in more crowded landscapes, they eradicated wolves whenever they could. Rulers and governments joined the fray. As long ago as the sixth century BCE the Athenian lawmaker Solon offered a bounty for every wolf that was killed. Wolves eventually influenced religious doctrine. Christian symbolism depicted the wolf as the devil, the evil being that pursued and suborned the living faithful. To protect flocks and herds, European kings paid bounties for wolves. Wolf packs were extinct in England by the end of King Henry VII's reign in 1509, hunted and trapped relentlessly as sheep killers. The vendetta crossed the Atlantic. By 1930, there were virtually no wolves left in the United States' Lower Forty-Eight and none in the West. Yet gray wolves remain the most widespread large mammals on earth after people and their livestock, although they now occupy but a third of their ancient range. Fortunately, generations of research have taught us a great deal about them and their impact on the landscape.

More on a Social Predator

GRAY WOLVES SOMEWHAT RESEMBLE German shepherds, but with larger heads, longer legs, and bigger paws. They are slender, powerfully built animals that move swiftly, their long legs allowing them to navigate through the deep snow that falls over much of their range. Wolves have no enemies except humans and, in the Russian Far East, Siberian tigers. After humans and lions, they were once the world's most widely distributed mammals, accustomed to living alongside people, with whom they shared common prey.

Like humans, wolves are social animals, which live in close-knit packs. Most groups consist of two parents and their offspring, with occasionally a sibling or some other individuals.[5] There's a strong dominance hierarchy in wolf packs, the two top-ranking beasts being the breeding pair. Subordinate, mature animals are subservient to them, but these usually disperse from their natal group and form their own breeding packs. The hierarchy changes constantly, dominance and submission being measured by body postures such as the position of the ears or tail. The packs are constantly on the move, usually traveling in single file. They can cover long distances when following in the tracks of game such as migrating caribou. When hunting, they rely on their acute sense of smell, which is said to allow them to locate a moose and its young over 7 kilometers (4.5 miles) away. They approach their prey silently, cautiously, and rapidly, chasing it at full speed, hoping to run it down within a short distance. Experts say that only about 10 percent of wolf hunts are successful, largely because animals such as moose and musk ox can defend themselves effectively while standing at bay. By contrast, caribou, deer, and reindeer rely on their speed to escape. The actual attacks involve the pack surrounding their prey and biting at it to bring it down. The wolves immediately start eating the dead beast, consuming as much as they can to compensate for long periods without food. Wolves are often scavengers, for they prey on older animals and young beasts and fawns, especially at times when their prey is weak and poorly nourished after a long winter.

Wolves are some of the most social of all predators. Such behavior may have originated with their adaptation to cooperative hunting of large ungulates such as bison or reindeer during the Ice Age, especially during the actual kill. In so doing, they behaved just like very early humans, who combined opportunism with scavenging. At first wolves were more successful than people, whose weapons were little more than fire-hardened or stone-tipped spears, at being able to get as close to the prey as possible. Judging from injuries found on Neanderthal skeletons, the hunters of fifty thousand years ago sometimes physically jumped onto the backs of larger animals to drive a spear into their hearts. There are analogies with wolves here, who rely on fast pursuit, then attack at close quarters.

With the appearance of *Homo sapiens*, modern people, in tropical Africa some one hundred fifty thousand years ago, the competitive gap between wolves and humans narrowed because of the gradually improving technology used by human hunters—the antler-tipped spear propelled by a spear thrower, which increased range and accuracy, then the bow and poisoned arrows. By thirty thousand years ago, humans and wolves were close neighbors in European and Eurasian landscapes. Both lived in tightly structured groups; both wolves and people raised their young as part of a small community. On many occasions, hunters and wolves may even have hunted together, in situations where both sides were familiar with, and not afraid of, one another.

If their cave paintings are any guide, hunters of thirty thousand years ago respected their prey and fellow predators. Wolves never appear in their rock art, but they were so commonplace that people must have respected their close neighbors and incorporated them both into their hunting lore and into mythic tales as important actors in the drama of cosmic origins. This is, of course, merely an assumption, but it has solid foundations in the ways in which modern northern hunters treat wolves. The Nunamiut Eskimos of Alaska admire wolves' hunting expertise when attacking caribou. Inuit hunters in the Arctic thought of them as guides, even as animals that were once people—and hence as brothers. But there were also tales of dangerous wolves, evil forces at creation. For the most part, the relationship between people and wolf was one of respect on the human side and, on occasion, of curiosity on the other. There were also advantages for both sides.

In the predator-rich landscapes of the Late Ice Age, wolves would have been commonplace, familiar beasts. Their human neighbors would have known, for example, that wolf packs move constantly in search of quarry except during the denning season of spring and early summer.[6] They would have been aware of the strategic locations where packs would track and hunt down migrating reindeer—often the very same places where humans ambushed the massed beasts. Both were intensely social animals accustomed to opportunism and scavenging, even from one another's kills. It would have been an easy step for wolves to scavenge discarded bones and meat from human kills carried back to hunting camps. Over the centuries, such scavenging would have become second nature, bringing human and beast into ever-closer juxtaposition. The wolves took advantage of human tolerance in supplying them with food. Both humans and wolves were accustomed to cooperation, cooperation in the hunt, in observing their surroundings, and in social relationships. Years of scavenging could have led to an easy familiarity, even to situations where some more sociable wolves lay close to feeding hunters, signaling, perhaps with their eyes or other gestures, that they wanted the leftovers. In time, too, one can imagine hunters and these same wolves tracking reindeer herds, the wolves acting as guides, perhaps surrounding the quarry, and the hunters, with their efficient weaponry, acting as the killers. A few wolves, or entire packs, may have associated themselves with hunting bands, perhaps warning against other predators, scouting game, scavenging meat. There would have been advantages on either side: more reliable food supplies for the wolves, a measure of protection and intelligence for the hunters.

Dog-wolves?

WHEN DID WOLVES BECOME dogs? Here we have to turn to scattered, very incomplete archaeological finds, the earliest of which create complex scientific challenges. Simply put, how does one distinguish the bones of a dog from those of a wolf? Most known remains of what may be early dogs are at best fragmentary, so one is working with inconspicuous clues. They provide us with a tantalizing portrait of animals that may have been part wolf, part dog.

The earliest possible domestic dog bones are a fragmentary skull from Goyet Cave in Belgium, claimed to date to about thirty-two thousand years ago, and a thirty-three-thousand-year-old tooth and jawbone fragment from Razboinichya Cave in the Altai Mountains of southern

Siberia, said to have a genetically "shallow divergence from ancient wolves."[7] Unfortunately, however, the Goyet cranium has no close association with human occupation, and the attribution is dubious. So Goyet is questionable at best. The geneticists working on the Razboinichya bones are rightly cautious about their findings, but it seems likely there was close interaction between wolves and humans much earlier than we now know.

Fortunately, there is more. Dozens of Late Ice Age archaeological sites with numerous mammoth bones occur in central and eastern Europe. Most lie on higher river terraces or in low, mountainous areas close to water. The huge beasts provided large quantities of meat, also materials for tools and ornaments. The bones formed stout frameworks for dome-shaped houses covered with mammoth hides. A hundred thousand years ago, the Neanderthals ate mammoth flesh but may have taken them only occasionally, perhaps in ambushes or when they were mired. After about forty-five thousand years ago, however, modern humans arrived with smaller, more effective weaponry that enabled them to attack mammoths from a greater distance. Pat Shipman, a specialist in ancient animal bones, theorizes that the hunters may also have used another weapon: fairly large, doglike animals morphologically distinct from wolves, whose much-fragmented bones lie among the game animals at mammoth kill sites. She calls them "dog-wolves," canines with an unusual mitochondrial DNA, unknown among modern dogs or recent or ancient wolves. Males within this haplotype may have interbred with female wolves, leading to a population ancestral to either modern dogs or wolves. This may have been an early attempt at domestication, which left few, if any descendants.

At the time of writing, Shipman's "dog-wolves" are a shadowy presence, known only from fragmentary bones across Europe. If they existed, they would have been invaluable to people pursuing larger game. Like wolves, they would have surrounded lumbering mammoth or other large game, howling loudly and enabling the hunters to approach closely for the kill. They would also have served as guard dogs, keeping other predators away from the fresh meat being butchered and from the nearby dwellings. Dog-wolves might not have been trained hunting animals, but their wolflike behavior of stalking and surrounding their prey in packs would have allowed effective hunting of mammoth and other formidable creatures, and better control of the resulting carcasses. The result could have been more food, then rising population densities, reflected in more mammoth kill sites. Perhaps, also, the larger-bodied dog-wolves could have transported meat from kill sites to camp, but this is pure speculation.[8]

The Shipman hypothesis, and the research of geneticists working on early dogs, assumes that there was a long twilight zone of wolf domestication that was more a matter of close cooperation than taming beasts that lived alongside people on a daily basis. The putative dog-wolves were extinct by the end of the Ice Age, for they differ significantly from later domesticated dogs. Whatever the closeness of their relationship to people, they offered clear advantages to their human neighbors in what must have been a loose relationship of interdependency based on respect and a need for meat supplies on both sides.

How Did Domestication Take Place?

DOG-WOLVES ASIDE, WE WILL never know exactly how full domestication came to pass. One obvious scenario has people adopting orphaned wolf puppies, which became pets and eventually dogs. They would have been fed alongside human babies, and then would have started breeding among themselves, producing "wolf puppies." As the generations passed, they would have become ever more doglike. This hypothesis assumes that people captured pups on a considerable scale. It takes little account of how wolves behave around humans, of their innate, profound curiosity as social animals.

Captured wolf pups reared by people can be tamed and socialized to some extent, especially between the ages of three and eight months. These are the months when both dogs and wolves form their critical social bonds. According to biologist Raymond Coppinger, tame wolves would eat in the presence of humans; wild ones would not—a critical difference.[9] This does not necessarily mean that tamed wolf pups became dogs, for this requires other major adaptations. First, the animals have to sustain their foothold in the domestic arena, which requires them to become very much more like family members than wild animals. At the same time, dogs have a much greater tolerance of stress, which means that only a few wolf pups would adapt successfully. But the initial rearing did not mean that they had to be fully tamed or prevented from escaping. Both humans and wolves have remarkably similar hierarchical social organization, which revolves around the family and effective communication. These biological realities helped adapt stress-tolerant wolves to domestic life with people. By no means would all young wolves have melded readily into a society dominated by humans rather than fellow wolves. More aggressive individuals that did not adapt must have been killed or driven away into the wild.

The process of wolves becoming dogs was as much social as biological. Part of the transformation involved changes in diet. Both dogs and humans are omnivorous, but young domestic wolves would have had to adapt to a diet of both meat scraps and plant remains. They wouldn't have learned the group hunting skills that were common to wolf packs in the wild. Their diet would have come in part from human hands, from casual scavenging, and from their own hunting of small rodents and other animals. This penchant for solitary hunting might well have become a critical skill for cooperating with humans. Acquiring a varied diet from diverse sources would have required both ingenuity and solicitation. Still, such a diet probably resulted in smaller body size, an adaptation that led to reduced nutritional requirements.

It's all very well for individual wolves to adapt a doglike life, but how would they have perpetuated themselves? Their opportunities to breed with members of wild packs would have been limited at best, especially since most packs discourage outsiders from joining breeding pairs and siblings. Almost certainly, then, breeding occurred between tamed wolves in a domestic association with humans. The first dogs entered a new habitat, where they spread rapidly to fill a new ecological niche, thanks to a premium on early sexual maturity. In strictly ecological terms, one could talk about an act of colonization of human society by wolves that evolved into what we know as dogs. Domestic dogs reach puberty much earlier than wolves in the wild, so the trend toward a smaller body size and more juvenile appearance than those of wolves accelerated with the expanding population. As anthropologist Darcy Morey eloquently puts it, the best strategy for early dogs would have been "have as many viable pups as you can, as fast as you can, and get them out there."[10]

Wolves joined humans, became domesticated dogs, and formed close bonds with them in many places and on many occasions over vast areas of Europe, Eurasia, East Asia, and even the Himalayas (see sidebar "Dogs, Wolves, and DNA"). Their domestication was a diffuse event that was a direct, and inevitable, consequence of people and animals living in close juxtaposition, depending on one another, and developing informal bonds cemented on the human side with rituals and attitudes of profound respect toward other living beings.

Dogs, Wolves, and DNA

Ever since the identification of the ABO blood system in the early twentieth century, genetics has played an important role in studying both animal and human evolution. Modern molecular biological techniques have made it possible to study the genetic information inside the nuclei of each cell in bodies of animals such as dogs, sheep, and cattle. This nuclear DNA is easy to study in living creatures, but degrades quickly after death. In recent years, studies of mitochondrial DNA (mtDNA) outside the cell nuclei in small structures called mitochondria, which passes through the female line, have cast new light on the ancestry of different animals. The mtDNA passes through generations, and changes at a steady and distinctive rate, and only through random mutation. Some of the remarkable findings include the fact that the genetic signature of chickens from the Andes dating to before Columbus is identical to that of Polynesian birds, hinting, perhaps, at contact between the two areas before the European Age of Discovery.

The genetic history of dog origins is still little understood.[11] A comparison between DNA from 27 wolf populations in Asia,

Europe, and North America and that of 140 dogs from 67 different breeds leave no doubt that wolves were dogs' ultimate ancestors. However, did domestication occur once or at many locations? One influential study in 2002 produced mitochondrial evidence for an origin in Southeast Asia, but the earliest archaeological finds there date to about seven thousand years ago, much later than those from Europe. A recent paper studied the Y chromosome (inherited through the male line) in 151 dogs from around the world and suggested a place of origin south of the Yangtze River in East Asia. A growing body of evidence points to a Southeast Asian population that spread throughout the world. Yet, the earliest known domesticated canines come from Europe and Southwest Asia. The geneticists point out that European and Eurasian dogs interbred with wolves for a long time, whereas Southeast Asian canines, once domesticated, lived far from them. Thus, they developed their own evolutionary path. By calculating the mutation rate of genetic markers on Y chromosomes from a sample of a hundred Australian dingoes, known to have appeared about forty-two hundred years ago, the researchers calculated that Eurasian and Southeast Asian dogs parted company about seven thousand years ago. Subsequently, Southeast Asian dogs evolved in such a way that their increasing numbers enabled them to replace western forms as they moved east at a time when agriculture was taking hold over wide areas.

The research and debates continue, but it seems certain that wolves and humans got together in many places, in some areas at least fifteen thousand years ago.

CHAPTER 3

Cherished Companions

Denmark, spring, 8000 BCE. The hunter crouches among the dense reeds, bow at the ready, and arrow hooked to the string. A pile of arrows lies to his right, ready for use. He watches the geese as they rest on the placid waters of the shallow lake after their arduous journey from the south. Feet in the mud, he remains motionless, waiting for some geese to swim within arrow's range. To his right, his black-and-brown hunting dog lies quietly, and completely still, panting gently, alert. Half a dozen ducks paddle slowly close to shore. Slowly, deliberately, the man draws his bow and takes aim. The dog remains absolutely still, watching intently. Zip, zip . . . the hunter releases once, grabs another arrow and shoots again. The startled birds take to the air, but two struggle in the water, impaled by razor-sharp flint-tipped arrows. A soft command: the dog points, then slips into the water. He swims to the struggling fowl, grabs them one by one, and carries them to shore. The hunter quickly wrings their necks and puts them in a netting bag. His dog wags his tail and looks up expectantly. A pat on the head, and maybe a scrap of food, then back to the hunt as the hunter moves slowly to a new vantage point in quest of more prey. Hours later, dog and master return to camp, the last bird gripped firmly in canine jaws.

AS WE HAVE SEEN, wolves and humans got together in many locations, some bitterly cold, others much warmer. Despite the growing, if incomplete, evidence for wolf-dogs, we still do not know precisely when people fully tamed canines. One certainly could not describe wolf-dogs as fully domesticated—if they existed at all.

What evidence do we have for actual dogs? The earliest unquestionable dog came to light in the grave of a fifty-year-old man and a twenty- to twenty-five-year-old woman unearthed at Bonn-Oberkassel, Germany, by quarrymen's picks in 1914.[1] The quarrymen shattered most of the bones before archaeologists investigated the burial with methods that were extremely crude by modern standards. Unfortunately, only a jaw fragment of the fourteen-thousand-year-old beast survives.

When I excavate a burial, I always wonder what events surrounded the interment, whether animal or human. Did the deceased perish from old age, from chronic disease, or a war wound? Was he loved or held in contempt? Did she have children and what rituals surrounded her passing? Many of these questions can be teased from the bones (from telltale signs of injuries caused by hard work, or of serious infections), and from DNA. The Bonn-Oberkassel burial is particularly fascinating, because the earliest-known dog in the world lay with two people, perhaps its master and mistress.

At fourteen thousand years ago, the Bonn-Oberkassel beast is a very ancient dog indeed. But was it a dog or its close wild relative, a wolf? Distinguishing dogs from wolves is notoriously difficult, especially when the surviving bones are fragmentary, as they usually are. Domestic dogs are generally smaller. Their teeth and skulls display minor differences from those of wolves. To tell the two apart is challenging at best, so the experts have turned to a statistical tool known as discriminant function analysis. The researchers have designed a classifier that combines measurements from the bones from known wolves and domesticated dogs to produce spreads of measurements around an average, so that a jaw such as that from Bonn-Oberkassel can be compared with the averages for both wild and domestic canids. Zooarchaeologist Norbert Benecke compared the Oberkassel jaw with other archaeological finds and with bones from Greenland wolves and specimens from zoos, even from Australian dingoes. He found that it belonged firmly in the dog category, making this find—alas, sadly incomplete after the passage of a century—the earliest-known domestic dog yet known.[2]

Is Oberkassel the earliest dog in the world? Certainly not, for the changeover took hold in many locations at a time when major environmental changes caused by rapid warming at the end of the Ice Age were under way. At present, the Bonn-Oberkassel beast is the earliest known and, lying alongside a human couple, suggests an intimate human-animal relationship, at minimum one of companionship. By fourteen thousand years ago, dogs begin to turn up in other places, among them, settlements in the Dnieper River Basin on the Central Russian Plain. Two nearly complete skulls are about the same size as those of modern-day Great Danes, large beasts that could possibly have been wolves held in captivity, or even wolf-dogs. There are other dog finds from the Ukraine, but what is striking is that the size of dog bones falls sharply after fifteen thousand years ago, especially among specimens from Southwest Asia dating to around nine thousand to ten thousand years ago, by which time domesticated dogs were commonplace and significantly smaller than wolves.

Eleven Thousand Years of STDs, Canine Style

Dogs suffer from a transmittable genital cancer, a sexually transmitted disease (STD) that causes bleeding genitals or forms grotesque tumors in canines wherever they live. This contagious cancer first appeared in a dog that lived about eleven thousand years ago. Unlike other cancers, which die with the patient, this sexually transmitted cancer passed to other dogs during the victim's mating activities while it was still alive. A team of researchers sequenced this cancer genome, which carries about two million mutations, far more than in most human cancers, which have between a thousand and five thousand.[3] They used an infected Australian Aboriginal camp dog and a spaniel from Brazil, two beasts separated by more than sixteen thousand kilometers (ten thousand miles). The genetic makeup of the tumors from both animals was remarkably similar. By using a single mutation, known to accumulate through time, they were able to estimate that the cancer first appeared about eleven thousand years ago, when agriculture was taking hold in Southwest Asia and the

Ice Age was in full retreat. They also compared DNA from modern tumor cells to the genotypes of 1,106 coyotes, dogs, and wolves. They believe that the original cancer-carrying beast may have resembled an Alaskan malamute or husky, with a short gray-brown or black coat. The sex of the animal is unknown, but most likely it was a relatively inbred individual.

Transmittable cancer is commonplace among today's dogs, but it existed among a single isolated dog population until about five hundred years ago. Since then, the cancer has spread widely around the world, perhaps carried by dogs that accompanied ships on global voyages during the European Age of Discovery. The tumor mutation rates showed that the Australian and Brazilian dogs' cancer cells separated about 460 years ago.

Cancers, both in animals and in humans, arise when a single cell acquires mutations that cause it to produce more copies of itself. The cancer cells can then metastasize to other parts of the body. But for them to leave the bodies of their original hosts and spread to other individuals is very rare indeed. The only other known transmittable cancer is a fast-moving facial cancer found in a carnivorous marsupial, the Tasmanian devil, spread by biting.

The unknown canine ancestor that hosted transmissible cancer has passed us a genome to help cancer researchers better understand the factors that drive the evolution of many types of cancer. Above all, these researchers have an opportunity to understand what processes cause cancers to become transmissible and that could, one day, arise in either animals or humans.

We'll never know why a man and a woman were buried with their dog fourteen thousand years ago, for the intangibles of the past vanish within generations. Was it a faithful companion, a protector, or a beast valued in the hunt? Was it killed to accompany its owners into the other world or did it die somewhat later? Once again, the archaeological record is silent. That it was cherished is a certainty, for the mourners took the trouble to inter it with those who were presumably its owners. At the moment, this is the earliest dog burial known, but more important, it is the first in a tradition of dog burials that survived through thousands of years in different societies, whether those of hunters or farmers.

After the Ice Age

IT MAY BE NO coincidence that the first domesticated dogs appear at a time when the grip of the last Ice Age cold snap was loosening. Within a few thousand years, rapid warming and environmental shifts had wrought profound changes in hunting societies over huge tracts of the world, from western and northern Europe, across Eurasia, and into Southwest Asia. Natural global warming rapidly shrank the great ice sheets that mantled Scandinavia, the Alps, and what is now Canada. Sea levels rose, continental shelves vanished under the ocean, and temperatures climbed. The northern world changed profoundly as ice sheets and open steppe retreated northward and gave way to more closed-in woodland and forest.

Thousands of hunters and foragers adjusted to these environmental changes in various ways. Some hunting bands moved northward from sheltered valleys in southwestern France and northern Spain and into the more open terrain of areas such as the Paris Basin and northern Germany, where they continued to hunt reindeer and other Ice Age animals, as they had always done.[4] Others moved to newly exposed coasts and to lakes formed by the retreating ice and became fisher folk and fowlers. Many groups stayed where they were and adapted to lives where wild plant food became as important as game. The prey they hunted was no longer reindeer and other cold-loving animals, but red deer and other forest beasts, taken by patient stalking and with bow and arrow. In a changing world where solitary prey, birds on the wing, and waterfowl assumed great importance, the dog came into its own and became far more than a companion—this at a time when no one cultivated the soil or herded animals. For the first time, it served as a true hunting partner in ways that overcame the limitations and size of the human hunter.

In an era of smaller, more elusive game, the dog's matchless sense of smell and silent tracking abilities paid rich dividends when the hunter was pursuing forest deer or small rodents. A well-trained hunting dog could flush waterfowl and recover shot prey from lakes and rivers. Today, there are numerous breeds of "hunting dogs" (among them hounds, retrievers, and terriers) or gun dogs. Some dogs track game by their scent. "Sight hounds" are breeds, such as whippets, that have acute sight and can run fast. They course prey from a distance, pursue, and kill it. Spaniels are adept at flushing out game for a hunter, while terriers are skilled at locating dens and capturing bolting inhabitants. Retrievers are excellent swimmers, which makes them ideal for retrieving waterfowl as well as birds on land. All these breeds, and many others, result from selective breeding by their owners.

There were, of course, none of these breeds twelve to fifteen thousand years ago, but constant association with hunters and patient training, almost certainly using rewards, would have adapted dogs into a useful tool for the hunt. The key word may be *companion*, for it seems unlikely that dogs did much of the killing. A hunter would have known his dog intimately and as well as, if not better than, his quarry. He would have recognized the telltale signs when the dog sensed a deer or some other hidden quarry, even a bear. However, in a world where more and more food came from birds of all kinds, especially waterfowl, dogs would have been invaluable for retrieving kills made among dense thickets or on the water. The hunters must have trained their dogs to remain under control, to wait quietly when sent to retrieve. Animals with "soft mouths," who were willing to please and obey, would have been ideal for retrieving game unharmed, without consuming it at once. Sometimes they would have watched the bird fall. At others, they would have listened for directions from the hunter, who would have stayed on shore as the dog swam into deeper water. The reward back at camp would have been, perhaps, a bird or parts of the quarry.

All this is a hypothetical projection back over many thousands of years, but it gains traction when one considers the hunting weapons of the day. The Cro-Magnons and other Late Ice Age hunters used antler and bone-tipped spears, but their descendants adopted much lighter

hunting weaponry that reflected both more forested landscapes and also
the need to hunt birds and other small game over land and water. They
developed lethal arrows tipped with small, razor-sharp stone arrow-
heads known to archaeologists as microliths (from the Greek *micros*,
for "small"; *lithos*, for "stone"). Thousands of microliths have come
from European hunting sites dating to between 10,000 and 6000 BCE. At
a long-used hunting camp on the edge of a glacial lake at Star Carr in
northeastern England dating to about 8500 BCE, the inhabitants hunted
a wide variety of mammals, including red and roe deer, as well as waterfowl, including ducks. From this settlement has come a dog skull whose
carbon isotope readings reveal a diet that may have included waterfowl,
fish, mollusks, plant foods, and deer meat.[5] At Vedbaek, across the
North Sea in Denmark, a well-known hunting site of 5300 to 4500 BCE,
the inhabitants were highly efficient hunters who relied on a very broad
array of game and plant foods, and on fish. Here again, microliths
were commonplace. Two dog skulls come from the site, one found in a
grave.

Over many centuries, dogs became companions and hunting partners in a world of wetlands and forests. They were also guards, and
some may even have carried or pulled loads, a common role for them in
ancient North America, but there are no signs of this occurring as early
as, say, ten thousand years ago. One should also note that dogs were
sometimes themselves eaten. There are many instances from Danish
hunting camps and other locations of dog bones being cracked open for
marrow and skulls exhibiting chopping marks.

The Ritual Dog

QUITE APART FROM COMPANIONSHIP or partnership in the hunt, or even
faithful service as a pack dog, dogs clearly had spiritual associations
in many ancient societies—if burials are any guide. Such connections
cannot be discerned in the mirror of the intangible after thousands
of years, but we know that dogs had powerful mythic associations in
Mesopotamia and Ancient Egypt, and among the Romans and in Greek
society. Hindus consider dogs as the guardians of Heaven and Hell.

The Dominican order of monks has adopted a black-and-white dog as its symbol—in Latin, *domini canes*, "dogs and hounds of the Lord." The Norse believed that a bloodstained watchdog named Garmr guarded the gates of Hell.

As we have seen, dog burials began at least fourteen thousand years ago. The Bonn-Oberkassel dog lay in a double grave. At Ain Mallaha, in Israel, an immature dog or possibly a wolf puppy lay in an eleven-thousand-year-old grave of an older person, whose hand rested on the chest of the small beast.[6] Another Israeli site, at Hayonim Terrace, yielded two dogs buried with people between 9000 and 8500 BCE. Dog interments became positively commonplace in later times. At Skateholm, in Sweden, fourteen dogs lay interred in a cemetery, four of them lying with people; one, with a deliberately broken neck, placed atop the legs of a woman. Some dog burials lay with grave goods and were scattered with red ocher.

Dogs arrived in the Americas with the first human settlers, some of the few domesticated animals available to the Native Americans. Their genetic diversity confirms that they didn't originate there, but they acquired powerful ritual associations, reflected, once again, in deliberate burial. Examples abound, among them three dog burials dating to about 6500 BCE from a long-occupied hunter-gatherer site at Koster, on the Illinois River in the Midwest, each deposited in a shallow pit apparently without much ceremony. The densest concentration of dog burials comes from archaeological sites in the Green River Valley of Kentucky, where at least 111 interments have come from 11 shell mounds, 28 of them with humans. There are also major concentrations in the central Tennessee River Valley in Alabama.

We know of canine ritual roles from carefully preserved oral traditions collected by anthropologists and others. The best known are those of the Cherokee of the southeastern United States, sometimes known as the Dog Tribe. The Cherokee's sacred dog restored order and harmony in the face of chaos. It rebalanced humans with the forces of their world. The same animal created a path to the spirit world, acted as a judge of ethical behavior, and ensured that rituals were carried out properly. Above all, dogs protected humanity and guided it on its way to the Underworld, which gave dogs a profound association with death and the West, the realm of the dead and the night sky.

The notion of restoring order and balance may well have been the reason for ancient dog burials in many societies. Sacrificing a dog to act as judge and to guide a deceased individual who had committed some form of ritual transgression might have restored spiritual balance to a community. To place a dog at the head or at the face of the deceased, where the soul left the body, would symbolize how dogs acted as ritual leaders. The Cherokee sometimes buried dogs with deceased shamans, perhaps to guide these especially powerful souls away from the realms of the living.

We've lived in close association with dogs for some fifteen thousand years, a relationship that began among hunters facing the challenges of a rapidly warming world. From the beginning, the close ties between dogs and people may well have forged even closer spiritual associations that were to endure in changing forms for thousands of years. Dogs and humans became partners in daily life long before widespread droughts and a variety of other compelling factors turned hunting bands in southwestern Asia, and soon afterward elsewhere, into farmers and herders about twelve thousand years ago. And it was then that the relationship between people and animals changed history dramatically as new domesticated animals assumed dominant roles in human lives.

The Farming Revolution

CHAPTER 4

Down on the First Farms

Hallan Çemi, eastern Turkey, c. 10,000 BCE. The village has remained at the same location for many generations. Circular huts squat around an open space, crowded in by hillsides covered with oak forest. Beyond the settlement, the forest gives way to more open woodland that extends to the Tigris River in the distance. Small wooden pens stand among the dwellings, where a few young sows and their piglets lie in the sun. Strips of drying deer and gazelle meat hang from nearby racks next to wicker storage bins filled with last year's acorns and pistachios. Two hunters return home, carrying the carcass of a wild boar suspended from a pole between their shoulders. A third hefts a bound and squealing female piglet, which he releases into a pen to join a sow and her young. The men quickly dismember the boar, adding strips of flesh to the drying racks and setting aside the head and neck for the evening meal.

Drought and Domestication

TWELVE THOUSAND YEARS AGO, a profound revolution in human life began in Southwest Asia, during a time of dramatic climatic change. For millennia, small bands of hunters and foragers had dwelt in an arid world, constantly on the move, their lives anchored to sparse water sources. The landscape was edible to people who knew it intimately— for food, such people had drought-resistant grasses and tubers, deer, rabbits. Above all, they preyed on the gazelle, a small desert antelope that migrated north in spring and south in fall and gave them a relatively predictable food supply. Then, about fifteen thousand years ago, global warming really took hold as the Ice Age loosened its grip. The climate became warmer and somewhat wetter. What had been semiarid scrubland now supported large tracts of oak, olive, and pistachio trees. Lush meadows nurtured dense stands of wild barley and wheat. So rich were the nut harvests, and so abundant were migrating gazelle, that many peoples settled in much larger communities of several hundred people, which they occupied year round for generations. This was a very different way of life from the existence of their highly mobile ancestors, but like that of their predecessors, it was a life brilliantly calibrated to the realities of their environment.

Between about 14,500 and 13,000 years ago, generations of hunters and foragers lived so well that they founded much larger settlements. They began to bury their dead in cemeteries. The deceased wore seashells and other exotic ornaments that may have reflected more elaborate social organization, as well as a profound reverence for ancestors, those who had occupied the same territory in earlier generations. The warmth and increased rainfall did not last long. About thirteen thousand years ago, a thirteen-hundred-year-long cold drought cycle parched Southwest Asia, known to climatologists as the Younger Dryas, named after an alpine tundra flower. Colder and drier conditions rippled across once well-watered, food-rich landscapes. Many groups responded to greater aridity and nut harvest shortfalls by abandoning permanent settlements and resuming mobile lifeways. The persistent droughts forced people to adapt to a world of more finite food supplies scattered over the landscape in irregular patches. Forests retreated in the face of aridity; wild grass harvests plummeted. Gazelle hunting and more intensive processing of grains and legumes kept society going. Grinding stones for processing plant foods now abounded. These were the centuries when communities across this region of diverse landscapes started cultivating wild grasses in a deliberate attempt to extend their range. They also turned to familiar gregarious ungulates, which relied, just as people did, on predictable water supplies. Again, close juxtaposition of animals to humans became more prevalent. This time the outcome was not companionship, but full domestication of some of the most commonplace of today's farm animals: pigs, goats, and sheep.

Hunters became farmers—no longer on the move, but anchored to fields, flocks, herds, and grazing ranges. The needs of animals transformed the familiar tenor of daily life. Human societies were never the same again. Climate change and drought were not, of course, the only factors behind what has been called the Agricultural Revolution, but they were powerful catalysts for a world in which animals ultimately transformed human society beyond recognition, made cities and civilizations possible, and helped create a global world. Permanent settlement, ownership of herds and individual animals, inheritance, and control of grazing ranges—all these were imperatives, partially imposed by the needs of animal management, that helped change the course of history.

Domesticated Pigs or Merely Managed Ones?

SOME TWELVE THOUSAND YEARS ago, the settlement known to archaeologists as Hallan Çemi lay in the oak-forested eastern foothills of the Taurus Mountains.[1] Here, the people relied not on wild cereals, but on nut harvests, forest game, and on the ubiquitous gazelle. They hunted both wild goats and sheep, killing mainly older beasts, as one might expect when stalking game among trees. But perhaps their most important quarry was the pig. *Sus scrofa* is a forest animal, adapted to hilly terrain covered with mature trees. Swine feed off leaves and branches, plow and tunnel in the soil, and consume the undergrowth. The hunters would, of course, have had a close familiarity with the home ranges and daily routines of wild pigs, with their eating and sleeping habits. They would have known that a sow with her newly born piglets retires to a leafy nest and remains there for about a week or more before rejoining the group. They would have been wary of fierce males, always formidable adversaries, defending their young. Once the male was out of the way, young sows were easier prey, especially in their nests. Any sow can suckle piglets, so to kill the mother and then capture the piglets and take them back home would have been relatively easy. Once penned, young piglets are soon tamed, and bond readily with humans. These may—and one stresses the word *may*—have been the first farm animals of all, because they were easily controlled when young.

Piglets are easy, but growing pigs are much harder to control than goats or sheep, especially the adult males, which can become danger-ously aggressive. So we cannot be absolutely sure that the Hallan Çemi pigs were fully domesticated. Inhabitants of the settlement were cer-tainly hunting pigs on a fairly large scale, but the bones from the site are an enigma in that they fall between the sizes of both wild and domestic forms. Unlike adult wild goats and sheep killed during hunting, 43 per-cent of the Hallan Çemi swine were slaughtered before they were a year old and 10 percent when they were less than six months. A strong eleven-to-four male bias dominated the culling—the pigs being slaughtered on site in the village rather than elsewhere—as with wild goats and sheep. Such data strongly hint at domestication, or at least systematic manage-ment, for tamed pigs have many advantages. They are fecund and fertile, grow fast, and produce protein more rapidly than other domesticated animals. But being difficult to control, they might have made a poor choice of farm animal, especially for people collecting or growing cereal crops such as wheat and barley, which pigs targeted voraciously.

We know from modern experience across the world that there are some relatively easy ways to manage pigs.[2] One is to let the animals roam freely, visiting them only occasionally. Another is to allow them free range during the day, then drive them back to the settlement at night. In both instances, the corralled pigs have contact with wild groups and with their boars, even if their loyalties now lie elsewhere and their diet is somewhat changed. As time went on, the people may have kept sows and their young but acquired new stock by allowing these to breed in the wild. Why would they have done this? These were difficult times throughout Southwest Asia, when droughts were devastating nut crops after centuries of abundance during which human populations rose. Deer and other game became scarcer as people competed for food, so to corral young pigs and find some way of increasing the food supply as a form of risk management may have made sense. The Hallan Çemi bones reveal systematic killing of the young, mostly of males, as if cull-ing of surplus breeding animals were commonplace, presumably for meat. But were these domesticated animals or merely closely managed beasts that were still partially in the wild?

We may never know, for there are limits to what fragmentary pig bones can tell us. Some tantalizing clues come from the other side of the world, from traditional pig management practices in highland and lowland New Guinea, where pig husbandry has been a central part of subsistence economies for many centuries.[3] The New Guineans manage pig reproduction in a variety of ways, but captive pigs are often the progeny of wild boars and domestic sows, with the surplus males being castrated. Breeding tame sows with wild boars would have been easier in earlier times than it is today, when agriculture was less intensified and more forested land was close at hand. Crossing domesticated boars and sows with no contact with the wild would have required much higher human population densities, many more pigs in village herds, and regular exchanges of animals from one community to another. Such transactions would have been laden with social consequences in societies where individually owned animals were a novelty.

Full domestication involving the exclusive breeding of domestic herds may have taken many generations to achieve, especially when people and pigs competed, as they did, for cereal crops that were the staple of farming communities throughout Southwest Asia. This may be why pigs—which were, after all, prized mainly for their meat and for their social value—came fully into their own only after goats and sheep had become the farm animals of choice from Turkey to Egypt and beyond.[4]

Mouflon and Bezoar

THE HUNTERS WALK OPENLY *across the grassy clearing in the morning sun, wrapped up well against the chill. Deep shadows give way to bright sunlight where the mouflon flock grazes peacefully, the red brown of their coats glowing softly in the still-tentative warmth. A ram with magnificent, curling horns looks up uninterestedly at the familiar visitors, who pass close to the nearest ewes. One of the females moves slowly up to the men and almost nudges a young man armed with a bow and arrow. He reaches down to pet her head, but she moves away, lingering a few meters off, totally unafraid. The flock moves closer, still grazing as the hunters walk slowly away. No one in the group remarks on the close*

encounter, for they see it virtually every time they approach the sheep in
clear view. There's an easy familiarity between mouflon and human.

NEITHER WILD GOATS NOR sheep are dangerous or frightening prey; nor,
as far as we know, did they inspire mythic tales of danger and fierce
attacks in the past. As with other ungulates, their defense was to flee,
and then only when they perceived an imminent threat. Those who
hunted them had observed their prey for generations and knew well that
walking unthreateningly in the open rarely alarmed the flocks.

Today's goats and sheep retain qualities that may have been more
marked ten millennia ago. John Mionczynski is a modern-day expert
on goat packing. He takes his beasts far into the backcountry of the
western United States—they are strong, hardworking, and disciplined
animals.[5] Above all, he says, they are friendly and very adaptable, comfortable in cold landscapes and in semiarid terrain. Goats are inquisitive
creatures, so much so that Mionczynski and many others have experienced wild goats and sheep walking right up to them in remote places.
Like humans, caprines are gregarious and intensely curious. They are
more intelligent than many people believe and also recognize both other
beasts and individual people after repeated encounters. These qualities could have enhanced close contacts between wild goats, sheep, and
humans at a time of drought and enhanced propinquity across desic-
cated landscapes. A form of easy coexistence could have developed that
led, almost inevitably, to domestication. No one knows why people
turned to sheep and goats, but like Hallan Çemi's pigs, they may have
created flocks and herds as a form of what we would call risk management against food shortages.

The ancestors of today's goats and sheep still survive today in remote
mountainous terrain, though it is decimated by centuries of intensive
hunting. The West Asiatic mouflon, the wild sheep, was a native of a
wide area of southwestern Asia, including Turkey and the Caucasus
Mountains, even the Balkans, where it disappeared three thousand years
ago.[6] Mouflon are agile beasts, predominantly grazers, well adapted to
steep terrain. In contrast, the stocky Persian wild goat, sometimes called

the bezoar, is at home amid cliffs and rugged slopes, using its climbing ability to escape predators. Bezoar are browsers and grazers, capable of exploiting a wider range of foods than the mouflon. Both wild goats and sheep are nonterritorial, gregarious ungulates that spend most of their time in hierarchical groups. Rams compete strongly for ewes, with a dominant male acquiring a harem of several females, which are generally smaller.

Close observation and daily familiarity are givens in any scenario for domestication. But what actually happened? Here, alas, scientific data are hard to come by, which means that we have to rely on what we know about the behavior of modern animals and wild ancestors. In other words, we fall back on intelligent speculation. We can be certain that there must have been numerous occasions when hunters would capture a young mouflon, perhaps several of them. What would be more logical than to corral them separately from their original flock as a convenient way of having food close at hand? We can be certain, too, that sometimes the corralling worked, but more frequently it probably did not.

We can develop the hypothetical scenario further. As generations unfolded, so wild goats and sheep lived out their lives within easy hunting range in landscapes where sparse water supplies nourished animals and people alike. Inevitably, the number of captures gradually increased. Corralling young beasts became a familiar routine in what one can only describe as a form of "predomestication." The imprisoned beasts were still technically wild, but now formed herds or flocks that spent most of their time close to human settlements, perhaps in simple enclosures that protected them from predators at night.

An imaginary situation, one admits, but the only one that fits what we know about goat and sheep behavior. This was something very different from the domestication of dogs, which was a much more social process. Here, in the final analysis, the primary interest on the human side must have been access to a reliable meat supply in a time of major climatic change, when both game populations and wild plant foods became much harder to find during prolonged droughts. Previously, hunting groups throughout Southwest Asia had harvested hundreds of gazelle during their spring and fall migrations to new pastures. People still relied heavily on gazelle, but goats and sheep were about to assume a central role in local life.

What about Gazelle?

WHY DIDN'T THE FARMERS just domesticate the ubiquitous gazelle? Gazelle (*Gazella sp.*) are some of the fastest-moving antelope on earth.[7] They are small animals, usually live in herds, and thrive on coarse semiarid vegetation. From the ancient hunter's perspective, they had one priceless and relatively predictable characteristic: They migrated in enormous numbers northward in late spring and early summer, when in prime condition, and then returned south in the fall. For thousands of years, hunters, then farmers, harvested migrating gazelle in mass kills that provided meat for the rest of the year.

A large enclosure of close-set wooden poles lies near a small stream. Gaps in the fence open into deep pits just outside. Every year, the hunters wait for migrating gazelle, which arrive in a packed mass to drink on their way to summer pastures where the young are born. The hunters watch for the telltale dust clouds raised by the approaching herd. The hunters, spaced out with their weapons, shout and wave their clubs and bows, while women stand and flap skin cloaks. Dogs bark at the terrified herd. The frightened antelope stampede into the enclosed space. They try to leap over the fence, crowd for the entrances, where they fall into the waiting holes, breaking their legs and struggling in agony. The hunters move in with clubs and spears, killing dozens of beasts. Meanwhile, others shoot razor-sharp arrows into the teeming herds inside the palisade. The butchery starts immediately. Animal after animal is skinned, then expertly dismembered, the flesh cut into strips and dried for use year-round.

FOR ALL THE SUSTAINED contact with gazelles, corralling them was nearly impossible, as they were jumpers. They also had a profound fear of all predators, including humans. We can be certain, however, that the hunters captured young fawns. None other than the famed African explorer

Sir Richard Burton observed of the Bedouin that they "so succeed in taming the young things that they will follow their owner like dogs, and amuse themselves by hopping on his shoulders."[8] Such casual pet keeping was very different from maintaining significant numbers of adult animals in captivity and breeding them, which was much easier with goats and sheep.

Sheep, Goats, and Survivor Curves

THE DELIBERATE CORRALLING OF young goats and sheep must have occurred in many places. We can only imagine what happened. At first the captures may have been casual, perhaps like those of young gazelle. But in the case of the bezoar and mouflon, cherishing a few newborns or abandoned young ones gradually turned into something quite different, once it became clear that these relatively docile and quite intelligent beasts flourished in captivity. Now the hunters separated young beasts from flocks and herds, selecting them carefully for their docility and daily behavior. Capturing such beasts would have been relatively simple, given the ease with which humans and wild caprines interacted on a regular basis.

Once the animals were penned, the ingredients of a founder herd were in place, probably within a relatively short time. Its members lived under very different conditions than those of the wild. Now the physical contact with humans was constant and intimate, the incentives for trust and mutual understanding greatly enhanced. Their new masters and mistresses controlled the animals' every movement in situations where their charges were already accustomed to hierarchy and leadership in the wild. The animals enjoyed immediate benefits: greater protection from predators, shelter from cold and heat when needed, and much better access to grazing grounds and very different foods. There were now immediate shifts in selection pressures from those in the wild.

Generations of researchers have excavated farming villages and early towns from Turkey and across Southwest Asia to the Nile Valley, yet we still know frustratingly little about the changing relationship between animals and humans after domestication. A palimpsest of

archaeological sites, fragmentary animal bones, and what zooarchaeologists call "survivorship curves" tells an incomplete story (see sidebar
"Studying Survivorship Curves"). Such research attacks fundamental
questions. What were the goals of herd management in the early millennia of goat and sheep domestication? Were animals kept for meat, which
would have meant that most young surplus males were slaughtered
when they reached an optimum weight? Alternatively, did the herders
manage their animals for their wool or hair? Under these circumstances,
male and female adults would have been culled, both being productive
in management terms. But if the herders were after milk, most males
would have been slaughtered at a very young age, to maximize the
amount of milk available for human consumption. Unfortunately, it's
very difficult to establish dairying practices from animal bones.

Studying Survivorship Curves

Can you tell a bison from a musk ox, an African eland from an
impala, or—and this is where it gets really challenging—a wild goat
or sheep from a domesticated one? Zooarchaeologists, the special-
ists who study animal bones from archaeological sites, find this hard
enough with complete body parts. But when the people who butchered the animals in the first place literally cut the skeletons into ribbons for flesh, marrow, sinews, and so on, the task becomes even
harder. Fortunately, distinctive body parts such as skulls, jaws, and
the articular end of limb bones make most identifications relatively
straightforward as far as wild animals and fully domesticated beasts
are concerned. The shadowy transition period between, say, wild and
domesticated sheep or pigs is especially challenging, owing to the
often subtle changes between wild and tamed beasts. This is without taking into account sexual dimorphism (size variations between
males and females) and other such factors. The most effective way
of looking at the changes in human behavior toward animals during
these millennia is to create survivorship curves, using large samples

of upper and lower jaws, where the teeth supply information on the age of individual animals at the time when they were killed or slaughtered.

Teeth provide an almost continuous guide to the age of an individual animal from birth to old age. Immature teeth appear first, followed by mature ones, which erupt in sequence. For example, if a group of hunters drives a bison herd over a cliff, the result will be what zooarchaeologists call a "catastrophic age profile," with few older individuals. An "attritional profile," with overrepresentation of young and old beasts and few prime-age animals relative to their abundance in living populations, could result from spear hunting. Both these profiles are different from those found with a domesticated herd or flock, where the meat supply is controlled. Here you might find an abundance of prime animals with newly erupted mature teeth and fewer older animals. This reflects the reality of too many surplus males. Some may have been castrated, with most consumed for their meat and by-products; older females might have been killed when they were no longer of any use for breeding, milk, or (with males, too) draft purposes.

The situation becomes even more complicated at the threshold of domestication, when you might find a combination of selective hunting and systematic killing of surplus domesticated males. The only way one can figure out the meaning of such profiles is by working with large samples and assessing their meaning in the context of the excavated occupations as a whole. Survivorship research, carried out on goats, sheep, and pigs, is still in its infancy, relatively speaking, but shows great promise for the future.

Many variables act on survivorship curves, especially for subsistence herders, who rely heavily on their animal for food and raw materials, while at the same time being well aware of the risks that could decimate their herds. They tend, for example, to space out the slaughtering of rams as a hedge against food shortages. Herders have to respond to a wide range of environmental, political, and social realities, which can change dramatically within a short period. For instance, just the movement of herds from summer to winter pastures can skew curves obtained from a single site. Circumstances also change dramatically when the herders are engaged in the business of supplying meat and other products to larger urban populations, which was the case in later times.

We can track some of the changes, at least in general terms, from a series of Turkish sites that have yielded large numbers of goat and sheep bones.[9] For instance, the inhabitants of Asikli Höyük, a large village in central Turkey occupied during the second half of the eighth millennium BCE, slaughtered caprines between the ages of one to three years. There are no signs of size decrease or other telltale indications of domestication. Perhaps the animals were not under intensive human management and still associated with wild breeding populations. At contemporary Süberde, the herders killed most animals between one and three years, most of these between twenty-one and twenty-four months. Süberde's sheep are smaller than wild sheep beasts, probably living and breeding under human management. The earliest definitive evidence for a deliberate strategy of culling young adult male sheep, especially larger rams, comes from Erbaba Höyük, northwest of Süberde, occupied during the seventh millennium BCE.

By 6000 BCE, farmers over wide areas of Southwest Asia followed a strategy of herding goats and sheep for both meat and dairy products, often in landscapes outside the natural habitats of their larger wild ancestors. Surplus rams provided tender flesh, but goats survived longer, perhaps because of their much-valued hair.

Changing Beasts

QUITE WHEN THE CHANGES that distinguished domestic from wild goats and sheep began, we don't know, but they were gradual and probably took hold around and after 9000 BCE, as flocks became larger.[10] The danger of predators receded dramatically. The need for camouflage, so important in the wild, would have vanished in founder herds. Colors would have become more variable. The shape and size of the animals changed as agility and large body size became less important. Short-limbed, smaller beasts would have had a much better chance of surviving when domesticated. Horns, once valued as defense weapons against attackers and in competition for mates, became smaller, more varied, and sometimes were absent altogether. Goats and sheep in the wild had a heightened awareness of danger and were more aggressive toward one another during mating season or when defending territory than were domestic beasts. The latter no longer needed the familiar defense mechanisms of the wild.

Both goats and sheep had been seasonal feeders, moving to different locales in spring and fall. Now the pattern changed as their human masters preferred more open terrain, which had previously exposed the beasts to predators. Humans also restricted herd movement, which led to changes in limb size and proportions, such as a shortening of the extremities. Both animals became somewhat more sedentary and therefore more easily controlled. With a less mobile existence, the availability of food and water differed greatly from that in the wild. Richer, more stable environments may have resulted in less herd competition, and to automatic selection for accelerated sexual maturity, greater fertility, and increased fat storage. From the beginning the herders may have culled surplus males over and above those needed for breeding purposes. For one thing, rams were more aggressive and harder to control. The age and sex composition of herds changed dramatically, with major variations in reproduction patterns. Rams could now start reproducing much earlier, long before dominance competitions in the wild allowed. They became smaller; their horns changed and became reduced in size.

Tracking the subtle changes that transformed wild into domestic beasts is extremely difficult. We have only fragmentary bones to document herding practices. It's an ineluctable fact of biological life that many more males are born in domesticated herds of all kinds than are needed for breeding purposes. This means that there are always fairly compelling reasons to cull surplus males before maturity, or to castrate them. However, other factors come into play. Was the herd merely a source of meat, or were its owners interested in milk or wool? Did the landscape provide sufficient winter feed to nourish both breeding stock and an excess of males? These were important questions when individual ownership and animal management were transforming farming and herding societies in profound ways.

The domestication of goats and sheep changed the dynamics of human life in fundamental ways from the beginning. Some values remained the same. Respect for animals endured, for flocks and herds were small. Every beast was valued, and each was recognized individually. These gregarious creatures became part of the family in a real sense. They were guarded carefully, driven to pasture daily, shorn for their hair and wool, with their surplus males culled for meat to control the size of the group, and their pens kept close to or even as part of human dwellings. There was a strong element of sustainability. Those who herded goats and sheep were well aware of the dangers of overgrazing, of stripping vegetation promiscuously from the landscape. At the same time, a profound sea change was afoot. For tens of thousands of years, game was there for the taking, the property of everyone; the hunter's only obligation was to share his kill with others. The animal-human relationship involved respect and ritual that treated beasts as vibrant players in the cosmos. Even when domesticated flocks and herds were small, they represented something new in the subsistence equation. Goats, pigs, and sheep became property in ways that game animals never were. They were owned and cared for and passed on to one's children and relatives. These were the creatures, other than game, that provided meat and raw materials and tied people to fields and grazing grounds. The investment of time for herders was entirely different, devoted as they were almost entirely to animal care and protection, activities that often dovetailed with cereal cultivation. Almost immediately, these new responsibilities caused changes in what were now village societies anchored to their land by their animals and crops. New undercurrents coursed through society—issues of inheritance, of grazing rights, and of ownership came into play. Inevitably, too, respected members of herds and flocks became social instruments used to seal marriages and other relationships. In due course, they became wealth, counted by the household head, and, inevitably, symbols of prestige and power.

CHAPTER 5

Working Landscapes

DOMESTICATION CHANGED THE WORLD, its landscapes, animals—and humanity. About ten thousand years ago—the precise date will never be known—numerous deliberate acts, such as the corralling of young ungulates, turned animal-human relationships on end. Over a surprisingly brief compass of generations what had been a symbolic partnership involving giving and taking became one of dominance, of mastership. Humans were now the masters, so the role of animals changed. They became objects of individual ownership, tangible symbols of wealth, and powerful social instruments. But in so becoming, they cast a profound influence on the nature of changing human societies. Let's explore some of the parameters. (I've left cattle until later, as they changed history, in the long term, in different ways. Being larger, sometimes ferocious beasts, wild oxen were harder to domesticate and far more demanding to herd.)

Gregarious Communities

MANY EARLY FARMING SETTLEMENTS engaged in subsistence herding, where the primary concern was feeding one's family and kin, as well as acquiring individual wealth in animals, with all the social implications that involved. At this point, the relationships between sheepherders and their flocks or herds were relatively intimate. Owners enjoyed a familiarity with a fairly small number of individual beasts, perhaps to the point of giving many of them names and recognizing them individually. Sheep are ardently gregarious and accustomed to close relationships. They tend to stay close to fellow members of their flock, for an individual sheep can become stressed if separated from the others. Flock behavior, which is the secret to managing sheep, develops with four or more sheep. The relationships within flocks are closest among relatives, so ewes and their descendants often form a unit within a larger group.

Unlike gazelle, sheep do not form territories, although they have home ranges. They are not only gregarious, but each flock also tends to follow a leader, often the first animal to move, despite well-developed dominance hierarchies among the members. Shepherds take advantage of this behavior. They know that their beasts can recognize individual human voices, as well as the cries of fellow sheep, and recall them for years. Most important of all, flocks can be "hefted" to a specific pasture, or series of pastures, small areas where they are comfortable grazing for long periods. Sheep are entirely herbivorous. They prefer grass and short roughage and do well in areas with uniform grass coverage, which makes herding them easier. Goats consume branches, leaves, and other vegetation some distance off the ground with ardent voracity. A combination of both sheep and goats could have devastating effects on the landscape, as they eat from dawn to dusk with only short pauses for digestion. So managing them carefully soon became a paramount concern. We can only imagine the ecological damage wrought on fragile, semiarid landscapes by uncontrolled grazing, which must have become apparent within short order to herders living in denuded landscapes.

In a sense, one's sheep flock was an animal community, not accessible to everyone, as was the case with game, but managed and owned by an individual, a family, or a kin group. Most early flocks or herds cannot have been much larger than a few dozen beasts, given the small size of villages, the limited number of shepherds to manage the animals, and the scarcity of winter fodder. In order to protect one's flock, one always lived with the realities of management: the need to keep constant watch when the animals were out during the day, to establish times for milking them, and to guard corrals carefully during the night hours.

Like growing crops, herding goats and sheep is a matter of carefully managed routines—overseeing seasons of breeding and giving birth, rotating grazing so pastures are never denuded, protecting the beasts against predators, culling surplus animals before winter or for important feasts. Behind this endless rhythm—dictated in large part by the passage of the seasons and, in warmer climates, by the availability of water and graze—were practical strategies that continued with virtually no change through thousands of years, regardless of the rise and fall of societies and civilizations. Human life revolved around the life and death of the animals, unexpected diseases that decimated flocks or herds, and the ever-changing demands of kin and social obligation. Simple, utterly pragmatic, and refined by countless generations of experience, subsistence herders, whatever their animals and wherever they lived, relied on practical experience when it came to their beasts. England's Fengate sheep farmers of thirty-five hundred years ago provide dramatic proof.[1]

Fengate and the Realities of Sheepherding

EASTERN ENGLAND, SUMMER, 1500 BCE. *The rising sun casts long shadows an hour after dawn. Light mist hovers near the ground, soon to vanish in the face of warm sunlight. Another long, hot day lies ahead for the herd boys clad in skin cloaks. Their charges huddle together in the byre, mothers and growing lambs crowded by the narrow gateway. One of the youngsters opens the hurdle. The flock pushes forward as the other herd boy urges them gently with soft calls; a dog hovers nearby. The sheep follow their leader, as they always do, to the small pasture, a familiar place where they know they can feed comfortably. As the sun sets hours later, the boys will steer the beasts back to the safety of the homestead in a routine that has never changed over many generations.*

FRANCIS PRYOR, BOTH AN archaeologist and a sheep farmer, has investigated Fengate, a thirty-five-hundred-year-old sheep farming landscape in the low meadows and wetlands of the Fens, in eastern England, near the cathedral city of Peterborough. He believes that the ancient sheep farmers lived amid a "landscape of the mind," a dynamic landscape peopled with the deeds of ancestors and the symbolic associations that populated fields and meadows with benign and hostile spirits, with the unpredictable forces of the supernatural world. Theirs was also a "working landscape," an ever-changing environment that encompassed both physical features such as ditches and hedgerows and intangibles such as the behavior of sheep, herding dogs, and cattle.

People modified the working landscape. They repaired hedges, deepened and maintained ditches, and kept fences and paddocks in good condition. The positioning of fields and trackways, and even of houses and yards, depended on far more than the altitude and slope of the land. Drainage, shade, and soil types were critical factors, so much so that most farmers kept a remarkably accurate map of their land in their heads—they do to this day. For instance, in the flat Fen country of eastern England, farmers had several types of land. Some was floodplain; other areas flooded regularly during the winters. You needed a diversity of land and soil if your beasts were to thrive on good summer pasture in flooded areas and keep dry in the winter. This led to often confusing arrangements for handling stock, which could include establishing and using droveways (trackways for driving animals) that followed field layouts and allowed animals to pass in an orderly fashion from one form of grazing to another.

The same droveways separated individual landholdings and served as boundaries that subdivided what eventually became an organized landscape, seemingly a patchwork of fields, ditches, hedges, and tracks, but easily decipherable to those who used and maintained it. The working landscapes of ancient times, wherever they were located, were both material and social landscapes.

Efficient stock raising relied on carefully monitored grazing that used barriers of all kinds. Hedges and ditches may have kept out wild animals and predators, but they were far more important as a means of controlling grazing, especially in crowded landscapes. Such devices would have allowed individual plots to recover, and permitted dung lying on the surface to break down and become incorporated into the recovering, grazed vegetation. Allowing land to lie fallow for a while also offers some relief from microscopic parasites, such as fluke, that can cause serious problems. If the quality of the grazing was good and abundant, then herds and flocks would have wandered quite widely, with only children or young men controlling them.

Enclosed grazing land tended to develop when flocks became larger, graze was of poorer quality, and land in shorter supply. Much closer control was necessary. For thousands of years, earthworks, sometimes including burial mounds—as was the case in southern Britain—may have served as territorial markers that delineated landholdings, perhaps by kin groups. These mounds, or tumuli, dotted an open landscape where herds and flocks grazed, tended by young men and boys, and watched over by the revered ancestors lying under conspicuous burial mounds. As farming populations rose in number, so the importance of boundaries increased, not just shallow banks and ditches, which even a young lamb can traverse, but substantial hedges. Francis Pryor believes that winter hardwood cuttings taken from nearby forests formed such hedges for thousands of years—tough, easily geminated, and often with their own natural protection in the form of thorns. He points out that such hedges were commonly used many centuries later, during the days of the infamous Enclosure Act of the early nineteenth century CE.

At Fengate, the herders practiced what Pryor calls a carefully "structured mobility."[2] The mobility was vital, but it was far from random. Each winter, the farmers lived on high, flood-free ground, in small farms dominated by a single round house. Both the land and the dwelling might have been occupied for only a generation or so. Come late April or May, the water levels in the nearby marshland fell slowly. Part of each family would move out into the lush, open fen pastures, taking most of their sheep and cattle with them. Young men and children would supervise the herds. In autumn, the now-fattened and well-fed beasts would be driven back to higher ground. This was the season of feasting and ritual, when people gathered from a wide area of surrounding countryside. Animals would be culled, marriages arranged, and livestock exchanged between different families.

The Fengate excavations revealed a landscape divided into a series of blocks separated by ditched driveways (or droveways) that ran perpendicularly down to the flooded land, giving each farmer access to both higher- and lower-lying ground, just as their descendants possessed in medieval times. At first the excavators were unable to follow a driveway to water's edge, but fortunately the construction of a large power station gave them a chance to trace two driveway ditches to the water, where the ditches bifurcated and ran along the boundary between wet and dry terrain. Here was convincing evidence that the people had driven their flocks. Phosphate analyses of the soil in what Pryor was now calling the Main Drove provided evidence of large quantities of deposited manure. This proved that large numbers of animals had passed through the Drove. There were clear signs of extensive trampling by animals where it terminated.

Francis Pryor manages his own sheep within small areas, so he has, effectively, firsthand experience of what it must have been like herding sheep in Fengate times. It was a crowded working landscape, but sheep and other stock are easier to manage when closely confined. This is why modern farmers jam as many animals as possible into a truck. Both cattle and sheep are herd animals, for being a member of a herd gives them a sense of security. Confining the animals within a small space also makes it easier to work with them, and to sort them into different categories. The methods of working different animals vary considerably. Pigs, for example, are often best handled individually, using a piece of wood to push their heads and to steer them in one direction or another. Sheep respond well to dogs, both in the open and in enclosed areas, where wild and domesticated sheep have a tendency to gather into close-knit groups when they sense a threat. Modern-day shepherds call the process of introducing a dog to a herd "dogging." Basically, the shepherd puts the fear of a dog into the sheep so they are clumped and easier to handle. The behavior is entirely natural for the dog and goes back to wolf-pack days, when the junior members of a pack would drive animals up to a top wolf, who would kill them, eat some flesh, and leave the rest for the pack. Pryor believes that dogging goes back deep into the past, to long before the days of medieval monks and the time when Britain supplied wool to much of the European world.

Most traditional ways of managing sheep and other farm animals take advantage of the beasts' instinctive behavior. Droving, batching, confining, inspecting, and sorting sheep was part of herding routine probably long before Fengate times, and surviving field systems reflect this. The farmers of thirty-five hundred years ago were, above all, practical managers who knew that well-nourished, carefully managed animals were the foundation of good stock keeping. Behind their expertise was an intimate knowledge of what sheep and other animals would and would not do, unless one tricked them. A case in point is the placing of gateways in fields. Place them in the middle of the edges, and the sheep will balk. Build the exit at a corner, where the converging fences funnel the animals through the defile, and the flock will pass through readily. From such an exit, the farmer, if he or she wished, could steer the herd into a narrow "race," funneled in by wooden hurdles or some temporary structure. There the flock could have been inspected for age, condition, and so on. The beasts would have passed through the defile and emerged in a three-way gate, which would have allowed the farmer to separate the herd into different categories, perhaps with the help of children using hurdles.

The size of the race would have depended on the number of sheep. Pryor uses a seven-meter (twenty-three-foot) race to handle some two hundred fifty beasts, but there is no means of estimating flock populations in Bronze Age times. He estimates that the entire Fengate field system handled "considerably less than ten thousand animals—even at the height of summer when all lambs were present."[3] The figure for the excavated area of the field system may have been between two thousand and three thousand animals. This, says Pryor, is a reflection not of small-scale subsistence farming, but of something more intensive, perhaps akin to the level of production during the height of the medieval wool trade.

This was an impressive achievement, possibly based on an ancient version of the small and hardy Soay sheep, which behave well in large flocks and yield excellent wool and high-quality meat.

All this worked because of the availability of seasonal grazing and extremely nourishing summer pastures. Between 1800 and 600 BCE, the margins of the Fens provided a superb environment for intensive sheep-herding, the farmers using simple methods that form the basis for much sheep farming to this day. This abundance of sheep might have triggered changes in local society, perhaps differences between individuals and kin groups in terms of wealth in head of sheep. Larger flocks gave their owner greater social influence, in that he or she had the ability to throw

Figure 5.1 *Excavations at Fengate showing the general topography. Courtesy of Francis Pryor.*

feasts, use gifts to reinforce obligations and ties with other people, and create advantageous marriages and other alliances. But when sudden epidemics could wipe out entire flocks in days, wealth in animals was volatile, often transitory. The only protection was to distribute animals across the landscape with fellow kin.

Social differences may have played out in numerous ways, especially in a context where meat consumption was a sign of prestige, and where feasting was an important part of the annual round. At Flag Fen, close to the Fengate field system, Francis Pryor recovered a remarkable series of bronze artifacts, including axes, swords, and a flesh hook that had been cast into the marsh as offerings; these were often bent before being cast into oblivion.[4] We'll never know the significance of these offerings, but they may well have been made to the powerful ancestors, guardians of the land, whose spirits lurked in the dark, symbolically charged waters of the Fenland marshes. Here, as elsewhere, the ties between the living and those who came before, between the supernatural realm and the material world, must have lain at the very core of human existence, defined in part by the flesh of beasts raised on farm and marshland.

Social Instruments

BOTH SHEEP AND GOATS were workaday animals. They provided meat, milk, skins, and wool or hair, plus tallow and other by-products. They were a reliable source of flesh, far more predictable than game, even if hunting continued to be part of the subsistence equation for thousands of years. Surplus males culled from the flock or herd provided a steady meat supply and also important social benefits in farming societies that, in their attitude toward animals, were totally different from hunting peoples. For the first time, people owned beasts other than dogs—not just a single animal, but males and females. These both formed breeding populations that maintained the herd and were also a vital source of social currency: surplus males.

Judging from modern subsistence societies, individual ownership of animals by family and kin transformed society in fundamental ways from the beginning. Those who owned animals possessed assets that passed from one generation to the next. At the same time, the size of a herd became a token of wealth, and often social standing, within a kin group or a settlement. A flock owner might know his animals individually and watch them closely at lambing time, but in the final analysis, the members of his flock were powerful social instruments. Within a very short time, the surplus males from a founder flock assumed important symbolism, especially as gifts, whether given alive or slaughtered for a communal feast. Owners with proliferating flocks or herds acquired social standing and prestige, as animals became wealth on the hoof.

At issue here were wealth and the delicate matter of the inheritance of animals and the pastures upon which they grazed. Unlike a hunter's prey, animals were now tangible property and wealth, as were dwellings and grazing grounds, which had to pass from one generation to the next. Property and rights to land passed through the father or mother's side, following what had to become well-established rules that affected both social and economic status. Land ownership and grazing rights were surely carefully guarded from the beginning, especially among people who knew from hard experience just how devastating voracious small stock could be on the surrounding landscape.

Kin ties had always been important in Ice Age hunting societies. Links between widely separated bands were of paramount importance for survival. Kin could take refuge with other groups after hunting accidents and could make use of another group's territories. But the dynamics changed profoundly with the domestication of animals, for, like cereal cultivators, each community was tied to its land, usually owned by kin groups. Cultural practices were often similar among farmers and herders. Many ancient farming communities possessed farm animals, for full-time herders are, and probably were, rare and almost invariably obtain some grain or grow it to survive in lean times. With both farmers and herders, farming and grazing tracts passed from one generation to the next down through a continuous sequence of descendants whose line of ancestors reached back far into the past. New rules for human existence accompanied the process of adapting to animal domestication, rules that defined the nature of inheritance and drastically enhanced the importance of marriage ties between different families and fellow kin in ways unimaginable among hunting groups.

Marriages and inheritance, whether through the male or female line, became serious business, cemented by careful negotiation and by the exchange of gifts, notably of livestock—bride price. This is where surplus males came in: as gifts to a new couple starting their own flock, as ritual offerings to be sacrificed during marriage ceremonies, or to honor important guests. Deep ties of sharing and mutual obligation were a necessity in all farming societies, especially those with animals, whose welfare often depended on people spreading their beasts widely over the landscape to avoid epidemics, drought, or even human raiders. Now, for the first time, animals became individual property— something to be cherished, valued, and counted—to be given as calculated gifts, not necessarily as currency in the sense we would use the word today, but as part of the equation of survival and wealth accumulation that became central to human life in ways unimaginable among hunters and foragers.

Sheep and goats were never prestigious animals, but their ties to the land, like those of farmers, formed another type of partnership, in which one side provided protection and food, and the other provided its meat and social leverage. Both sides were members of farming societies with deep ties to the landscape, to the spiritual realm of the ancestors. A striking example of this partnership comes from twentieth-century New Guinea.

And Then There Were Cats

Cats were domesticated at least ninety-five hundred years ago, probably from *Felis sylvestris lybica*, the wildcat of western Asia. How domestication occurred is, as always, a mystery, but it may have resulted from wildcats hunting mice and rats feeding on stored grain. The oldest known example is a large eight-month-old cat that lay alongside a deceased man in a grave dating to about 7500 BCE, from a large farming village at Shillourokambos, near Limassol on southern Cyprus.[5]

Unlike other early domesticated animals, independent-minded cats are not highly social. Their relationship with people is more commensal (sometimes commensual) than anything else, but their body shape, especially while kittens, appeals to the nurturing instincts of humans. (A commensal relationship is one where one species benefits, while the other is unaffected.) Cats were known as early as 3700 BCE in Egypt, where they became household pets valued for their successful hunting of both rodents and snakes and were sometimes buried carefully.[6] They were known as *miu* or *miut* ("he or she who mews"). By the New Kingdom (1530–1070 BCE), they appear in tomb paintings hunting with their masters, retrieving bird and fish, or sitting by their mistresses' chairs.

Cats had powerful supernatural associations in Egypt. The cat goddess Bastet protected pregnant women and was patroness of dance and music. She was believed to protect people from disease and demons. Bastet was the personification of the warming rays of the sun, usually depicted as a woman with a cat's head, holding the ankh, a type of cross symbolizing life. Her cult center and temple center were at Bubastis, in the Nile Delta. Many dead pets were mummified and buried, sometimes in a huge Bubastis catacomb, and elsewhere. A tomb discovered at Beni Hasan, in central Egypt, in 1888, contained an estimated eighty thousand cat burials. The Greek historian Diodorus noted in the first century BCE that deceased cats were "treated with cedar oil and such spices as have the quality of imparting a pleasant odour and of preserving the body for a long time."[7] To kill a cat meant a sentence of death, as one unfortunate Roman, who killed one by accident, discovered in 47 BCE, when he was stoned to death.

The Romans also revered cats, sometimes considering them household gods; indeed, they were the only animals allowed into temples. Romans respected them as rodent hunters and also considered them symbols of liberty. Roman armies carried cats with them through Gaul and eventually to Britain, to protect their grain supplies. Today, Rome is home to at least three hundred thousand feral cats, which live in the city's monuments and were granted protection as part of Rome's "bioheritage" in 2001.

Pigs and Ancestors

No ONE KNOWS WHEN people in New Guinea acquired pigs, but they are now a fundamental prop of local traditional societies and a classic example of how animals loom large in human existence.[8] Some seven thousand Maring-speaking farmers live in the New Guinea Highlands. Back in the 1960s, anthropologist Roy Rappaport lived among the Tsembaga group, whose lives were dominated by ancestor worship, warfare, and pig keeping. They formed part of a tapestry of allies and adversaries, their lives governed by the supernatural forces of their ancestors. Without the ancestors' assistance, there would be no success in pig raising and other aspects of daily life. Tsembaga life, and that of their neighbors, revolved around an unfolding cycle of warfare and a ritual observance known as a *kaiko*, which culminated in a huge pig feast.

Once a *kaiko* ends, with its gargantuan pig feed, there are few male beasts left. Warfare ceases. The living now direct their thoughts toward raising pigs. A rumbim shrub is planted, and grows until there is a renewed abundance of animals, at which point it is uprooted and the cycle begins anew. *Kaikos* occur about every twelve years, but the Tsembaga have no way of measuring time, so the timing of *kaikos* depends on social factors. The women grow yams, taro, and sweet potatoes, and also raise the pigs. Once weaned, piglets are trained to walk behind humans like dogs. At four or five months, they are released into the forest to scrounge for themselves until called home to be fed a daily ration of substandard yams and sweet potatoes. As the pigs mature and their numbers increase, the women have to work harder and harder to feed them. They have to enlarge their gardens to raise more pigs as soon as possible so that the group can hold a *kaiko* before their enemies do. When Rappaport observed a *kaiko* in 1963, the more ambitious Tsembaga women were taking care of about six 61-kilogram (135-pound) pigs each, a demanding job over and above childrearing and other household tasks. Social tensions rose as the women cleared new gardens and hungry pigs ravaged even the fenced, cultivated land. Eventually the women's complaints bore fruit. The men felled the rumbim shrub, and the moment for a *kaiko* arrived.

The price in pigs was enormous. Rappaport's 1963 *kaiko*, with its repeated feasts, had the Tsembaga killing off three-quarters of their pigs by number and seven-eighths by weight. Much of the meat went to allies and in-laws. At the climactic rituals in November 1963, ninety-six pigs were slaughtered, their meat and fat distributed to about two or three thousand people. The Tsembaga themselves ate about 5.5 kilograms (12 pounds) of meat and fat per person over five days of unconstrained gluttony.

All this slaughter and preoccupation with pigs, as well as the elaborate costumes, dances, and rituals, fulfilled practical needs. *Kaikos* satisfied the Tsembaga's craving for pork, something that is normally rare in their diet. Their environment, with its humidity and damp shade, is ideal for raising pigs, which obtain much of their food by free-ranging. However, too many pigs overburden the women and endanger the Maring gardens. This is when the *kaiko* comes into play, as the ancestors ensure that pigs do not destroy the women or their gardens. A *kaiko* keeps the ancestors happy and helps keep the pig population under control. No one can set formal limits, for circumstances change radically from year to year, depending on the size of the local population, the fortunes of individual clans, the intentions of enemies nearby, and the amount of secondary forest available for expansion. The Tsembaga and their neighbors are all engaged in a struggle to validate their varying claims to the earth's resources. Warfare and the mere threat of it validates these claims, giving the ancestors an insatiable pig craving. At the same time, by banking large quantities of nutritionally valuable pig flesh, the Maring can attract and reward allies in times of imminent war. As a *kaiko* unfolds, allies and enemies alike can assess the strength of their and their hosts' ability to defend territory. The entire system affects distribution of plants, animals, and people over a large area of the New Guinea Highlands. The Tsembaga pigs truly serve as a social lubricant.

To own and manage a flock or herd, however small, as an ancient subsistence farmer or herder, changed one's life dramatically—and one's relationship with animals. Even goats, sheep, and swine were far more than just flesh and hides. As sources of wealth and social obligation, they shaped human society in new ways. And as we will see with cattle, once herding began, humanity was never the same again.

CHAPTER 6

Corralling the Aurochs

AUROCHS CAVORT ON THE walls of Lascaux Cave in southwestern France—black, drawn in outline, always with menacing, lyrelike horns. Seventeen thousand years ago, these great wild oxen would have flickered and moved in the soft light of fat lamps, symbols of primordial power and the challenges of the hunt. Wild bulls were dangerous prey, the stuff of hunting legend and mythic tales, nimble adversaries capable of killing a hunter with a quick flick of a horn.

The aurochs (*Bos primigenius*) was one of the largest European herbivores to survive the Ice Age. Some weighed in at around 700 kilograms (1,550 pounds). With their massive, forward-facing horns; large, elongated heads; and quite long, slender legs, these were athletic, fast-moving beasts when aroused. At least three subspecies flourished in India, Europe and Eurasia, and North Africa. All are now extinct, the last European aurochs dying of natural causes in Poland in 1627. Efforts to recreate *Bos primigenius* have produced animals closely resembling them, but complete success still eludes the experts. Once encountered, the aurochs were rarely forgotten. Roman general Julius Caesar encountered them during his campaigns in Gaul. He described them as "a little below the elephant in size. Their strength and speed is extraordinary; they spare neither man nor beast." He added, "Not even when taken very young can they be rendered familiar to men and tamed."[1]

Caesar was wrong. Some eight thousand years before his time, farmers in South and Southwest Asia tamed the wild ox almost as early as goats and sheep. The historical consequences were momentous. Bulls rapidly became symbols of leadership, cattle a desirable form of wealth.

They plowed fields and intensified agricultural production, helped cities and civilizations come into being. Oxen hauled plows in Mesopotamia as early as the sixth millennium BCE. They gradually replaced the back-breaking digging sticks and hoes used by earlier farmers and increased agricultural productivity significantly.

Domesticating a larger animal such as an aurochs would have been much harder than taming smaller farm animals. Just its size and unpredictable ferocity would seem insurmountable obstacles. Apparently, however, a small number of people in both Southwest Asia and South Asia succeeded in managing and taming a few large, aggressive, and by nature territorial beasts as a more reliable food source than game. And, in time, they apparently learned how to milk the cows. Just corralling a few aurochs would have been a major challenge. Perhaps neighboring villages exchanged information, and even partially tamed beasts. We will never know. It's certain, however, that such animals would have had important symbolic value in societies where hunting fierce beasts and carnivores was a central part of cultural ideology. Today, cattle are the most important domesticated animals in the world, 1.3 billion of them cows. They provide dairy products, leather, meat, and manure for fertilizer. We couldn't live life as we know it today without them.

An Excursion into Cattle Handling

HOW DID PEOPLE TAME such a seemingly formidable beast? As with smaller farm animals, here we enter the realm of intelligent guesswork, for we will, of course, never know the details. However, we can glean some clues from modern studies of cattle behavior and stock management procedures. The animal scientist Temple Grandin points out that cattle are always alert for predators.[2] Their brains operate like sentries against sudden movement. When threatened, they bunch together and seek safety in numbers, or they turn and fight with their horns. Many people who are unfamiliar with farms don't realize that most beef cattle aren't tame. They offer a contrast with pet cows and working oxen, and with dairy cows that are milked two or three times a day. Such animals enjoy a close association with people and have fewer fear genes. For

instance, the well-known Holstein dairy cow is almost certainly genetically farther away from her wild ancestors than other domesticated
cattle, as she has been selected for milk production. On large ranches,
beef cattle are habituated to the sight of people, but again, they are not
fully tame. Grandin writes of "flight zones," the distances that wild
animals will allow you to approach before they flee. Domesticated cows
have a small-to-zero flight zone compared with range beef cattle.

A great deal depends on how people handle cattle. Yelling, someone
or something's sudden appearance, or fast-moving objects, such as a
galloping horse, cause fear to kick in. The beasts' nervous systems are
attuned to detect predators and threats, as they are prime targets in the
wild. All cattle are afraid of heights and sudden movement. They learn
fear from one another. As a friend of Grandin's aptly expressed it, they
are "curiously afraid" when confronted with something unfamiliar. The
curiosity and uncertainty cause mild anxiety and vigilance. They want
to investigate something new but are afraid of the possible outcomes.
Forced novelty just doesn't work.

Cattle are likely to be upset when they have to be moved. Tame
cattle will follow buckets of grain. They will even move into new pastures by truck if they know there is food at the end of the trip. They
are familiar with the handling procedures. Herding cattle over longer
distances is much harder, especially on an open range, where there are
no intensively managed pastures. The most successful moves are those
that cause as little fear in the animals as possible. The old stereotypical
cowhand drives in Westerns, with shouting and whistling cowboys and
galloping steeds, are dead wrong, for such behavior causes cattle to run
and panic. The most effective way to move cattle over longer distances
is by pressuring their flight zones with gentle movements, where you
back off when they move in the right direction. Once the cattle bunch
instead of scattering, they can be quietly moved as a herd. Their loosely
arranged formation coincides with your giving them more protection
as they graze. This is common behavior with other animals, such as
antelope. In wide-open spaces like the Serengeti Plains in East Africa,
for instance, antelope feed calmly even when a pride of lions is nearby.
When the lions stalk them, they know it. *Bos primigenius* had similar

hardwired predefense behaviors. By using gentle herding methods, the modern-day cattle herder invokes these behaviors. Once the cattle are bunched, he or she can move deeper into the flight zone and move them along, using their natural defense instincts. This is not true of dairy cows, which are used to being led toward pasture or a corral.

Cattle handling probably reached its greatest skill level during the nineteenth century CE, when cowboys drove thousands of head of cattle over enormous distances of the American West between 1866 and 1886. Twenty million cattle traveled from Texas to railheads in Kansas such as Abilene, for shipment to stockyards in Chicago and points farther east. The cowboys moved the cattle slowly and quietly, for they knew that stress from rough handling would kill hundreds of animals along the way. On average, a Texas-to-Kansas drive numbered about three thousand head, with at least ten cowboys driving and watching the cattle day and night, moving them about twenty-four kilometers (fifteen miles) a day. It could take as long as two months to complete a drive. Not that such drives were unique to the American West. In medieval Europe, Hungarian Grey cattle traveled across the Danube to the beef markets of western Europe. The Swiss drove cattle across the Alps and into Italy, until sedentary dairy farming became more profitable. In the American West, the expansion of railroads throughout the country (also chronic overgrazing) tolled the death knell for much long-distance driving. All kinds of other research has relevance to early cattle herding. For instance, cattle herds should be larger than four head, for larger groups are more peaceful, housed as they are in bigger pens, which allows attacked animals to move away. It's important, too, to keep cattle together with beasts they know, as a way of reducing aggressive behavior.

Much of the behavior of range cattle during the nineteenth century and, for that matter, today seems to mirror what we know about the habits of *Bos primigenius*. A placid beast when calm, it can display aggressive and violent behavior with sudden movement or an unexpected noise. Hunting such a formidable, easily angered quarry required consummate stalking skills. However, if African game or range cattle are any guide, people moving quietly within clear sight of an aurochs might well have triggered no emotional reaction from a grazing wild ox whatsoever. I've walked quietly among herds of antelope with no obvious threatening intent. They merely looked up, and then went on grazing. But if I'd suddenly appeared from among the trees or high grass, they would have bolted at once, feeling threatened. This is very different behavior from that of a beast that is aware it's being stalked and then attacked. And this may be a clue as to how cattle were first tamed.

Hunters survive and are successful in the hunt because they know their quarry at close quarters, at every season, at night and by day, at first light and dusk. They've learned when not to approach them, and how to allay their fears; they've watched how wild oxen protect their young. One can imagine a hunting group living in close juxtaposition to a small aurochs herd, even walking around them in the open with no plan for a kill. Perhaps a young calf or a juvenile bull became separated from the herd. The hunters, who probably knew different beasts individually, would gently herd the stray into a large enclosure, and then make sure it had fodder and water. And so the slow process would unfold until a few captive animals became habituated to humans and bred within their corral, or grazed nearby and were corralled at night. The hunters, now herders, would protect their charges against predators. The process must have taken years before the lumbering animals became accustomed to captivity and management, or to being milked. Regular milking must have developed a close bond between tamer and tamed, which may account for the intimate relationships that subsequently developed between cattle and their owners in many pastoral societies.

Exploitation, breeding, and nurturing—these practices resonate in modern experience with animal husbandry, which began during the eighteenth century (see chapter 15). Early cattle herders were concerned above all with acquiring docile beasts that were easily managed. They must have soon learned that castrating surplus males produced more manageable beasts. This also allowed a herder to choose which animals to breed. Within a relatively short time, domesticated cattle were smaller, almost juvenile (a condition known as neoteny), more docile, and less wary around humans.

Wild cattle may have been dangerous prey, but they offered important advantages to those who tamed them. Nutritionally, they are highly desirable, supplying 2,360 calories per kilogram. Almost certainly they were tamed initially not for their milk, but for their meat. As societies in Southwest Asia turned to cultivation, their predominantly carbohydrate-laden diet created both long-term health problems such as osteoporosis, and needs for protein to compensate for cereal-based diets. In the final analysis, it was easier to protect, breed, and cull herds than to hunt reliably—and we humans develop attachments to large mammals and their young. Domestication was a symbiotic process to which both animals and humans contributed.

Domesticating Bos

NOW LET'S LOOK AT the archaeological data. Most authorities believe that *Bos primigenius* was domesticated at least twice, perhaps three times. The Cro-Magnons of Europe never tamed *Primigenius*, which was first tamed in more arid, less-forested environments. There, perhaps, the beasts were easier to approach when they could see people clearly. Humpless cattle, sometimes called taurines (*Bos taurus*), were first corralled in the Taurus Mountains region of what is now Turkey, the place where the greatest genetic diversity of cattle occurs. If the molecular biologists are to be believed, cattle domestication may have involved a mere eighty beasts.[3] Mitochondrial DNA from ancient and modern sources tell us that only a limited number of cattle lineages was involved in a domestication process that may have taken as long as two thousand years, perhaps along the upper reaches of the Tigris and Euphrates Rivers in what is now Syria and Turkey. Dja'de and Çayönü, both villages of the ninth millennium BCE, lie less than 250 kilometers (155 miles) apart. Between 8800 and 8200 BCE, the inhabitants relied more and more on cattle at the expense of hunting. Hundreds of fragmentary bones from the two villages may document a gradual process of domestication.

Once domesticated, these cattle spread rapidly across Southwest Asia, a consequence, in part, of the need for nutritious grazing, and, perhaps, of trading. They may even have been tamed in northeastern China as early as 8700 BCE, but the evidence is not unequivocal. What is certain, however, is that cattle were in widespread use in China, Mongolia, and Korea by 3000 BCE, when the first cities and civilizations appeared in Mesopotamia and along the Nile. Domestic cattle abounded in the Nile Valley well before founding of Egyptian civilization in 3100 BCE and are known from sites occupied at least two thousand years earlier. Farmers brought cattle and other farm animals with them as they spread across Europe in about 5500 BCE. The humped zebu (*Bos indicus*) was domesticated, most likely in the Indus River Valley of South Asia, by about 5000 BCE and spread widely into southern China and Southeast Asia.

"Goods to Think With"

BY 7500 BCE, FARMING villages, even some small towns, flourished over a wide area of the Near East. One of the larger settlements, Çatal Höyük, on Turkey's Anatolian Plateau, gives us a clear portrait of the increasingly sophisticated relationships between cattle and humans.[4] Here, every aspect of daily life, whether secular or ritual, unfolded not in great public buildings, but in houses occupied for many generations. They were literally "history houses" that commemorated ancestors, lavishly decorated with wall paintings that displayed elaborate symbolism. There were paintings of humans. Dangerous animals and bulls were everywhere. Ox skulls modeled with plaster features adorned houses from their moment of first occupation. Bull's horns projected from walls and benches. Plastered skulls of revered ancestors and ancestral burials lay under the floors. Çatal Höyük's history houses were vibrant archives with a status that involved control of history, religion, and interaction with ancestors. They may also have played an important role in ceremonial feasts involving wild bulls that had mythical and spiritual associations. Ancestors, animal and human, protected the occupants of the house, part of a strong motif of continuity that permeated early farming societies throughout Southwest Asia, where farming life revolved around the endless passage of the seasons (see sidebar "Disengaging from Nature?").

Disengaging from Nature?

Domesticating animals was most emphatically not a one-sided relationship, where people were in charge, set the conditions for taming, and then exploited their beasts. Rather, humans were participants in a broad process, part of a profound shift in the human relationship to the natural environment. Some French scholars such as Jacques Cauvin argue that farming settled people on the land and "disengaged" them from nature, making them distinctive and, as it were, on a higher plane than animals.[5] Cauvin believes that a dramatic shift in human consciousness resulted.

There was a florescence of animal imagery just before farming began, which endured for some time, reflected in shrines like those of Göbekli Tepe and Çatal Höyük, with their routine depictions of foxes, vultures, and other ferocious beasts.

Göbekli Tepe, in southeastern Turkey, lies on a hill where a series of circular structures were cut into the underlying limestone in about 9600 BCE.[6] They are almost cryptlike, adorned with rectangular stone pillars up to 2.4 meters (8 feet) high, bearing carvings of aurochs, gazelle, wild boar, snakes, and birds. There are no domesticated animals, just game and predators. Göbekli Tepe may have been a shrine where ancient rituals involving both predators and familiar animals unfolded for many generations, perhaps attracting visitors from communities with similar structures at least a hundred kilometers (sixty-two miles) away.

The wild animals persist for a long time, including in scenes at another site, Nevali Çori, near the Euphrates, where a bird perches on a human head and a figure with a human head stands near a bird. Everywhere, they may be tangible symbols of rituals that connected hunters with the hunted, people with animals, just as they had done for thousands of years, and did in some regions right into modern times. Then something changed: after about 7500 BCE, only depictions of human females and bulls persist, as if these two had become part of a symbolism of life and death when humans became separated from the natural world. And from there it was a short step to feelings of dominance and superiority over nature and its beasts. There was a sharp break from the intimacy with the natural world among Ice Age hunters that coincided with the domestication of the farm animals so familiar to us today.

Cattle herding and its values permeated farming societies over a large area of Southwest Asia. The same values continued to shape the customs of these societies long after they had changed profoundly and moved away from any emphasis on herding. The French anthropologist Claude Lévi-Strauss once remarked that animals, among them cattle, were goods to think with—and think their owners did. Cattle became wealth, accumulated, displayed, fought over, and sacrificed with reverence. But they were also the focus of human behaviors and values deeply embedded in animal husbandry. The herders manipulated their herds, their control helping both animals and humans to thrive. Milk and cheese, provided by cows year after year, formed a powerful bond between people and their cattle, which was expressed in a reluctance to kill animals, except in a sacrificial setting. It followed that slaughtering herds for their meat was a problem, partly because killing beasts reduced the herd, but also because of the conflict between necessity and social values.

Cattle, power, wealth—the close relationships between cattle and their herders developed in the earliest days of domestication, thanks to the close bonds developed between corralled animals and their guardians, especially with cows. From this interdependence developed distinctive social values that permeate subsistence cattle herding societies to this day. The relationships they forge with their beasts are profoundly emotional and sometimes border on obsession.

Cattle herders range their beasts over considerable distances, especially in semiarid environments where even a small amount of rainfall can make a dramatic difference to animals on the land. The number of hectares required for such grazing was enormous. One estimate has it that had not the herds of the Maasai of East Africa been decimated by an epidemic of rinderpest (cattle plague, now extinct) in the late nineteenth century, their cattle would eventually have required all of Kenya, Tanzania, and Uganda for their range. Such landscapes are like giant sets of lungs, sucking people in when rainfall encourages plant growth and creates standing water, pushing them out when conditions are drier. Herein lies a central dynamic of history triggered by animals—the often hostile relationship between farmers anchored to their fields and nomadic herders on the margins. In drought years, marauding nomads would drive their beasts onto better-watered farmland, seeking water and forage for them. Sumerian cities, such as Ur, in what is now southern Iraq, lived in constant fear of raiding nomads, especially in times of drought. In 2200 BCE, so many herds moved downstream that the city's ruler built a 180-kilometer-long (112-mile) wall, named the "Repeller of Amorites," to keep herder immigration in check. His efforts were to no avail. The population of Ur increased threefold, and the economy collapsed.[7]

Cultivated, settled lands symbolized order and continuity at least to their settlers, constantly under threat from those without, who possessed animals but no land. Such beliefs permeated ancient Japan, Egypt, the Greeks, and the Romans, who considered Corsican shepherds from island mountains to be brigands and savages, effectively wild beasts. As Englishman Edmund Spenser was to write in Elizabethan times, "Loke into all Countries that live in suche sorte by keeping of Cattle and you shall finde that they are bothe verie Barbarians and uncivil, allsoe greatly given to warre."[8] The fourteenth-century Islamic geographer and historian Ibn Khaldun described Arab camel herding groups as defiant of authority. "They are the most savage human beings that exist. Compared with sedentary people, they are on a level with wild untamable [animals]."[9] For all these derogatory remarks, the relationships between humans and nomadic herders shaped key ideas and values that were fundamental to people in many parts of the world.

Domestication means a shift in focus from the dead animal to the living one. Unlike communally owned game, open to be killed by all, domesticated livestock is owned and maintained. Slaughtering an animal diminishes the herd, so the owner has to take into account all manner of other factors, not only costs such as food needs and herd requirements, but benefits of all kinds, such as meeting social and ritual obligations. These factors are particularly important with large, slow-reproducing animals like cattle, which are harder to replace. Without access to storage or drying facilities, one family alone cannot consume the amount of meat such animals produce, which adds another layer of complication to daily life. Modern-day anthropological studies of traditional cattle herders find that they behave toward their animals in ways that are very different from those of modern owners, concerned only with price, protein, and calories.

Managing the Herd

HARDLY ANY TWENTIETH-CENTURY CATTLE herders (pastoralists) lived entirely off their herds. They relied on cereals and even cultivated the soil themselves if they had to, which they usually considered a demeaning activity. The blood, flesh, and milk from their beasts were inadequate for true self-sufficiency. Most likely, ancient herds were small, for cattle breed more slowly than goats or sheep. This makes it harder to recover losses from slaughtering, drought, or disease. Judging from recent traditional practice, documented by anthropologists, each herder had his own management strategy, which depended to a considerable extent on the size of his or her herd and wealth. Right from the beginning, herding households would have measured their wealth and social status in head of cattle. Both small stock and grain also had value, but not as wealth in the social sense. Land was communally owned by clans or other kin units, so about the only currency was beasts. And cattle have the advantage that they are social animals that thrive in groups and can survive off natural vegetation without fodder; otherwise, the cost of raising them in corrals alone would be unsustainable. In many African societies, cattle effectively served as "money." The same must have been true in many other ancient cattle-owning cultures.

As cattle became more important as wealth, a conflict would arise between the quest for riches and the need for subsistence. If ancient societies were like recent ones, the management strategies would have changed. Cattle became stored wealth, often exchanged for grain. In more arid environments with a high risk of drought, wealth on the hoof was never permanent riches. Owners would try to reduce risk by lending out animals, distributing them with relatives over wide areas, or loaning them to obtain goodwill and help fellow kin. Those without livestock would often have attached themselves to wealthy households in exchange for their labor and a few animals that allowed them to build up a herd. A great deal of energy and thought went into building ever-larger stocks of cattle wealth. Then there was the bride price (sometimes called bride wealth), a payment from the groom's side to the bride's to seal a marriage, a fundamental dynamic in many cattle-herding societies.

"The Parasite of the Cow"

UNTIL RECENTLY, CATTLE-HERDING SOCIETIES thrived in widely scattered parts of the Old World, in both Africa and Asia. Fortunately, a series of classic anthropological studies described some of these societies before population growth and industrialization encroached on their lifeways. Given the conservatism of herding societies, we can learn something from them about the realities of cattle management in the more remote past. We know, for example, that subsistence cattle herders developed extremely close relationships with their beasts, almost to the point of what we would describe as eccentricity.

Among the best-known pastoralists are the tall, long-limbed Nuer, who grazed their beasts in the swamps and open savanna on either side of the Nile in southern Sudan. The British anthropologist E. E. Evans-Pritchard, who lived among them during the 1930s, wrote that they "regard horticulture as toil forced on them by poverty of stock . . . The only labor they delight in is care of cattle."[10] Families owned cattle. Kinship formed powerful bonds, defined in part by payment of bride wealth. Evans-Pritchard defined the movement of cattle from family camp to family camp as the equivalent of lines on a genealogical chart, so carefully were such movements traced.

So important were cattle in Nuer life that both men and women often bore names that referred to the form and color of their favorite beasts. Every owner established contact with spirits of the lineages of the owner. By rubbing ashes along the back of a beast, one could get in touch with the spirit or ghost associated with it, and ask for assistance. The Nuer also contacted the dead through sacrifice of oxen or smaller animals. This obsession with their cattle—it was nothing less—was due in part to the beasts' great economic value, but also because the people defined their social relationships in terms of them.

In subsistence terms, the Nuer prized their cows for their milk, the most valuable beasts being those that yielded the most. Like other East African cattle herders, the Nuer extracted blood from the necks of their beasts, especially during the dry season, when milk was in short supply. No Nuer herd was maintained for slaughter, much as the people liked meat. But they did consume animals that died, even those of which they were inordinately fond. Cattle were sacrificed rarely, and mostly on important occasions such as funerals or marriages.

Above all, the Nuer valued their beasts for display and because of the prestige that a large, fat animal brought, especially those with large humps that wobbled when the animal walked. As Evans-Pritchard remarked, "The Nuer might be called the parasite of the cow."[11] Their herds lived lives of indolent leisure, while the people catered to their every need—lighting fires to keep off mosquitoes, moving them to ensure their good health, fashioning ornaments to adorn them, and guarding them against human raiders and animal predators. Every herder knew each animal in his herd: its color, the shape of its horns, its peculiarities, its history, ancestry, and the amount of milk it provided. He knew which beast bellowed in the evening, which liked to lead the herd back to camp, and which were restless during milking. The more an owner could display his ox, walking among the docile herd at night with an ox bell, the happier he was. The symbiotic relationship between the Nuer and their cattle was one of common interests, and of close physical contact.

During the 1930s, the herders ranged over an enormous tract of open country, their movements determined by variations in the vegetation and water supplies. During the rainy season, from April to August, the people moved out into small camps. During the height of the dry season, they congregated in larger settlements near permanent water. During the flood season, camps lay on low mounds or on higher ground with enough space for humans and animals, as it is dangerous for cattle to stand in water for long periods of time. Today, Nuer cattle herding is a shadow of its former self, a victim of rising populations, political and social unrest, civil war in southern Sudan, and rampant modernization. Many Nuer now live in Nebraska.[12]

Change was afoot long before the twentieth century. Stock raising for cities, especially of goats and sheep, developed on a rapidly growing scale during the fourth millennium BCE. The ancient stockyards that supplied the relentless maw of cities, temples, and rulers became places where animals were statistics of numbers and weight rather than measures of social importance. As subsistence herding of farm animals gave way to a tapestry of religious ideologies, we find an ambivalence about humans and their relationships with beasts that would have been unthinkable for the Nuer.

CHAPTER 7

"Wild Bull on the Rampage"

"HE WALKS AROUND IN the enclosure of Uruk / Like a wild bull he makes himself mighty, head raised [over others]." Thus reads the mythic Sumerian hero Gilgamesh, commemorated in an epic that is one of the classics of ancient literature. He was "the brave scion of [the city of Uruk], wild bull on the rampage." His genealogy proclaimed him "suckling of the august Wild-Cow, the goddess Ninsun." He "lords it over the men like a wild bull," capable of shattering established order, while at the same time he is shepherd of the people.[1] *The Epic of Gilgamesh* is far more than a tale of heroes. It's an ideological document, an exploration of a king's role in society where the divine and the human are interconnected and where rulers and priests sacrifice to the deities and appease them, using their unique knowledge and ritual acts to do so. Many of the ideas about animals laid out in the epic reflect the then-still-close links between animals, humans, and the forces of the supernatural world.

By Gilgamesh's time, there was an emerging symbolic ambiguity expressed in the daily life of cattle herds. Cows were symbols of the nurturing earth mother, sustainer of life. Lions and griffins had long been symbols of leadership, of prowess in the chase and in war. Inevitably, the bull was also seen as icon of masculine power, a fierce beast but the protector of its herd. Its ferocity implied connections with the powers of the wild and the unexplained. Such thinking became critical to the ways in which early rulers such as Gilgamesh projected their authority. Bulls possessed explosive power. They became the avatar of gods and rulers; the divine power of the bull reinforced that of the king. These beliefs shaped the religious ideas of Mediterranean society for many centuries. At the same time, the development of the wheeled cart and the plow, perhaps in the fourth millennium BCE in Mesopotamia, introduced another element: the use of cattle as draft animals.

Divine Kings, Holy Bulls

BY THE FOURTH MILLENNIUM, we can discern a divergence between cattle as numinous—symbols of power and sacrificial victims—and their more pragmatic role as draft animals pulling plows and transporting loads, and as sources of meat. The identification of rulers with bulls provided the leaders with respect and uncontrollable might. Egyptian pharaohs identified themselves with the divine bull. The Egyptians revered bulls through the cult of Osiris, with special festivals in honor of Hapi (the Greek name is Apis), known as the Running of Hapi, as early as the First Dynasty, around 2900 BCE.[2] But cattle cults go back much further in Egyptian history, perhaps to the time when herders from the increasingly arid Sahara Desert brought their cattle cults and notions of leaders as strong bulls to the Nile long before 3000 BCE. Hapi may have started as a fertility god connected to grain and herds. The sacred bull symbolized the strength and virility of the pharaoh, who was often called "strong bull of his mother Hathor," the cow goddess and mistress of the West, the realm of the dead.

Over the centuries, the cult of the sacred Apis bull, the personification of the god Ptah, creator god of Memphis, became deeply ingrained in Egyptian life. The great pharaoh Ramesses II (who reigned 1279–1213 BCE) elevated the Apis cult to new heights. He ordered the construction of the Serapeum, an underground maze of burial chambers for Apis bulls near the royal capital at Memphis in Lower Egypt, which remained in use for many centuries[3] (see sidebar "Rediscovering the Serapeum"). Every living Apis bull had the same coloring: black with a white diamond mark on the forehead. A bull born with such markings lived a pampered existence in Ptah's temple. Apis was an oracle and a prophet, a source of wisdom, attended by priests who monitored its every move. When an Apis bull died or was sacrificed in its mid- to late twenties (the age of the god Osiris when he perished), the state plunged into mourning. The discovery of a new Apis bull with the correct markings was an occasion for rejoicing.

Rediscovering the Serapeum

In 24 CE, the Greek geographer Strabo mentioned that the Apis bulls were buried in an underground sepulcher known as the Serapeum, at the end of an avenue of sphinxes that was constantly buried by drifting sand. Apis was an oracle and a prophet, so powerful that his cult survived until almost 400 CE, into late Roman times. Once the popular cult passed into oblivion, the Serapeum, with its mummified bulls, was effectively lost until 1850, when a twenty-nine-year-old Frenchman, Auguste Mariette (1821–1881), became curious about fifteen sphinxes adorning the gardens of wealthy Alexandrians and Cairenes. At the time, Mariette worked for the Louvre, in Paris, which had sent him out to acquire Coptic and other historic manuscripts. While waiting for permission to export his collection, he inquired about the sphinxes, learned they came from the Saqqara necropolis, on the west bank of the Nile. Mariette remembered Strabo's words, set thirty men to work and uncovered 140 sphinxes, on the very avenue described eight centuries earlier by the ancient geographer. At the end, he found the entrance of the Serapeum, buried in sand that was "so to speak fluid." It was like excavating water. The discovery caused an international sensation.

The tomb of Apis lay behind a magnificent sandstone door. Inside stood the great sandstone coffins of the Apis bulls, their lids removed by tomb robbers centuries earlier. A great deal of material and numerous precious artifacts remained, however. The terms of Marquette's permit required that he hand over his discoveries to the Egyptian authorities, so he quietly packed the cases destined for the Louvre at the bottom of a dark pit at night, while showing disappointed Egyptian officials the empty tombs in daytime.

Mariette spent four laborious years recovering a multitude of artifacts and parts of mummified bulls. He was lucky enough to find one undisturbed Apis burial in a sealed niche, dating to the time of

Ramesses II. The fingerprints of the worker who'd put the last stone in place could still be seen in the plaster. Even the footprints of the funerary workers had survived in a dusty corner. The sarcophagus contained both the undisturbed bull mummy and rich offerings of gold and jewelry. In his rough-and-ready fashion, Mariette used gunpowder to open the lid.

Auguste Mariette devoted the rest of his life to Egyptology and became the country's first "conservator of monuments." Among other things, he developed the plot for Verdi's opera *Aida*, first performed in Cairo, and supervised the scenery with its Ancient Egyptian themes.

Nevertheless, at the same time, tomb paintings depict workers butchering animals and herding them on noble estates. Cattle worked and were slaughtered in thoroughly pragmatic ways. It was inevitable that beef would become an important food source in a society where the state paid noble and commoner alike in rations and kind, not with currency. The Pyramids of Giza, erected at vast expense by the pharaoh Khufu and his successors after 2550 BCE, required veritable armies of laborers, who had to be housed and fed. One pyramid builder's settlement is estimated to have required more than eighteen hundred kilograms (thirty-six hundred pounds) of meat daily—from cattle, sheep, and goats.[4] Only about half the protein for the ten thousand workers who lived in the settlement for the pharaoh Menkaure's pyramid came from fish, beans, and other nonmeat sources. One estimate has it that about 11 cattle and 37 sheep or goats were butchered daily. To maintain this slaughter level would have required herds of 21,900 cattle and 54,750 goats and sheep. To graze these animals would have required about 400 square kilometers (154 square miles) of pasture, probably in the fertile Nile Delta. Farm animals were an integral part of the Ancient Egyptian economy, used for draft, as rations, and for their milk and other byproducts. Scribes counted herds and flocks, whose members were as much commodities as dried fish and grain.

Palace Monopolies and Bull Leaping

IN GREECE, DOMESTIC CATTLE arrived from Anatolia: beasts with long, lyre-shaped horns, much prized as drinking vessels. Herds were small; there was plenty of land to go around; oxen were important for hauling plows. This was low-intensity cattle herding, based mainly on mountain pastures where abundant forage could be found. By 1700 BCE, however, cattle had assumed great importance in the Minoan civilization of Crete, where they played an important role in both economic and symbolic life. Minoan civilization revolved around a network of palaces, the most elaborate being Knossos, near the modern city of Heraklion, a sprawling complex of courtyards, shrines, workshops, storehouses, and residential quarters inhabited by between thirteen thousand and seventeen thousand people.[5]

Knossos prospered on wool and textiles, so much so that its flocks may have numbered as many as a hundred thousand sheep, grazing on 200,000 hectares (494,000 acres) or more of pasture. Clay tablets inscribed with Linear B script tell us much about the Minoan economy. The tablets tell us that cowherds gave individual beasts names such as *aiwolos*, "nimble," or *kelainos*, "black." Almost invariably, palace tablets inventory cattle when they were sent out from Knossos. Some *we-ka-ta*, "working oxen," left Knossos for dependent settlements and other palaces, sent in pairs for work at the plow. But most beasts departed alone, high-value goods perhaps destined for sacrifice. Such a present had great value, not only in ritual terms, but also as a source of meat, hide, and other by-products. It may be no coincidence that copper ingots were shaped like ox hides when traded, perhaps a symbolic indication of the beasts' value.

Almost all Minoan cattle herding appears to have been under tight palace control, a monopoly that formed part of an elaborate network of connections with other palaces and communities. The wealth implied by cattle allowed rulers to assert political authority by means of providing sacrificial beasts that were ancient symbols of power and by demonstrating a regal largesse that cemented domination over others.

According to Greek legend, the Minotaur, a creature with the head of a bull and the body of a human, dwelled in a special compound near

Knossos. This fierce beast was born of King Minos's wife, Pasiphaë, who mated with a white bull sent to Minos by the sea god Poseidon as a sign of support. Minos corralled the monster near the palace, where it is said to have been killed by the Greek hero Theseus, sent as a sacrifice to the Minotaur by the ruler of Athens as part of an annual offering of young men and women as tribute to the Cretans. We know nothing of this remarkable beast beyond legend of the Minotaur—the word is a Greek combination of *Minos* and *tauros*, or "bull." Perhaps it was a priest wearing a bull's head who carried out the human sacrifices. We will never know.

The Minotaur is a striking reminder of the importance of bulls in Minoan society. Minoan palaces teem with them. Ceremonial bronze axes, rings, terracotta figures, stone seals, and frescoes all commemorate these powerful animals. Frescoes on Knossos's walls, and in Minoan buildings as far away as Avaris, in the Nile Delta, depict bulls and human figures leaping over them. Most impressive of all are ceremonial containers known as rhytons, which are perforated at the base and designed to dispense blood from sacrificial victims. The most famous rhyton, from Knossos, is in the form of a bull's head carved from steatite and decorated with rock crystal and gold. A formal libation from a bull's head rhyton at the feast where the sacrificial beast was eaten would have reenacted the bloodletting, replacing slaughter with formal ceremony.

Friezes depicting young men leaping over bulls adorn the walls of Knossos. Bull leaping itself is a contested subject among scholars. Whether it was a reenactment of an ancient cosmic drama or simply a way of demonstrating human mastery over bulls is a mystery. Perhaps it was a ceremony at which young participants somersaulted or vaulted over a charging beast's back, a movement akin to the *saut de l'ange* and other movements performed by modern-day bull leapers in southwestern France.[6] Certainly bull leaping, which also took place elsewhere in the eastern Mediterranean world, was a centerpiece of Minoan life, and perhaps a way of affirming the power of the elite over society as a whole. Cattle were unique symbols of power in Minoan society and also special commodities in the intricate realm of trade and exchange.

Figure 7.1 *A bull rhyton with golden horns from Knossos. John Copland/Shutterstock.*

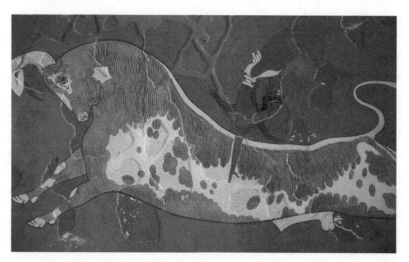

Figure 7.2 *Frieze depicting a bull leaper from Knossos, Crete. Superstock.*

Minoan civilization gave way, after 1450 BCE, to Mycenaean control of Crete, a mainland society where cattle wealth was of central importance. As Mycenaean influence grew, so bull leaping vanished into history. Now the elite used cattle in more pragmatic ways, as they controlled access to breeding stock, draft animals, and food. Ceremonial feasting became an important instrument of exercising political authority. Some of these feasts were on a large scale. Linear B tablets from the Mycenaean palace at Pylos, in western Greece, come from the same room as a rich deposit of cattle bones, the remains of five to eleven head of cattle. These beasts would have provided enough meat to feed many more people than a small elite group. At another Mycenaean site, Tsoungiza, near Nemea, most of the surviving bones from a deposit of cattle remains are those from the heads and feet, as if the rest of the carcasses were butchered and the flesh-carrying bones carried elsewhere for numerous celebrants.

Sacrifice, ceremonial feasting, and food distribution—the Minoan and Mycenaean treatment of cattle was a way of acquiring and confirming prestige. The cattle wealth became social capital through feasting and the distribution of flesh to people, who subsisted, for the most part, on cereals. At Pylos, in the eastern Peloponnese, where cattle herding was far more important than at Knossos, Linear B inventories tell us that economic imperatives and religious beliefs were closely interwoven. Everyone in the Mycenaean world was bound together by sacred bonds: stockbreeding, sacrifice, and ceremonial feasting. Bulls were symbols of power, associated with gods such as Zeus and Poseidon. Thus it was that Homeric king Nestor of Pylos sacrificed "sleek black bulls" to Poseidon, "god of the sea-blue mane who shakes the earth."[7]

The Mycenaeans took cattle out of myriad economic activities and made them a central element in their social and political organization. This legacy passed down the centuries to the classical Greeks, whose small agricultural communities prized their autonomy but engaged in both manufacturing and trade on a broader canvas. But dedications, rituals, and sacrifices to supplicate the gods remained a central part of Greek life and colored people's relationships with the remote descendants of *Bos primigenius*.

The Enduring Dilemma

HEREIN LAY A DILEMMA for the Greeks. Cattle were not only a specific form of wealth, but also the focus of human behaviors and values that arose from animal husbandry. The herders manipulated their herds, their control helping both animals and humans to thrive. Milk, provided by cows year after year, was a powerful bond between people and their beasts, expressed in a profound reluctance to kill animals, except in a sacrificial setting. Sacrifices were ritual occasions, a means of connecting with the supernatural realm and revered deities, a moment of profound ritual significance, which usually ended in a feast, in itself a social outcome.[8]

There's a contrast here, between the hunter, who preyed on *Bos primigenius* opportunistically, and the herder, who nurtured the herd, sheltered it, then made sure the animals had water, and led them to pasture. He or she was in effect the herd leader, not a predator, until the moment when the beasts were killed in what can be seen as an act of betrayal. This was something that the Greeks took very seriously. As the historian Plutarch once famously observed, "They considered the sacrifice of living animals a very serious matter, and even now people are very wary of killing an animal before a drink-offering is poured over him and he shakes his head in assent."[9] The herder had a greater power to take life than a hunter ever did, because he controlled his herd. As the philosopher Plato once pointed out, piety is the human nurturing of the gods. Likewise, cattle herders nurture their beasts.

All this came out in the ritual of sacrifice. The Greeks garlanded sacrificial bulls, washed them, and adorned them with flowers. The victim processed to the altar, where the knife lay hidden in a basket. Grain showered on the beast caused it to nod and agree to the sacrifice. The sacrificial rite moved the act of killing to the realm of the holy, the divine, and the supernatural.

The classicist Jeremy McInerney points to the importance of what he calls the "bovine idiom," the familiarity with pastoralists that marked Greek life from deep in antiquity.[10] This common idiom helped the Greeks to navigate centuries of tumult and to search for a common identity, something never fully achieved. These were the centuries of Archaic Greece (800–480 BCE), when great sanctuaries such as Delphi, Olympia, and Nemea emerged to become shrines of significance to all Greeks, whatever their local loyalties. As the practices of classical culture took shape, cattle were always important during an era when the pantheon of Olympus came into prominence.

Greek deities personified the mind-set and values of stock-breeding societies, capable of turning themselves into bulls, possessing cow's eyes like the goddess Hera, or acting as herders. The gods were tauriform, yet were involved and appeased through cattle sacrifice, while the people ate the flesh of the victims. Meat was a source of nutrition as well as a medium of contact with the supernatural. Smoking altars, lowing cattle, and bloody knives—these were an important part of ceremonies associated with the Olympic Games and at Delphi festivals, apart from sacrifices carried out in Greek cities. Cattle shed their blood for the benefit of the community, this in a society where agriculture became increasingly important, with pastoralism pushed to the margins except for draft animals. Yet the institution of sacrifice demanded an increasingly large supply of sacrificial animals.

The continual emphasis on sacrifice caused severe economic strain in farming societies.[11] The more animals that were needed for sacrifice, the less land there was for farming—this in landscape with rugged terrain. Fully one-third of the Athenian year was taken up with communal sacrifices and feasting. When the major gods were involved, the offering had to be cattle, to the tune of an estimated sixty-five hundred annually in Athens alone. The major sanctuaries in more rural settings had grazing land around them. The real problem was for cities, so Athens leased land outside the city. Calculating the amount of meat produced by a major festival such as the midsummer Panathenaia in honor of the goddess Athena, celebrated every fourth July, is nearly impossible, but this particular event coincided with the best time for culling surplus beasts. As what one can only call the business of sacrifice became ever more elaborate, so the purchase of cattle moved from the sacred economy into the secular one, especially the market in hides. And as the centuries passed, Greek stock raising became a practice that straddled the religious, private, and public domains. In a modest way, and never on a large scale in a predominantly agricultural society, cattle became a commodity.

Roman Plow and Pasture

ARISTOTLE WROTE THAT NATURE had made animals for humankind, "both for his service and his food." Beasts possessed no virtue or vice, for "bestial badness is different in kind from vice."[12] Animals were subservient to human needs; they were unable to tell us their needs. From there it was but a short step to considering uncivilized people as beasts and equating them with animals. The Greek geographer Strabo wrote of Corsican mountaineers brought to Rome: "[You could] see and marvel at the degree to which the nature of wild beasts and grazing cattle is manifested in them."[13]

The Romans took a more pragmatic approach to cattle than the Greeks. Author Marcus Terentius Varro wrote in his eighty-fifth year that the ox "is still man's hard-working ally in the cultivation of the soil."[14] Varro distilled a lifetime of farming experience into his *De Res Rusticae*. His credentials were impeccable—a lifetime of owning stud farms for horses and mules, produced to generate maximum profit for capital outlay. He farmed on a large scale and ran hundreds of oxen strictly as working animals, so he knew of what he wrote. Much depended upon slave labor, and here again Varro had strong opinions. He recommended older slave foremen, who could read and write. "They are not to be allowed to control their men with whips rather than with words."[15]

Beef never loomed large in Roman diets, except for flesh from sacrificial animals. Oxen were strictly working beasts, raised for hauling carts and plowing. However, every farmer bred a few head for sacrificial purposes, chosen for their fine appearance. Invariably, breeders sought robust animals, their characteristics varying with Italy's varied environments. Authors such as Varro mention six Italian and four overseas breeds, including small Alpine cattle, said to be excellent milkers and hard workers. Swiss cattle are still some of the finest dairy animals in the world. Not that the Romans drank fresh milk. They used it to make cheese, especially in the rich pasturelands of the Po Valley.

Greek and Roman farmers had to be efficient, for they fed large and rapidly growing urban populations. The populations they supported were equal to, if not larger than, those of early nineteenth-century Greece and Italy.[16] Most people ate a remarkably varied diet that included cereals, some meat, wine, olive oil, and fruit. Their skeletons offer eloquent testimony to the efficacy of food production. Romans averaged 168 centimeters (5 feet, 6 inches) in height, a stature regained by Italians only after World War II. Hellenistic Greeks were taller than any modern Greeks until the late 1970s. In dramatic contrast, the mean heights of Spaniards, Italians, and Austro-Hungarians during the eighteenth and nineteenth centuries shrank to those of Ancient Egyptian peasants during the Old Kingdom of 2500 BCE. The blame lies with the malnutrition caused by protein- and calorie-deficient cereal diets consumed by western Europeans after the decline of the Roman Empire.

Fortunately, the Islamic agronomists of al-Andalus, formerly Roman Spain, absorbed the rich agricultural knowledge set down by authors Cato, Columella, Varro, and others now lost. Intensive agriculture did not reappear in Europe until cities grew rapidly in thirteenth-century Renaissance Italy. After the fall of Rome, throughout much of western Europe agriculture remained at the subsistence level for centuries. Many centuries later, the eighteenth-century English farming writer Adam Dickson pointed out that Roman agriculture was superior to that of England even in the midst of the Agricultural Revolution unfolding during his lifetime.[17]

Cattle lay at the very center of Roman agricultural endeavors. The farmers handled their livestock carefully, because they were valuable— money on the hoof and a source of backbreaking labor. Above all, they prized them for their nitrogen-rich manure, which enhanced crop yields dramatically. Even smallholders anticipated many innovations in modern agricultural practice, including seed selection and crop rotation. They planted alfalfa, most of the modern fodder crops for their herds, and lesser-known fodders, such as drought-resistant trefoil, a form of alfalfa ideal for sheep and goats. Roman wheat yields matched or exceeded the best performance of medieval farmers.

Without cattle, the intensification of Greek and Roman agriculture would never have achieved the success it did in supporting prosperous urban markets and underpinning burgeoning trade in such commodities as olive oil and wine. The city-states of Greece, Roman Italy, and Carthage were as highly urbanized as much later Dutch or Italian city-states. They were also powerfully democratic, which led to greater prosperity and a rising demand for luxury products, while the authorities imported cheap grain from Egypt and North Africa for cheap staple foods for the general population. This encouraged greater agricultural intensification, and much greater livestock production.

Cattle were, in large part, the engines that drove this agricultural economy. Farmers purchased the stock they needed, and then maintained their herds from their own resources, selling off weak or barren cows and replenishing the breeding stock from time to time. Everything was carefully managed, even the use of barren cows as draft animals. "Because of their sterility they can work just as hard as bullocks," adjured Cato. Working cattle spent their lives on the farm, for the system required that they work regularly throughout the year. The critical care periods were in late autumn, when all fresh forage was used up, and March, when spring plowing was in full swing. By spring, the oxen were weak, having been fed for the most part on dry fodder and even acorns and refuse from wine presses. A wise farmer developed a mix of hay and mash, which was quite adequate by modern standards. The most important feed was green fodder, such as legumes or horse-barley, said to be "better food than wheat for all farm animals." Most farmers had to stall-feed their herds. Above all, oxen preferred green fodder. As Cato remarked, "You mustn't put them to grass except in winter, when they are not ploughing; when they have once eaten green fodder, they are always expecting it, and they have to be muzzled when ploughing to keep them from going for the grass." A conscientious farmer branded his herd with a personal mark to keep track of them, took care they were watered twice a day in summer, and watched them grazing to prevent crowding. The rewards were strictly financial, in good prices for crops and for beasts when one sold them. Varro added, "Dogs must be kept as a matter of course, for no farm is safe without them."[18] Brigands and cattle rustlers were a constant problem in many remoter areas.

There was a real partnership between human and beast. But this was not teamwork based on emotion, as was the case of the Nuer, who cherished and loved their beasts for both economic and social reasons. Roman owners, many of whom sold grain to Rome and other cities, thought of their cattle in purely economic terms. They may have handled them with care and gentleness, and performed the prescribed rituals before plowing, but in the final analysis, they regarded their beasts as workers who generated profit of all kinds.

The relationship began with training one's beasts for the plow or to haul carts. Such training required gentleness and patience, especially with aggressive beasts. The farmer would often tie the animals to horizontal posts, tethering them with ropes that severely restricted movement to accustom them to the yoke. Unruly beasts might require up to thirty-six hours of such treatment. After this somewhat brutal breaking-in period, which could last several days, the animals had to be taught how to walk slowly and steadily so they could haul plows or wagons. Equally matched pairs of oxen learned "to walk for a thousand paces, in an orderly manner and without fear."[19] From the beginning, a pair alternated between hauling on the left and right side, to lessen fatigue. After three days, the animals were usually ready to don the yoke, a process that ended up with their towing an empty wagon. The same step-by-step process applied to plow oxen, with the animals first towing a plow over already tilled ground. Sometimes the trainer teamed up an experienced beast with a newcomer. Columella argued against the use of any form of goad or violence to secure obedience. Just like the first farmers to domesticate the aurochs, the Romans knew well that gentle persuasion worked with their charges.

But ambivalence lingered in a society that took sacrificial rituals very seriously. Sacrifices permeated Roman society—involving everything from crumbs thrown into a hearth to offerings of chickens, sheep, and oxen. Public sacrifices in city forums like that in Rome sometimes involved large numbers of oxen, often with gilded horns. Just as in

Athens, the sacrificial beast processed to the altar, where a priest would scatter grain upon it and then drink a libation. He would then pour the remainder of the wine between the beast's horns, some hair from the area being burnt on the altar as an offering to the gods. The animal was then stunned with a mallet before its throat was cut and the carcass disemboweled. An augur carefully examined the body so predictions could be made from the entrails. With the exception of the vital organs reserved for the deities, the meat was consumed by those attending the ceremony. Every detail of the ritual had to be absolutely correct, or the ceremony and the sacrifice had to be repeated.

Many centuries were to pass before animal sacrifice gave way to Christian ritual, and the symbolic offering of wine as the blood of Christ replaced ambivalent sacrifices of beasts.

How the Donkey Started Globalization

CHAPTER 8

"Average Joes"

"LYING THERE LIKE THE dead, he made no effort to rise. Clubs couldn't budge him, nor goads, not the yanking of his tail and ears every way which way." The ruthless bandits refused "to enslave themselves to an ass."[1] They hamstrung the helpless beast and flung him into a nearby ravine. The *Metamorphoses* of the Roman writer Apuleius, which none other than St. Augustine referred to as *Asinus aureus*, the "Golden Ass," is the only Latin novel to survive in its entirety. The protagonist, Lucius, is insatiably curious about magic. He tries to perform a spell to transform himself into a bird, but accidentally turns into an ass instead. After suffering dire hardships as a pack animal and grinder of grain, Lucius the donkey becomes a human once more, and a devotee of the goddess Isis. "Immediately the offensive form of a brute beast fell from me. . . . My enormous ears resumed their original paltry proportions."[2]

The Golden Ass epitomizes our cavalier and often cruel attitudes toward these remarkable beasts. Donkeys have worked alongside people for more than eight thousand years—but "alongside" actually means in the background, for they have always been inconspicuous players in history. Plodding asses carried food and water, exotic luxuries, and essential commodities across mountain passes and through deserts, in city streets and at the behest of great rulers. They walked in the background of events both stirring and prosaic, almost completely below the historical radar. Often a sentence in a history books suffices: "The Egyptians used donkey caravans to reach desert mines." "Black donkeys carried tin to Anatolia from Assur." Then the donkeys vanish once again into the oblivion of the past, just like illiterate peasants planting the fields. This humble pack animal was a silent partner to humans, sometimes working in the fields or grinding grain, sometimes even consumed as meat. Hardworking and adaptable, donkeys were among the most important players in the development and spread of civilization. For some reason they come across the pages of history as stubborn, mere beasts of burden, and capable only of loud braying. In fact, they are the unsung heroes of the long human relationship with animals, and we have never given them the credit they deserve. The more we uncover their story, the more significant their quiet roles in history become.

Saharan Origins

THE SOUTHERN SAHARA DESERT, *winter, 5000 BCE. Four emaciated donkeys plod steadily along the pebbly trail. Heads slightly down, heavily laden, they look neither to the left nor the right at the featureless aridity on either side. Firewood and water—the donkeys carry heaped bundles of dried shrubs or leather water bags suspended on either side of their coarse saddle blankets, collected at a small oasis over the horizon. Wizened, animal-skin-clad women and their beasts find their way with subtle landmarks such as a long, dried-up watercourse, a large boulder, or an unusually conspicuous dune—familiar signposts to people born to desert life, but the travelers never relax. It's easy to get lost in this featureless landscape of sand, gravel, and boulders. The small caravan picks its way across the desert, its destination a large clump of palm trees barely visible on the horizon, where cattle graze. The herders' traditions tell of better-watered times in the past, when springs and shallow lakes abounded and the people moved over short distances. For generations since, humans and their animals have ranged far and wide for sustenance, relying on their donkeys to bring water and firewood to temporary camps.*

QUITE WHEN AND WHERE people domesticated donkeys remains somewhat of a mystery.[3] One likely ancestor is the now nearly extinct African wild ass, *Equus africanus*. Most likely, wild asses were tamed in several areas of North Africa, one of which was the Sahara, where the donkey's unique qualities came into play at a time of increasingly erratic rainfall and much greater aridity, after about 5000 BCE.

For thousands of years after the Ice Age, the Sahara enjoyed regular, if sparse, rainfall. The desert supported broad tracts of semiarid grassland. Shallow lakes, springs, and oases provided ample water supplies for hunters and, later, cattle herders. By at least 6000 BCE, probably earlier, hunters in the southern Egyptian desert and to the west had domesticated *Bos primigenius*, the formidable wild ox. They lived off their herds, and off game and wild plant foods. Both water supplies and grazing were dependable enough that the herders could survive comfortably within relatively limited areas.

Life was good—until the Sahara began to dry up, around 5000 BCE. Both grazing and water became harder to find, except in widely scattered locations across the arid landscape. Instead of staying in small territories, the herders now followed food and water, which meant they had to cover long distances and move at frequent intervals. Cattle are demanding beasts, for they dehydrate easily and require water at least once a day, especially in hot environments such as the Sahara. Each group would have relied heavily on younger men, who would have moved adult beasts to outlying grazing and water supplies. The groups would have turned to the donkey to transport families, firewood, and other essentials.

No one knows how Saharan pastoralists, and others, first tamed donkeys, but it was perhaps a consequence of seasonal corralling of wild asses. The practice was still commonplace throughout the Saharan Sahel, the southern margins of the desert, as recently as the nineteenth century, and it is still used with reindeer by the Saami of Lapland. Perhaps domestication began with young animals who bred in their corrals and became familiar with human behavior. Perhaps, too, they were first tamed for their meat and milk, both little used today. However, those who corralled them soon became aware of the donkey's remarkable qualities, which made them perfectly adapted to an existence in increasingly dry environments.

Donkeys, with their efficient gait, walk faster than cattle, especially over rugged terrain. This quality alone offered huge advantages to cattle people confronted with the need for much greater mobility, with regular journeys of many kilometers to grazing grounds now widely separated over the landscape and to increasingly elusive water supplies. There were other advantages. Donkeys have labile body temperatures and tolerate desiccation readily, to the point that they can be trained to expect water only every two or three days. They dehydrate more slowly than cattle and rehydrate rapidly, do not need to rest for rumination, and can digest food while dehydrated. The donkey is said to be relatively easy to train and, above all, is a consummate load carrier.

Firewood and water, domestic possessions, young children and animals—all were suitable for a donkey's back. In many of today's societies, donkeys are considered "women's animals," used for domestic tasks—animals of lower status than cattle, sheep, or goats, which had important social roles in herding societies. But they were the load carriers of Saharan cattle herding. They carried things over an enormous area of northern Africa, the Sahara, and, soon, farther afield.

Donkeys of the Pharaohs

AT SOME POINT, THESE utilitarian pack animals came into use in the Nile Valley. Whether this was the result of pastoral groups moving to the edges of the settled lands along the river or because the Egyptians domesticated donkeys independently, we don't know. The earliest Nile Valley donkey bones come from villages in the Nile Delta and in the northern Sudan by at least 4000 BCE. Donkeys appear at the small town of Maadi, now on the outskirts of an expanding Cairo, during the first half of the fourth millennium. This important settlement was a key link in a major trade network that brought commodities from the eastern Mediterranean coastal region, and perhaps even from Mesopotamia, to the Nile.

Contacts between people living inside and outside the Nile Valley expanded dramatically after about 3500 BCE, both through river trade and via caravans of pack animals over neighboring deserts. Within a thousand years, donkeys appear in inscriptions and wall paintings. By then, they were in common use as beasts of burden; even, on occasion, buried near pharaohs.

Abydos, about 480 kilometers (298 miles) south of Cairo, is the burial place of the earliest pharaohs of about five thousand years ago.[4] A great embayment of cliffs provides a dramatic setting on the west bank of the Nile. Royal tombs and mortuary enclosures surrounded by high-status burials commemorate the departed kings in a symbolic landscape associated with the legendary Osiris, ruler of the realm of the dead. One ruler's tomb lay close to some buried lions, an ancient symbol of kingship. Fourteen large funerary boats accompanied another enclosure, ready for the journey to the Other World. One of the very early rulers went to eternity accompanied by donkeys, laid to rest adjacent to his funerary enclosure. Unfortunately, we don't know who he was.

Ten donkeys lay in three carefully prepared brick tombs with wood-and-masonry roofs. Each beast lay on its left side on a reed mat, as carefully buried as high officials. The donkeys were apparently in good health and well looked after, but the cartilage of their major joints at hip and shoulder display signs of heavy wear from overloading. The same areas display signs of arthritis, also caused by load carrying. Why did the mourners lavish such care on dead, or sacrificed, beasts? Presumably the donkeys' importance came from their qualities as pack animals, capable of surviving on little water and poor forage as they tramped across arid terrain carrying precious loads for the king.

The Abydos donkeys were larger and finer limbed than today's familiar beasts. They display some features of domesticated donkeys, others of wild asses. However, the pathological conditions of their backs clearly identify them as domesticated pack animals, the earliest unequivocal evidence for human use of such animals anywhere, even if we know from fragmentary bones that donkeys were in use along the Nile earlier. The physical changes and smaller size of the donkey developed over many centuries, which, among other things, made them slower than the revered beasts at Abydos.

Donkeys played a lowly part in Egyptian iconography, beyond being a symbol of the Sun God Re, for they were pack animals, not much else. They soon assumed a vital part in overland trade, so much so that wealthier members of Egyptian society were said to own more than a

Figure 8.1 *A man guides donkeys. From the tomb of Mereruka, VI Dynasty, c. 2349 BCE. Saqqara, Egypt. De Agostini/Superstock.*

thousand donkeys each by 2500 BCE, used for agriculture and carrying loads or people, and for meat and milk. They traveled up and down the Nile, but above all, they ventured into the arid lands on either side of the river, to the Red Sea and deep into the Sahara.

Why would donkey caravans have ventured into the unforgiving desert? The pharaohs craved lapis lazuli, gold, and other raw materials found in desert outcrops. They also traded extensively with distant kingdoms in what they called Nubia, now southern Egypt and northern Sudan, far upstream of the First Cataract, where their domains ended. During much of the Old Kingdom (2750–2180 BCE), the desert nomads were hostile, which made journeys along the Nile dangerous, especially when valuable cargoes were involved. So the Egyptians operated donkey trails far into the Sahara, well clear of hostile marauders. Few traces of these ancient caravan routes survive for modern investigators, for they lie in some of the most forbidding desert on earth.

Trackways to the West

THE DAKHLA OASIS LIES about 300 kilometers (186 miles) from the Nile Valley, in Egypt's Western Desert. In 1947, a sandstorm revealed what was probably the westernmost outpost of Egyptian civilization as early as 2600 BCE. Judging from strategically placed watchtowers, Egyptian knowledge of the desert to the west of Dakhla dated back to at least the time of the pharaoh Khufu (2589–2566 BCE). Rock inscriptions tell us that parties of at least four hundred men penetrated sixty kilometers (thirty-seven miles) into the arid landscape to acquire mineral powder used in paint. Apparently, people in Dakhla were familiar with the harsh, completely arid desert farther west, even if systematic journeying began later.

In 1999/2000, a German desert traveler, Carol Bergmann, discovered a chain of staging posts that once marked an ancient donkey trail that ran about 400 kilometers (248 miles) southwest into the desert from Dakhla to the Gilf Kebir Plateau in the Libyan Desert. Since then, German scholars have worked on the ancient donkey trails.[5] Clay vessels and other artifacts along the trail clearly link it to the administrative center in the oasis as early as Sixth Dynasty times (2345–2181 BCE). The terrain between Dakhla and the Gilf Kebir Plateau had but sparse vegetation and was almost waterless. Undeterred, the Egyptians organized donkey caravans along a much-used trail so wanting in food and water that provisions and water for human and beast had to be carried in and stashed at intervals along the way. Remarkably, donkey droppings and even traces of the trail itself survive in this remote landscape. Strategically placed stone cairns still mark the route. So do small stone circles, places where the caravaneers watered their beasts. Special supply caravans dumped food and water in carefully located caches. So far, archaeologists have located about twenty dumps of some three hundred clay jars along the route, just a fraction of what must actually have been used. Mineral stains inside the jars are characteristic of evaporating liquid, presumably water. Some have yielded barley seeds, perhaps food for donkeys and their drivers. Many of the vessels have eroded outer surfaces, as if they lay empty for some time before being refilled. The jars were probably sealed with leather covers.

Figure 8.2 *An ancient Egyptian donkey trail leading toward Abu Ballas, "Pottery Hill," on the caravan route between the Dakhla Oasis and the Gilf Kebir Plateau. Courtesy of Dr. Rudolph Kuper.*

In some places, the caches were larger, with hearths and other structures nearby that speak of somewhat longer stays. Some have vats for preparing bread dough, presumably the staple ration of the drivers. The men who stayed there may have guarded the provisions and water and also baked large amounts of bread for passing caravans.

Assuming that the donkeys covered about twenty-five to thirty kilometers (fifteen to nineteen miles) a day, the caravans would have stopped at large halts every third day, when the beasts were watered. Thus the journey from Dakhla to Gilf Kebir would have taken about two weeks, probably best undertaken in winter, with its cooler temperatures and chances of at least some forage from irregular rainfall.

The logistics of the trail must have been formidable, even under the most favorable circumstances. Distributing jars and water at regular intervals along the trail would have required numerous donkeys. Perhaps some beasts carried out four empty jars each, to reduce the danger of losing a precious load, while the water traveled in two light goatskin bags per beast, about 60 liters (16 gallons) per load. A 3,000 liter (793-gallon) stash at a major station would have required twenty-five donkeys to transport a hundred jars and fifty more to fill them.

What was the trail used for and where, ultimately, did it lead beyond the Gilf Kebir? There's no evidence that the Egyptians penetrated deeper into the Sahara, but they certainly maintained contact with nomadic herding groups far west of the Nile. Perhaps the trail was a bypass that allowed the pharaohs to skirt hostile groups along the river and maintain their valuable trade with Nubia. The elaborate logistics to provide food and water for animals and people required enormous effort, but the potential rewards in gold, ivory, semiprecious stones, and African products such as leopard skins were enormous. With hostile tribes along the river and a constant danger of raids, the caravans passed south and north through the desert, via routes far west of the Nile. Here, a well-armed donkey convoy, which would have required a secure, water-plentiful base to be successful, was safe from surprise raids. The strategy appears to have worked. During the twenty-third century BCE, Harkhuf, the governor of the southern part of Upper Egypt and overseer of caravans for the pharaoh Merenre (2283–2278 BCE), made at least four journeys to Nubia (see sidebar "Harkhuf and His Donkeys").

Harkhuf and His Donkeys

Harkhuf's travels give us momentary insight into the scale of the Egyptian donkey trade. The inscriptions on the walls of his tomb at Aswan, near the First Cataract, tell us that Pharaoh Merenre charged Harkhuf's family with exploring Nubia upstream, where gold abounded. As a young man, Harkhuf accompanied his father along a desert route to a kingdom named Yam, deep in Nubia. They traveled by donkey, the first of four expeditions that took Harkhuf far upstream. We do not know whether such donkey journeys were routine or whether Harkhuf traveled in unusual luxury. The accounts of his trips come from his tomb, a place for boasting if ever there was one. Most likely few people traveled in such elaborate style, but donkey caravans to Nubia were certainly routine for many centuries. Harkhuf was, after all, an important official at the royal court. His four trips southward took him not up the Nile itself, but along the so-called Oasis Road. This overland route led from Upper Egypt through a chain of four desert oases before regaining the Nile Valley at Toshke, in Nubia. Given the hostile terrain and unsettled conditions along the river, Harkhuf and his parties traveled on hundreds of donkeys. This enabled him to complete one successful journey in seven months and to travel on other occasions deep into Nubia to the kingdom of Yam, which was centered on the town of Kerma, south of the Third Cataract, well over 500 kilometers (311 miles) upstream of the First Cataract, near Aswan.

Harkhuf's inscriptions tell us that he exchanged gifts with the ruler of Yam and returned with "three hundred donkeys laden with incense, ebony . . . elephant tusks, throw sticks, and all sorts of good products." Just the logistics of this caravan beggar description. One estimate has it that a third of the donkeys would have carried goods, another third provisions, and a final third water through arid stages of the journey. An armed escort accompanied the caravan.

Harkhuf's entourage included a dancing dwarf. Harkhuf had sent a courier ahead to the court to report on his doings. The youthful pharaoh Pepi II wrote back in his own hand in great excitement: "Come north to the residence at once! Hurry and bring with you this dwarf whom you brought from the land of the horizon-dwellers live, hale, and hearty, for the dances of the god, to gladden the heart." When traveling on the Nile, men were to guard the dwarf lest he fall into the water. Twenty were to watch over him as he slept in camp, lest he come to harm. "My majesty wishes to see this pygmy more than the gifts of the mine-land [Sinai] and of Punt [the Red Sea lands]."[6] The royal message, originally preserved on papyrus, would have perished almost immediately had not Harkhuf caused it to be inscribed on the wall of his sepulcher after years as a prosperous senior courtier.

For centuries, donkeys by the hundred plied well-trodden tracks between the Nile and the Red Sea and deep into the Western Desert. The Theban

Desert Road Survey, a project of Yale University, has traced some of the desolate caravan routes that crossed forbidding terrain to the Kharga Oasis, 177 kilometers (110 miles) west of the Nile.[7] Thebes (modern-day Luxor) became an important hub for trade east and west, especially during a turbulent period in approximately 1800 BCE, when Hyksos invaders from Southwest Asia occupied the Nile Delta. The pharaohs marooned in Upper Egypt responded by controlling desert caravan routes that led east and west and trading with the Nubian rulers of Kerma upstream. In about 2000 BCE, the Theban ruler Mentuhotep II annexed the western oasis region. So successful were Egyptian donkey caravans that, for centuries, the desert effectively became a fourth power in the Egyptian equation.

The well-watered Kharga Oasis extends ninety-six kilometers (sixty miles) north and south along a limestone ridge in the Western Desert. The oasis became a major caravan crossroads both for the well-trodden Girja Road from the Nile and for routes to Nubia and places to the north. Umm Mawagir ("mother of bread molds" in Arabic) was a large permanent settlement of several thousand people at the end of the Girja Road that flourished between 1650 and 1550 BCE. Its excavators, John and Deborah Darnell, found an administrative building, grain silos, storerooms, workshops, and enormous numbers of bread molds, all protected by a military garrison. Anyone wanting to trade in the Western Desert had to deal with the people at Kharga, whether they were driving a handful of donkeys or hundreds of beasts. From the oasis, the archaeologists are mapping ancient trails, using potsherds (pottery fragments) from an enormous area, including Nubia. Umm Mawagir and the earlier oasis settlement at Dakhla Oasis, to the south, were the bases that allowed the rulers of Thebes to control donkey caravan trade over an enormous tract of arid landscapes.

Donkeys were everywhere in Egypt, as commonplace as people working in the fields. At the tomb workers' village at Deir el-Medina, on the west bank of the Nile, opposite Thebes, dozens of ostraca (pot-sherds, or smooth limestone flakes used as "writing pads") record medical remedies, love poems, and the transactions of the donkey trade, written between 1500 and 1200 BCE. The Deir el-Medina workers were unusually literate and quite prosperous. Their ostraca record the trading of donkeys, people borrowing them, owners commonly renting them out—the Ancient Egyptian equivalent of a rent-a-car. Owners leased out their beasts for an average of a month, sometimes longer, with the transactions faithfully recorded. The records preserve the inevitable problems: failure to pay, disagreements over prices, and the unexpected death of what were valuable animals. Water carriers, woodcutters, and policemen rented donkeys, for which they paid about three and a quarter sacks of grain a month, about two-thirds a worker's salary. This must have been a profitable business. Records one ostracon: "Year 3, second month of winter day 1. This day, giving the donkey for hire to the policeman Amen-Kha: makes 5 copper *deben* for the month. And it spent 42 days with him." (A *deben* was about a quarter pound of copper.) Leases were sometimes guaranteed against potential disputes, and occasionally terminated early, especially if the animal fell ill. "Year 31, fourth month of winter, day 17. Giving the donkey to Hori in place of his father," records another document. Ten days later "[the donkey] died, although his lease was not [complete]."[8] Situations like this were hard on the owner, perhaps, but the business was lucrative, with so many donkeys used for agriculture and load carrying.

Egypt's contacts with Mesopotamia were of little economic importance compared with the gold and tropical products obtained from Nubia and the semiprecious stones, copper, and other vital commodities packed in from the Sinai. Some official caravans, sent to obtain copper and other strategic commodities, involved hundreds of people and thousands of donkeys. Apart from riverboats and coastal merchantmen, all diplomatic ventures and trading expeditions relied on strings of donkeys, which plodded stoically along arid trackways far from the Nile. These "average joes" linked temples and oases; cities, towns, and villages hundreds of kilometers apart. Their arduous journeys globalized much of the eastern Mediterranean world.

CHAPTER 9

The Pickup Trucks of History

FOUR THOUSAND YEARS AGO, no one living along the Nile or in eastern Mediterranean lands would have given a laden donkey a second glance. A nineteenth century English traveler in Syria remarked of the beast that "It will maintain an easy trot and canter for hours without flagging, and always gains on the horse up the hills or on the broken ground."[1] Obdurate, certainly, occasionally troublesome, these versatile beasts linked cities and civilizations over thousands of kilometers of arid, often rugged terrain. There was little glamor attached to donkeys in the early days. They were the ancient equivalent of pickup trucks long before they became marks of rank and dignity. We've forgotten that these self-effacing beasts helped create the first truly global world. They linked the Euphrates with the Mediterranean, the Upper Tigris with Central Turkey, quietly broke down Egypt's geographical and cultural isolation, and provisioned military campaigns. A more powerful instrument of globalization is hard to imagine.

Donkeys Become an International Asset

DONKEY CARAVANS CONNECTED COURTS and cities long before Ancient Egypt's greatest pharaohs cast their eyes on more distant lands. The tempo of long-distance trade, of globalized commerce, picked up dramatically throughout Southwest Asia after the nineteenth century BCE. Caravan trails led from coastal cities such as Ugarit and Tyre, on the Mediterranean coast, to the Euphrates and Tigris. Donkey routes linked Egypt and the Levant. Virtually everywhere, the terrain was rough, the trails narrow and sometimes hazardous. Only donkeys, heavy oxcarts, or human porters could carry loads from city to inland city, until the

Figure 9.1 *A modern-day donkey caravan in Mali transporting Saharan salt. James Michael Dorsey/Shutterstock.*

introduction of the camel in the centuries before Christ. The sheer volume of the mercantile caravan trade turned the donkey into a major economic asset, an instrument of widespread prosperity. Gifts for rulers, mundane commodities such as textiles or salt, mining caravans using hundreds of beasts—loads of all kinds traversed desert and river valley alike in a world where urban economies were becoming more interdependent, more global.

Some respect for these humble beasts developed as well. They served a small but well-documented ritual part in an increasingly complex mercantile and political world. Numerous examples of donkey burials lie with the graves of high-status individuals or warriors. They occur in pairs, even occasionally in larger numbers, their bones sometimes disarticulated as if they were part of ritual feasts or sacrifices. Judging from Egypt's Abydos burials, such sacrifices were symbolic of wealth and economic power. One well-documented donkey burial lies in the heart of the sacred precinct at Tel Haror, a city near Gaza, dating to around 1700 to 1550 BCE.[2] The four-year-old donkey, a young beast, came to light in a temple courtyard, lying on its left side, its limbs neatly bent. A well-worn, defective, copper bridle bit was still in its jaws, but was just placed in the animal's mouth. There are no signs from the teeth that the donkey was ever ridden or carried loads, but the bit gives it a special status: a beast too young to be trained for caravan use. Significantly, too, copper fittings for saddle bags survive on either side of the ribs, again a symbolic acknowledgment of the importance of donkeys in the economic lives of the rich and powerful.

Still, donkeys were mainly economic assets. The impatient, aggressive Sumerians, in southern Mesopotamia, who first made extensive use of donkeys forty-five hundred years ago, portrayed them as slow, stubborn animals. One saying preserved on a cuneiform tablet remarks that donkeys ate their own bedding. Another owner rebuked his donkey for not running fast, but merely braying. (The loud and prolonged bray was an excellent adaptation for arid landscapes, where wild asses were often widely separated.) In later times, the Jewish *Wisdom of Sirach* talks of "Fodder and a stick and burdens for the ass; bread and discipline and work for a servant."[3] Even when ridden, donkeys were humble beasts. Witness the prophet Zachariah, who portrayed Israel's future king as arriving not on a war horse, but "humble and riding on an ass."[4] Some donkeys denoted dignity and prestige. In Judges, the prophetess Deborah addresses the judges: "Speak ye that ride on white asses, ye that sit in judgment."[5] For the most part, however, donkeys were the proletariat of the ancient animal world.

Emarum Sallamum: *The Saga of Assyrian Donkey Caravans*

IF ONE WERE TO ask for an example of obscure, highly specialized scholarship, one would need look no further than the esoteric, but very challenging, task of studying Assyrian donkey caravans. The few experts on the subject pore over dozens of cuneiform tablets from an important trading post at Karum Kanesh, adjacent to a major ancient city at Kultepe, in what is now central Turkey. The often highly personal letters and records from both Kanesh and Kultepe provide a compelling story of an enduring and prosperous international trade that could flourish only because of donkeys (see sidebar "Archives in Clay Envelopes").

Archives in Clay Envelopes

Karum Kanesh (Assyrian, meaning the "merchant colony of Kanesh") yielded more than a thousand cuneiform tablets when the Czech archaeologist Bedrich Hrozny dug into its earthen mound in 1923. Excavations resumed in 1948, in the hands of Turkish archaeologists, and continue today. Five hundred meters (1,640 feet) across and standing about 20 meters (66 feet) above the surrounding plain, Kanesh and its twenty-three thousand cuneiform tablets provide us with a complex portrait of a thriving commercial settlement just under four thousand years ago.

Fortunately for archaeologists, but not for the inhabitants, two fierce conflagrations destroyed the colony twice. The people fled, leaving their possessions and their archives behind. Thousands of burnt tablets, many of them still sealed in clay envelopes, reveal the complex transactions and sometimes convoluted personal lives of the merchants. The tablets are extremely fragile, many of them impregnated with high concentrations of soluble salts from the local soils, so just conserving them is a challenging task, often involving careful heating to bake them slowly. Then comes the intricate detective work of decipherment. Cuneiform is a wedge-shaped script; the writing used at Kanesh is Old Assyrian, which is relatively simple to learn. Although there were obviously trained scribes, the literacy level at Kanesh seems to have been unusually high. We know this from painstaking studies of correspondence on a wide range of subjects, written by both men and women. To tease out the complex transactions and hidden meanings of many tablets requires not only fluency in Old Assyrian and cuneiform, but also the same deep reserves of patience needed to assemble jigsaw puzzles.

The Kanesh tablets preserve an extraordinary range of correspondence. On one tablet, sealed in an envelope, a twenty-five-line letter written by Assur-lamassi, a copper trader, informs Su-Belum in Kanesh that he is shipping him silver carried by Iddi[n]-Su'en as payment for seven talents, thirty minas of copper. A shekel of silver purchased sixty-two and a half shekels of copper. The copper traders mentioned on the tablet are known from the karum archives of a well-known copper trader, Ada-S.ululi. Assur-lamassi considered the message so important that he sealed it eight times. Other tablets record ownership disputes involving merchant houses, the exchange of textiles and tin from Assur for precious metals, the dangers of bandits, and the need to provide grazing for donkeys. Women were active correspondents, concerned not only with the management of houses and servants, but also with commercial transactions. Tarisha, daughter of Alahum and sister of Assur-taklaku, maintained an archive of tablets for her husband. Wrote one man, "Extract for me my tablet concerning one mina of silver that Shat-ishtar, the wife of Assur-taklaku, wrote." This was a sophisticated, carefully monitored donkey trade that shaped economic life over an enormous area of the eastern Mediterranean world.

The city of Assur lies on the western bank of the Tigris River in what is now northern Iraq, far upstream of Sumerian domains in fertile Mesopotamia. Assur's rulers shook off the yoke of their southern masters at Ur, in Mesopotamia, during the twenty-first century BCE. They prospered because their city lay at the hub of a web of trade routes that extended over an enormous area. The city enjoyed a lucrative overland trade in textiles and tin, encouraging traders from elsewhere with minimal taxation.

Assur flourished at a time when bronze technology was of enormous importance, both for utilitarian artifacts and weapons and for ornaments and ceremonial vessels of all kinds. Bronze, an alloy of copper and tin, was a currency of imperial gifts and diplomatic exchange, prized for its durability and lustrous glow. Copper was relatively commonplace, but tin was a rarity, highly prized, and a staple of Assyrian trade. The city's merchants purchased the metal from Babylonia, but it originally came from modern-day Uzbekistan and Tajikistan in Eurasia. Who controlled the mines and to what extent Assur monopolized the tin trade is a mystery, but shipments of the metal passed westward by donkey caravan to the Anatolian Plateau. Assur's merchants also handled both locally woven textiles and highly prized Akkadian fabrics from the south. One expert has estimated that the ratio of donkey loads of textiles and wool to tin to pass west was in the order of three to one. However, one load of tin was five times as valuable as one of textiles.[6]

Assyrian commerce with Anatolia depended on trading colonies. For centuries, an Assyrian quarter of merchants and soldiers, known as a *kârum*, an Akkadian word for "port" or "quay"—Akkadian was the lingua franca of the time—prospered outside the city of Kultepe in central Turkey. Karum Kanesh was the terminus of a caravan trade in tin and textiles that lasted between about 1895 and 1715 BCE. The merchants of the *kârum* maintained contacts with a much larger set of trading networks through Anatolia and farther afield. The entire region was a patchwork of city-states and shifting alliances, which required adept diplomacy. The Assyrians with their tin and much-coveted textiles kept a strategic advantage by executing sworn agreements with local rulers. Tolls and tribute were important sources of income for such worthies. The cuneiform tablets from the *kârum* contain frequent references to payments made by caravans along the road.

Like so much ancient trade, the Assur caravan trade was in the hands of powerful family-run merchant houses, in this case Assyrian, within a framework of carefully administered and financed partnerships that depended on agents in Kanesh. The entire enterprise relied on the hardworking donkey. (The Assyrians also possessed mules, or *perdum*, which were used for riding, especially by more prominent individuals.)[7]

The Assyrian donkey was a dark-colored pack animal—*emarum sallamum*, or "black donkey"—apparently a larger animal than the modern equivalent, with a long body and ears. They were plentiful, sturdy, and generally docile. As far as the merchants were concerned, donkeys were merely a means of transport to be used as efficiently as possible, so their life expectancy was relatively short. Heavily laden Assyrian donkeys must have been tough beasts, operating as they did in rough terrain. The Kanesh tablets tell us that many caravans arrived without losing any animals. Others suffered casualty rates of 50 to even 70 percent, but whether this was because of disease or weather conditions is unknown.

A donkey caravan—*ellatum*, a word approximating to "traveler"—was the terrestrial equivalent of an ocean convoy. Most people preferred to travel in company, with caravans leaving once there were enough individuals wanting to reach a specific destination, perhaps several times a month. Apart from security considerations, caravans lessened labor expenses and, perhaps just as important, were an invaluable source of intelligence on conditions along well-traveled routes. Like Egyptian caravans, an *ellatum* moved slowly but steadily, apparently traveling about twenty-five kilometers (fifteen miles) a day, what one might call a donkey pace. (A British army manual from modern times states that a donkey carrying a full load would travel about 3.4 kilometers (2 miles) an hour for six hours a day, which provides a yardstick.) (Also see sidebar "Xenophon Once Again.") The journey from Assur to Kanesh, some 1,000 kilometers (621 miles) took about six weeks through rocky desert, mountain passes, dense forest, and flat plains.

The caravans required large numbers of strong beasts, so much so that breeding and training centers (*gigamlum*) sold them in many places. Assur in particular required a regular supply of male donkeys for load carrying; females were used for breeding. A caravan pack animal cost about sixteen to seventeen shekels in Assur, a few shekels more for saddles and panniers. Those sold in Anatolia fetched between twenty and thirty, so the profit margin was virtually nonexistent, once one took into account the costs of feeding the animal. Its care was minimal—the tablets speak of straw as fodder, the beasts being permitted to graze in spring, sometimes in rented paddocks along the way.

The vehicles of the caravan trade were just that, disposable pack animals worked to death or sold at the other end with the hope that one would break even. Few of the beasts made the return journey. The gold and silver carried eastward required many fewer pack animals. Hundreds, if not thousands, of donkeys plodded along the caravan routes, in convoys large and small—we have no means of estimating the precise numbers. As Assyriologist Gojko Barjamovic remarked in an e-mail to the author, "Someone must have been mass producing donkeys somewhere. The animals were not exactly cheap . . . about the price of a . . . female slave. These were not exactly Mercedeses, but at least the Dodge Ram trucks of the day. And people drove them in a comparably heinous and destructive manner."[8]

Each donkey carried about 75 kilograms (165 pounds), loaded on a pack saddle, perhaps a leather- or cloth-covered wooden frame over a saddle cloth. Tin lay in two goat hair or leather half packs, one on either side of the beast, textiles in leather bags atop the pack saddle. With relatively standardized loads, merchants could be charged costs per load, which made the logistics of the trade somewhat easier to control.

Just how large Assyrian caravans were is a matter of debate, but groups of forty donkeys or more were not uncommon. A cuneiform tablet from the archives at the city of Mari in Syria tells us that one *ellatum* organized by local merchants comprised some three hundred donkeys and three hundred men, presumably the drivers, at a rate of about one per beast. Junior members of the merchant family often served as caravan leaders. They were responsible for the administration of the convoy and its safe arrival, and for the letter tablets in clay envelopes that formed part of the cargo. Tablet after tablet pleads for messages to be sent with the first available caravan; at the typical pace of twenty-four kilometers (fifteen miles) daily, each day truly counted.

Just the provisioning of caravans was a major task. As a result, the caravan routes changed little over the generations, proceeding from staging post to staging post, using agreements with local rulers to ensure safe passage. Inns along the routes fulfilled many functions, including storage of goods as well as providing food, fodder, and water. The last was an important consideration, especially with large caravans of three hundred beasts or so, which could consume six tons of water daily. Just growing and processing the fodder at such inns would have been a full-time job involving significant numbers of workers. Everywhere, the Assyrian caravan trade had a lasting effect on communities through which it passed.

We will never be able to reconstruct the full details of the caravan trade from surviving clay tablets. The primary sources are too incomplete and leave out many telling details of what was a very profitable, if sometimes risky, trade. The weary pack animals earned huge sums for their owners. Profit margins for tin (about 100 percent) and textiles (200 percent) were enormous. Just to give an impression of the value of the textiles, one standard-size cloth would buy about 3,600 loaves of bread, 7 kilograms (15 pounds) of copper, or 12 sheep. A single length of fine textile was even more valuable than a slave. One family's tablet records a caravan of thirty-four donkeys that carried about 600 kilograms (1,322 pounds) of tin and 684 textiles, a mere smidgen of the wealth that traveled from Assur to Anatolia on donkey's backs. If one arbitrarily estimates one donkey load of tin per Assyrian family annually, about two tons' worth traveled west over a thirty-year period from 1889 to 1859 BCE, a staggering figure.

Global Beasts

MERCHANTS, TRAVELERS, PILGRIMS—EVERYONE IN the eastern Mediterranean used donkeys and sometimes mules, before horses and camels became people movers. Cities such as Damascus prospered because they lay at the crossroads of strategic donkey caravan routes. Convoys of beasts wended their way from central and southern Mesopotamia, traveling north along the Tigris and Euphrates before heading west rather than traveling straight across the arid and dangerous Syrian Desert, where brigands lurked. The caravans supplied the markets of Aleppo, Hamath, and Damascus, where they linked up with other groups from the north. From these hubs, the donkeys headed south to Egypt and places near the Red Sea. Some of the largest caravans are said to have involved three thousand beasts, many of them carrying fodder and water for the other pack animals.

Donkeys also carried loads deep into Armenia and eastward, along what became known as the Silk Road, linking Europe and China. They came to Greece as early as the tenth century BCE, where they found work in every aspect of daily life—packing loads from mountain villages to ships, hauling logs from forests, laboring on construction sites, grinding grain, and carrying baskets through rows of vines on hillside vineyards.[9] Without them, classical Athens would have lacked firewood, been chronically short of food, and its workshops and stores without raw materials or items to sell.

The Greeks made a clear distinction between the noble horse and the "servile" donkey, which corresponded in broad terms with that between people who were free and slaves. The ass was a menial laborer, a source of ribald humor, one of the unfree, despite being ridden by people of wealth or spiritual importance such as Christ and the Prophet Muhammad.[10] However, donkeys developed strong ties with Christian symbolism as a result of Christ's triumphant ride into Jerusalem. Christianity helped raise the status of the donkey, which supported the Savior when others ignored him.

"Sturdy, Sound in All Parts"

ROMAN DONKEYS WORKED HARD throughout their lives, both on the farm and in pack trains. Like Greek beasts, they pulled plows on lighter soils, crushed olives, ground grain, and carted manure. Their panniers carried grain, oil, wine, and all kinds of other merchandise. Farmers kept only as many as they needed, while traders assembled their herds depending on the loads to be carried. Heavily laden, straining donkeys caused traffic jams in narrow city streets, polluted the roads, and filled the air with their loud braying. But they were tolerated because they were uncomplaining load carriers that required little maintenance. Donkey breeding was a major industry throughout the empire. Beasts that were "sturdy, sound in all parts, full bodies, and of good stock" served as the best breeding donkeys.[11] Pregnant jennies were never worked. The young were weaned only partially after a year and were trained at age three for specific needs. Beasts destined to become pack animals were castrated when two years old, to ensure they were as tractable as possible.

Mules assumed increasing importance, especially in Roman times. Sumerians were probably the first to breed hybrid equids, perhaps during the third millennium BCE. By Assyrian times, *perdum*, the mule, was commonplace, ridden by people of status as well as serving as a pack animal. Mules came into their own during Roman times as powerful and resilient pack animals, so much so that they became the primary baggage and draft animal of the Roman army and the *cursus publicum*, the official courier and road service based on the empire's network of highways.

Throughout the Roman Empire both donkeys and mules were essential to the transport of goods and people. Pack trains helped maintain military supply lines, especially over relatively short distances in remote areas without roads and away from rivers, which were the best way of hauling bulk cargos such as grain and wine amphorae. Both beasts hauled wagons wherever the terrain was not too challenging and roads were passable. Over short distances, mules were superior. A string of twenty mules could carry as much as five ox-drawn wagon loads.

Mules occupied a kind of intermediate role between the humble donkey and the noble horse. Like horses, mules had many personalities. Some were spirited animals that could give an aristocrat a lively ride, while more placid beasts carried common folk. (The best mules were probably the size of small horses, some fourteen to fifteen hands—one hand equals ten centimeters, or four inches—just over a meter [3.2 feet].) Mule breeding was highly profitable. According to the Roman author Columella, mares "should be big and handsome and well able to endure toil."[12] Each mare produced about five foals between the ages of four and ten, and gestation periods were just over a year. This, and the difficulties of breeding, made for expensive mules, which were carefully trained. For example, trainers drove mule foals into the mountains in summer to harden their hooves against their eventual use on rough road surfaces.

These tough and undemanding animals tackled rugged terrain and mountain landscapes, were surefooted, and carried heavy loads. They crossed into Gaul with legions conquering Celtic and Germanic tribes and served as pack animals and mounts for auxiliary troops defending the Rhine frontier. The remains of at least four mules came from a large garbage dump of 160 CE, at the Biriciana frontier fort near the Bavarian town of Weißenburg.[13] Dogs gnawed the bones of the carelessly buried animals. Using serial stable isotope analysis on one of the mule teeth, German researchers were able to show that the mule was probably bred in northern Italy. From its eighth year onward, the beast frequented higher altitudes, probably packing across the Alps, silent testimony to the importance of mules to Roman garrisons.

Bartholomeus Anglicus and Others

THE ROMANS INTRODUCED DONKEYS to Europe, but they became more common after the Norman Conquest of Britain in 1066. Several appear in the Bayeux Tapestry. According to the thirteenth-century scholar Bartholomeus Anglicus, they were harshly treated. Older asses were "melancholy," also "unlusty and witless and forgetful." Their owners beat them and starved them until they died after "vain travails." They had "no reward after death for the service and travail of their lives."[14] When horses were requisitioned for war during the sixteenth century, donkeys took their places in the field, but by the eighteenth century they worked mainly in expanding industrial cities, where emaciated and neglected animals crowded the streets. Just as they had been in Greece, asses were considered inferior beasts.

Mules fared much better, especially well-bred animals that carried such worthies as fifteenth-century Cardinal Wolsey. He went forth on a white mule richly adorned with gold. Eminent churchmen such as bishops habitually used mules, a tradition going back to biblical times, when King Solomon rode King David's mule. Fourteenth-century popes residing in Avignon habitually rode well-bred mules. After the Reformation, the horse quickly replaced the mule as the animal of kings and the nobility, partly, perhaps, because their fathers were humble donkeys with no pretensions toward aristocracy. Meanwhile, the donkey carried loads and working folk, just as it had always done, silently, the subject of ridicule and abuse.

The Golden Ass set the tone. Almost invariably, people transformed into donkeys play comic roles, such as that of Bottom in *A Midsummer Night's Dream*, who wears an ass's head and lusts for a bottle of hay. There's Robert Louis Stevenson, who beat his overladen donkey, Modestine, and of course A. A. Milne's Eeyore, with his taste for disagreeable thistles and delight in being miserable. Few have ever credited the donkey with great intelligence, except perhaps Robert Graves, who commented in his introduction to *The Golden Ass* that "asses are really far more sagacious than horses."[15] All this is over and above the pejorative expressions so common today, of which "you are a silly ass" is one of the milder examples.

The Beast That Interconnected

EVERY DOMESTICATED ANIMAL TRANSFORMED human life in some way or other. Goats and sheep were the daily currency of many subsistence farmers. Cattle became powerful symbols of royal power. None of them had such an impact on the course of history as the donkey, with the possible exception of the horse, a creature of the steppes. Horses were faster, but lacked the ability of donkeys to traverse arid landscapes. The ass was hardier, cheaper to maintain, and more reliable in the challenging, work-a-day world of the caravan trade. Tough and easily trained, donkeys have labored alongside people for at least five thousand years, perhaps longer. They were catalysts for change, with an ability to traverse some of the driest terrain on earth that separated Egypt from Mesopotamia, the Indus Valley from what is now Iraq. They carried gold and textiles from Assyria deep into Anatolia, hefted supplies for armies, and transported food and raw materials for cities with an efficiency that linked rulers and states hundreds of kilometers apart. Their repetitive marches created the first truly international commerce throughout the eastern Mediterranean region and far beyond. Tin from Uzbekistan, lead from Turkey, textiles from cities between the Tigris and Euphrates—hundreds of donkeys and their drivers helped merchant ships (a much higher-risk form of transportation) to create a multicultural world that would have been unthinkable without them.

Donkeys are routine, self-effacing animals, valued by farmers, generals, merchants, and priests for thousands of years, and in many parts of the world to this day. For the most part, but not invariably of course, they carried trade goods rather than people. Civilizations rose and fell; royal dynasties collapsed in the face of conquering armies; kings reigned and were then forgotten. There was often turmoil as armies trod the land, but two eternal verities survived cataclysms of disruption and violence. Subsistence farmers tended their fields in the shadow of great events, as they had always done in an unchanging routine of planting and harvest, life and death. And across remote desert landscapes and arid valleys, donkey caravans plodded along at a measured pace, looking neither to left nor right in another unchanging routine, this time of cultural interconnectedness.

Xenophon Once Again

Many of the lessons learned by packers in the past have vanished, but the use of pack animals in military campaigns has resumed in the rugged terrain of Afghanistan during the early twenty-first century and helped revive basic skills. U.S. Special Forces units fought alongside Afghan Northern Alliance soldiers using donkeys in 2001. Donkeys and mules have become commonplace in campaigns against Taliban foes since then, for they can operate effectively at high altitudes, where helicopters have difficulty. "Tough, compact, sturdy, and well-formed"—these words describe the qualities sought by U.S. Special Forces for the donkeys and mules they use in Afghanistan to carry loads along narrow trails and across rugged terrain. The military's *Use of Pack Animals* manual can be consulted online, and reinforces what we know about the practices of ancient pack animal handlers. The manual "captures some of the expertise and techniques that have been lost in the United States Army over the past 50 years."[16]

The authors stress that the effectiveness and mobility of pack animals depend on their selection and training. Friendly, gentle personalities and comfort with humans are also essential. Handlers must never lose their tempers with their donkeys or use brute force. Confidence and trust between animal and handler leads to task completion. States the manual, "Donkeys have a strong sense of survival. If they deem something as dangerous, they will not do it. It is not stubbornness—it is Mother Nature, and they are smart enough to know when they cannot handle something." Donkeys will "generally freeze if frightened, or run a little way then stop to look at what startled them." The manual calls a donkey "a strong, calm, intelligent worker."

Mules are remarkable for their intelligence, agility, and stamina. They carry 55 percent of their weight on their front legs, which makes them surefooted and well balanced in rough country. Although people sometimes refer to individual people as being "as stubborn as a mule," in fact these beasts merely have a strong sense of self-preservation. Nothing a packer may do will change a mule's mind if it senses danger. Fortunately, mules are easy to control, as they will follow a mare. The manual recommends a bell for the lead mare. All a packer has to do is to control the bell mare. The rest of the file will follow. At night, mules can wander freely if the bell mare is picketed. Breaking in young mules requires kindness and patience. The manual has strong echoes of Xenophon's wise words from over two thousand years ago.

"Common sense, preparation, and good planning" are the mantras for pack trains operating under war conditions, among enemies who also use donkeys and mules. This raises concerns about safety. When on the move, pack detachments form columns, which present a long, linear target for the enemy. The manual urges the use of scouts and outriders for flank security, just like those used by the Romans to protect marching legions. In hostile territory, a pack detachment has to avoid skylines, stay within the tree line at higher altitudes, contour the terrain, camouflage loads, and avoid open areas as much as possible. If attacked or ambushed, "quickly escape in any feasible direction." In a modern twist unknown in the past, "dispersal and continuous movements are the keys to survival when attacked from the air."

The manual covers every eventuality, from training, to riding and saddles, to loading the animals with a maximum weight of 72 to 77 kilograms (160 to 170 pounds), to watering and feeding the beasts. There are esoterica, too. A handler can lead two animals to drink, but should not withdraw them from the water when they have raised their heads for the first time. "Animal transport systems can greatly increase mission success when hostile elements and conditions require the movement of combat troops and equipment by foot." Such movements reduce fatigue. According to the manual, a mule or horse can travel thirty-two to forty-eight kilometers (twenty to thirty miles) a day.

*The Beasts That
Toppled Emperors*

CHAPTER 10

Taming Equus

The Eurasian steppe, early autumn, seventeen thousand years ago. Fur-clad young men lie motionless in the stunted grass near the watering hole, their eyes cast watchfully, narrowed against the constant, dusty wind. A small wild horse herd grazes close upwind, the beasts' backs to the gusts, mares and their foals, the stallion feeding protectively close by. He tosses his head and mane, flicks his tail. Reassured, he resumes his graze. None of the hunters move, oblivious to the mosquitoes swarming overhead. They know the herd well, have counted the foals, are looking for strays. With stoic patience, they wait and wait. As the shadows lengthen, the herd moves away along a well-used, dung-lined trail. The hunters return empty-handed to camp. Hunting in this arid terrain requires infinite patience and relentless opportunism, the patience of the proverbial Job.

THE STEPPE WAS INHOSPITABLE country, an endless landscape of open plains and occasional shallow valleys where scrub brush hugged the ground and cold winds from arctic ice sheets raised great clouds of fine glacial dust high above the earth. Summers were short, mosquito-ridden, and sometimes very hot. For nine months of the year, cutting northerly winds lowered temperatures far below zero for weeks on end. Mere handfuls of people hunted in this desolate world, ranging cautiously over the steppe in summer, hunkering down in shallow river valleys during the subzero months, their dome-shaped sod and mammoth bone dwellings dug partially into the ground. They preyed on cold-loving animals such as the mammoth and bison, on saiga antelope, and on a fleet, often dangerous quarry: the wild horse (*Equus ferus*), ancestor of the domesticated equine of today.

Tarpans, Przewalski's, and Larger Beasts

WILD HORSES WERE FAST and aggressive, dangerous when cornered. The hunters would have watched stallions fight one another in vicious competitions for mares.[1] They also knew that mothers would turn against predators and protect their foals with flailing hooves. But this potentially ferocious animal provided nutritious meat and thongs and hides, and was so profoundly valued that Cro-Magnon artists painted it alongside the aurochs on the walls of Lascaux Cave, Pech Merle, and elsewhere.

Both large beasts with upright manes (up to 142 centimeters, or 56 inches, at the shoulder) and smaller horses coexisted in Europe and Eurasia during the last cold snap of the Ice Age.[2] The smaller horses, collectively known as tarpans, were up to fifty-seven centimeters (twenty-two inches) at the shoulder, survived after the ice retreated and temperatures rose. They flourished in large numbers across a broad swathe of the north, from southwest Europe deep into North and Central Asia. Unfortunately, they are now extinct. Hunters killed the last tarpans in the Ukraine in 1851. The only surviving zoo-based individual died in 1919. Tarpans had dun coats, black limbs, and short tails, very similar in appearance to the famous Przewalski's horse of Siberia, which is grayer. Judging from what we know about modern wild horse behavior, tarpans probably lived in small herds: harem groups of five or six mares, their stallion, and their foals. Male offspring reaching sexual maturity left the herd and lived alone or formed small bachelor groups. As they gained strength, the young stallions would have tried to steal young mares and form their own harems. Each herd had its own limited home range, which it traveled through along well-defined trails. They would have returned to reliable water sources virtually every day. The dominant mare invariably led the herd, including the stallion, which followed in single file. When frightened by a predator (or humans), they would take flight with the foals in the middle, the stallion staying on the side of greatest danger.

The tarpan, with its flailing hooves, was more dangerous prey than medium-size ungulates such as reindeer. Ancient hunters may have focused on harem groups, whose movements were easier to predict and, because of their young, slower than those of bachelors. They would ambush well-used trails or lie in wait for the beasts at watering holes, especially in early fall, when herds congregated in the same sheltered locales. Sometimes, as was the case at the famous horse kill site at Solutré, in France, the hunters would drive the herd into a natural cul-de-sac, kill the stallion, and then kill the mares.[3] Solutré was a strategic kill site for thousands of years. More than eighty thousand horses perished there before 16,000 BCE. Large-scale hunts produced enormous quantities of meat, much of which must have been dried for later use. In many cases, the hides and tendons may have been more important than the flesh, there being other plentiful sources of meat on the hoof.

As the climate warmed up after fifteen thousand years ago, forage became more plentiful and water more abundant. Horse hunting may have intensified, as other Ice Age game either moved far northward or became extinct. Tarpan abounded in the transitional zone of southern Eurasia, where forests gave way to open country, the so-called Pontic-Caspian Steppe. Wild horses were, above all, steppe animals, accustomed to long, frigid winters. They could survive subzero cold by virtue of their tough hooves, which enabled them to scrape snow away to obtain feed or to break through ice for water. Cattle and sheep have difficulty pushing their noses through snow and ice, and are soon incapacitated, making it necessary to maintain them with fodder. Thus, horses were an important meat source, especially for hunters who needed to consume copious amounts of fat. Horseflesh is high in polyunsaturated fats, amino acids, minerals, and vitamins, which may be why people attributed unusual medicinal and nutritional properties to it and to horse's milk.

Prelude to Domestication

WARMER CONDITIONS BROUGHT NEWCOMERS and profound changes to Eurasian life.[4] Around 5600 BCE, cereal farmers and cattle herders spread eastward from the fertile Lower Danube Valley. They brought with them both cattle and small stock, and also copper metallurgy. Soon local hunting groups adopted the new economies, but both agriculture and herding were risky propositions in these borderlands. Intensive hunting, especially of horses, served as a form of risk management.

Despite the challenges of a hostile environment, the newcomers prospered over the next seven centuries. More elaborate farming societies thrived over a wide area from the Carpathian Mountains in eastern Europe to the Dnieper River in the Ukraine. Their wealth came from trade in copper and gold, which passed from hand to hand over long distances. By 4500 BCE, farming populations had risen sharply in the river valleys north of the Black Sea. The following centuries were the moment of truth as far as the horse was concerned. Horse hunting intensified still further. Wild herds must have become scarcer. The stage was set for a new partnership with the most abundant of wild prey.

I use the word *partnership* deliberately, for what ultimately changed was not only the management of horse herds in place of hunting, but also the entire relationship between horses and humans, in ways that were to revolutionize history.[5] At issue here was one fact of life on the steppes: the quest for mobility.

The steppe extends to the far horizon, often featureless, dissected by occasional shallow river valleys. People are diminished in these vast landscapes, where distances are enormous and about the only food is game on the hoof. Hunting one's quarry was a challenge. Antelope and wild horses fled rapidly from danger, grazed in herds, and ranged over large territories, far more extensive than those of the humans who preyed upon them. Speed was preys' greatest protector, the ability to cover distances in a few minutes that would take people hours to traverse. For thousands of years, hunters preyed on these animals, most often when the latter congregated near watering holes or in shallow river valleys, where fertile graze was to be found, and shelter in winter. Success in the hunt depended on ambushes, on careful observation of vulnerable beasts, on constant opportunism that enabled people to cull strays and vulnerable animals. A timeless routine developed. In winter, hunting bands hunkered down in camps of dome-shaped houses, living much of the time off salted or dried meat. During the summer months, the bands would fan out over the plains in search of game. It was an isolated life at the best of times, for the land could support but handfuls of people. Most folk encountered only a few dozen others during their entire lives.

Much the same realities confronted the farmers who settled on the edge of the steppe. Their immobility hampered them. Survival depended on their stock and cereal crops, always a gamble in these climates of extremes, and on their ability to hunt wild horses. Their mobility, even under the most favorable conditions, was that of the walking distance between camps on the steppe. Then they tamed horses and rode them— and everything changed. For the first time, steppe people conquered distance. They could hunt more efficiently from horseback, drive cattle to distant pastures, transport loads on their mounts' backs. In a way, the effect historically was somewhat akin to that of the donkey in lands to the south. For the first time, a community could maintain links with settlements and people who had been out of range a few centuries earlier. The social effects were dramatic. People could marry into distant communities, which fostered kin ties over large distances. Now prominent individuals and kin leaders could maintain personal ties with potential allies dozens, even hundreds, of kilometers away. Mobility brought contacts and connections, those of trade and exchange in everything from basic commodities to luxuries such as ornaments. Ideas spread, too, creating relatively uniform cultural traditions, religious beliefs, and values over enormous areas of the steppe.

With mobility came quests for power—for cattle and conquest—in societies where horses were objects of devotion and close affections, forged in bonds strengthened by travel and war in very tough environments indeed. The horse cultures of the steppe were highly mobile, their prosperity depending on changing pasturage, climatic shifts that altered grazing grounds, and on success in war. Volatile, riven by factionalism and cemented by powerful, ever-changing loyalties, the kingdoms that developed on the steppe owed everything to their relationships to the horse, which made their survival possible. In the end, the horse and steppe nomads changed history, tumbled civilizations, and created mighty empires.

Taming Horses

CAPTURING OR CONTROLLING SUCH fast-moving, potentially ferocious animals as tarpans would never have been easy, especially on the open steppe, where close stalking is difficult at best for someone on foot armed with only a bow and arrow or a spear. So the hunters often turned to carefully orchestrated ambushes and cooperative drives. Such hunts required dealing with horses at close quarters. Such circumstances must have been commonplace enough, so much so that hunters may have gotten into the habit of corralling some of the trapped mares alive or even hobbling them, allowing them to feed in captivity until it was time to kill them. They may have focused on slower-moving pregnant mares, which would then give birth in captivity. Their foals would have been more amenable to control if brought up in captivity from the beginning. This may have been how domestication took hold, through loose management of growing herds of mares, who still bred with wild stallions.

This was not, of course, the first time that people had wrestled with the problem of domesticating large, often frisky animals. The first groups to domesticate horses were accustomed to cattle management. Like cattle, horses travel in bands. As with cattle, too, there's a lead female, who decides the route for the day. The others follow. Cattle and sheepherders had known for centuries that to control the leader was to control the herd, whether a flock of sheep or a small group of cattle.

As with bulls, rams, and boars, stallions were more unpredictable, even irascible, so nascent horse breeders may have captured more docile females that they would then have added to the harem of an already domesticated, relatively tractable male. Like cattle herders, they may also have faced the problem of surplus males, a problem solved by castrating many of them when young. Such gelded beasts were never a threat to the stallions, so the owner could graze the herd as a unit. It was probably no coincidence that cattle herders domesticated both donkeys and horses. One can envisage a scenario of close familiarity with local tarpan herds, and generations of close association with cattle, combined with growing populations and persistent meat shortages. Whatever the details, domestication almost certainly took place as a result of circumstances that varied from one place to another. In the final analysis, the herders knew what to do.

When Did It Start? Sredni Stog, Dereivka?

NO ONE KNOWS PRECISELY where horses were first domesticated, but if genetics is any guide, they were tamed in many locations between eastern Europe and the Caucasus. We'll never find a genetically ancestral mare, the "Eve," as it were, of *Equus caballus*, for crossbreeding with wild stallions was commonplace. With genetics inconclusive, we have to fall back on archaeological clues. These are contradictory at best. As is the case with cattle, it's a question of interpreting slaughter curves compiled from jaws and teeth. They can tell us the ages of slaughtered beasts, but not necessarily what the patterns mean. Unfortunately, too, there was so much size variation in wild horse populations that diminishing size is an unreliable criterion.

Between the Ingul River in the Ukraine and the Middle Volga River in Russia, the focus on horses became ever more intense around 4200 BCE, in the hands of the so-called Sredni Stog culture, a society where more elaborate burials signal more elaborate social hierarchies and the emergence of chieftains. By this time, households were three times larger than before, in a period when people sought food over much larger areas and moved frequently over the landscape. The earliest possible domestication at the time of writing—and this could change overnight—is from the Dereivka site, on the right bank of Ukraine's Dnieper River, where people hunted horses, and maybe domesticated them, between 4470 and 3530 BCE.[6] The inhabitants slaughtered nearly a quarter of all horses before the age of eight. Such a slaughter pattern is typical of Mongol horse herders to this day, but were these domesticated beasts? The zooarchaeologists debate back and forth, but it's interesting that one Dereivka ceremonial deposit contained two dogs and a horse—not, perhaps, a surprising association, since dogs may well have been used to herd horses. Dereivka also yielded perforated antlers that closely resemble Bronze Age cheek pieces found in later occupations at the site. This constellation of finds hints strongly at horse domestication in this region, and probably over a much wider area, during the fourth millennium BCE.

What Does One Do with Domesticated Horses?

WHAT DID THE DEREIVKA people do with their horses? Did they keep them purely for meat, milk, thongs, and hides? Were they using them as pack animals? Or, most important of all, did they ride them? Look at this from the perspective of moving around. A band of walking hunters seeking game on foot was a mere dot on a featureless landscape, amid animals such as the saiga antelope or the tarpan, both of whom annihilated distances at a gallop. Finding one's way across endless steppe would also have been a challenge, a matter of close knowledge of subtle landmarks like small gullies, clumps of bushes, and watering holes. Sun, moon, and stars would have been signposts in the great arc of the sky overhead, just as they were to canoe voyagers in the Pacific for thousands of years.

People engaged in herding and farming would have spent almost all their time anchored to river valleys and permanent water supplies. Herding cattle or sheep on foot across the steppe would have been near impossible, even with dogs. Except for fleeting contact between neighbors and occasional summer gatherings or the passing of exotics such as sea shells and metal objects from hand to hand, village to village, the isolation would have meant that one encountered few people in one's lifetime. The people had cattle, but these lumbering beasts cover but short distances daily and must drink every day, which made them vulnerable in arid landscapes. Donkeys were unknown on the steppe, which left only the horse. Once domesticated, the horse had open-ended potential, both as a pack animal controlled with a simple halter, or an animal to be ridden as a matter of routine, something entirely new in human experience.

Quite when people first rode horses is the subject of unending academic debate, largely because it's virtually impossible to tell from archaeological finds. At first, people rode their beasts with some form of noseband of leather, rope, or sinew, which rarely survive in archaeological sites. Bits, bridles, and other equipment came into use centuries later than initial domestication. (The earliest bits date to about 3500 to 3000 BCE, made of rope, bone, horn, or hardwood. Metal bits appear between 1300 and 1200 BCE, originally made of bronze and later of iron.)[7] But just how big a step was this? Perhaps the transition from herding to riding was much less than we think, accustomed as we are to bucking broncos and rodeos, also to terrified pedigree animals whose every instinct is to flee, flail out savagely, or bite. We shouldn't forget that the first people to ride horses had almost certainly sat on the backs of oxen, which already plowed fields and served as occasional pack animals. Also the first horses to be ridden on the steppe were much smaller than some later breeds. Even more important, those who domesticated them were intimately familiar with the behavior of agitated horses confronted with the unfamiliar.

Hunting with spears and the simple bows of the day required that one approach a wild horse, corralled or not, closely, to the point that on occasion the hunter might have jumped on the back of his prey to deliver a lethal blow into the heart. One can imagine a scenario where a bold young man leapt onto a horse's back, then held on to the mane as the horse reared and galloped. One can also imagine an individual hunter and a specific horse slowly developing an understanding of each other, even ways of communicating with each other, by voice or simply by touch. The process may have taken a long time, as riders gradually learned that their steeds would react to a gentle touch of a spear or even a finger. Hunters must have realized the importance of training, of established routines based on experience, developed through individual relationships with their mounts that may have begun when both rider and horse were young, with much to learn. Finger-light communication was the secret, perhaps first passed through lines and nose rings, and simple halters. Once the farmers rode horses as a matter of routine, the entire dynamic of human life on the steppes, and indeed history, changed fundamentally. Sedentary agriculturalists and herders became nomads, their lives tied to and revolving around, the horse, a creature that was to acquire near-mythic status in steppe culture over the ensuing centuries.

Again, we fall back on limited archaeological evidence. Judging from distinctive artifacts, Sredni Stog people spread as far west into what are now Hungary and Romania, and eastward beyond the Volga, a distance spanning some 1500 kilometers (930 miles). This is a staggering range for any stockbreeding society, probably beyond the capability of people traveling only on foot, given the severity of the environment. We know from burials that as farming and stockbreeding societies spread eastward, the treatment of horses changed. As early as 5000 BCE, many groups buried portions of both cattle and small stock with people. Within a few centuries, horse bones joined grave offerings across the entire region. The people who buried them relied on farm animals for much of their diet. By adding horses to mortuary rituals, maybe they commemorated an addition to the mix of managed animals that served humans. Thus, apparently, was born the powerful role of horse rituals over the steppe. Some early settlements on the Middle Volga have yielded human burials associated with pits containing heads and lower limbs of cattle and caprines. There are horse head and hoof offerings from graveside depressions heavily stained with red ocher. The consistency of these finds foreshadows ancient traditions of sacrifice where the flesh of the beast was consumed, but the hide, skull, and hooves were set aside and then suspended on a pole over the grave, a practice that became commonplace over a wide area of Eurasia and survived into modern times among nomads in the Altai Mountains.[8]

Horses at Botai

HORSES HAD COME TO the forefront of local economies by the mid-fourth millennium, especially in the eastern Urals and around Botai, in what is now northern Kazakhstan, in the heart of tarpan country.[9] Here, harsh winters and thin soils made agriculture impossible. For many centuries the sparse population relied on hunting and foraging, mostly in small river valleys, while remaining constantly on the move. Before about 3500 BCE, a tiny settlement of four houses flourished at Botai. Suddenly, what had been a mere hamlet ballooned into a large village of at least 158 houses that thrived for four to five centuries, inhabited by people who relied heavily on horses (see sidebar "Horses at Botai"). More than three hundred thousand animal bones, nearly all from horses, testify to a dramatic change in lifeway.

The finds from Botai portray a steppe society that practiced a form of mobility unheard of in earlier times. Gone were the days when people lived in one spot, tending herds close to home. Now they could roam freely, graze their animals over much larger ranges, and move them from one widely separated pasture to another. Horses became symbols of wealth, of prestige, with connections to the spiritual world. Botai saw the dawning of a dramatically different, horse-driven world, where constant movement, teamwork between animals and humans, and prowess in war became the dynamics of human life on the steppes.

Horses at Botai

The evidence for, at minimum, close horse management and, most likely, at least partial domestication at Botai is compelling. Of the three hundred thousand animal bones there, 99 percent come from equines. Slaughter curves derived from their teeth tell us that most of them were beasts slaughtered between three and eight years of age, mature adults rather than juveniles. They were generally smaller animals, perhaps around sixty centimeters (twenty-four inches), close to the size of later domesticated beasts, as if the herders were selecting and breeding wild horses for their physical attributes. Apparently, they managed their herds carefully. The males were slaughtered somewhat younger, perhaps young stallions in excess of breeding and other requirements. Some of the actual slaughter seems to have involved poleaxing. Judging from modern practice, two people would hold the horse's head steady with thongs, while a third struck a devastating blow between the eyes that killed the beast.

The Botai may have used their horses as pack animals, but they almost certainly rode them as well. The riders may not have used bits, but relied instead on thongs to control their mounts, presumably for bridles, hobbles, lassos, and whips. The jaws of no fewer than 135 horses from Botai became the smoothers used to process thongs.

Judging from the thick deposits of horse dung, the people kept their beasts in corrals adjacent to their houses, using some of the manure to insulate their homes. The Botai herds were a valuable meat source, but they also provided milk. Highly sophisticated isotope analyses of the minute residues on the walls of Botai clay pots have yielded traces of the fats in horse milk. This is the earliest evidence for the drinking of horse milk, which was fermented and turned into a slightly alcoholic beverage known as koumiss, consumed in Kazakhstan to this day and a staple for steppe nomads for thousands of years.

The Botai preferred horses to cattle and small stock, largely because they were steppe adapted and could feed through snow during cold winters without the need for fodder that had to be collected during the summer. The Botai's survival depended on horses and their mobility, on widely separated grazing grounds, and on their ability to control widely ranging herds from horseback. They seem to have treated their beasts with respect as steeds, but also revered them as connections to the supernatural world. Dozens of horse skulls and articulated neck vertebrae lie in ritual pits around Botai houses. In many Eurasian societies, horses had powerful ritual associations with the chief deity, the Sky or Sun God. Some of the finds may represent beasts sacrificed facing southeast at the time of the winter solstice. Given the featureless landscape, the cardinal directions and changing heavenly bodies were of great significance in Botai society. The only human burial from Botai (that of two men, a woman, and a child) lay surrounded by the remains of fourteen horses placed in an arc. There are signs, too, of a close ritual connection between dogs and horses, the dogs being used both to hunt wild animals and to control herds.

Riding horses opened up the steppes and provided a degree of mobility to people living in undeveloped country that had been unimaginable even a thousand years earlier. It also transformed the partnership between animals and humans in fundamental ways. Now the connection was far more than a working relationship; it became a bond between two individuals: a horse and its rider. A successful rider enjoys a close relationship with his or her steed, reinforced by gentle words and familiar commands. With careful training, the two form a close-knit team whose effectiveness comes from cooperation, not cajoling. With so many horses in the villages and with the realities of long distances and cattle herding on the steppe, riding horses had so many obvious advantages to people with close familiarity with their beasts that it would be astonishing if riding didn't take hold relatively soon after domestication during the fourth millennium. At first, it may have been somewhat of a rarity, but an explosion in the numbers of horse bones in archaeological sites after the fourth millennium may also have coincided with the beginnings of horse burial, where an owner journeyed to the next world with his steed, even with much of his herd, as individual wealth in horses and exotic treasures assumed ever greater importance in steppe society.

Lumbering Carts

BY 3400 BCE, SEMINOMADIC herding societies thrived over a wide area of the western steppes. Descended from earlier societies such as Sredni Stog, they occupied grasslands extending from the Danube River east to the Ural River. This was the moment when another defining innovation arrived on the steppes: the ox-drawn cart. Heavy vehicles with solid timber wheels appeared almost simultaneously between 3400 and 3100 BCE, over an enormous area from Mesopotamia in the south to the Russian/Ukrainian steppes and Central Europe.[10] A thousand years later, carts lumbered along the Rhine Valley and came into use as far east as the Indus River in South Asia. They were cumbersome vehicles at best, hauled by laboring oxen using yokes modified from plowing, and moving along at about 3.2 kilometers (2 miles) an hour—under favorable conditions. (Compare this with chariot horses in later times, which could reach 10 to 14 kilometers, or 6.0 to 8.7 miles, an hour at a trot, possibly 30 kilometers, or 18.6 miles, an hour at a gallop.)

Lumbering oxcarts added another element of mobility to steppe society, carrying people and manure to the fields and increasing farming efficiency dramatically. They also transported vital supplies for herders scattered widely over the grassland and living with their animals for long periods of time. Grave finds tell us that some carts had arched matting roofs, making it possible to sleep in them. Wheeled carts allowed some settlements to thrive as far as eighty kilometers (fifty miles) from the river valleys that anchored their society. Almost simultaneously, too, carts became far more than utilitarian vehicles. They became artifacts of prestige, for the mobility and the evidence of wealth they conferred on their owners in life and after death. Dozens of graves between the Danube and Urals contain sacrificial offerings of cattle, sheep, and horses, and actual wagons or clay votive offerings of them. But why did people use cattle for hauling carts when horses offered significant advantages as pack animals? Equines were faster, able to ford deep streams, and capable of either hauling or carrying significant loads over rugged terrain, especially when pulling two-wheeled carts. The problem was the harness. Equine anatomy was unsuitable for ox yokes, which reduced traction. Centuries were to pass before the Chinese, who had acquired horses from the steppes, developed, between the third and fifth centuries CE, the rigid collar and cart shafts, a technology not adopted in Europe until some three centuries later.

The horse and wheeled transport opened up the huge expanses of the Eurasian steppe, hitherto virtually inaccessible to any farmer or herder. Much of the expansion west of the Ural Mountains resulted from growing demand for precious metals. Nomadic groups penetrated territories inhabited by but handfuls of hunters and foragers, discovering new metal outcrops in the Altai and elsewhere as they moved into desert Central Asia. After 2000 BCE, the migration patterns were so complicated and multidirectional that a series of local societies came into being from the Urals as far northeast as the Yenisei River in Siberia. Thus it was that advanced wheeled technology reached China.

By the second millennium BCE, rich horse- and cattle-herding societies thrived in Central Asia. The leaders among them formed an impressive elite, who acquired prestige and wealth through trade and warfare—or, more accurately, raiding. They traveled to the next world in splendor, men and women being buried with carts, but this was the oxcart's last hurrah, as the horse-drawn chariot with its spoked wheels came into the hands of powerful chieftains. Soon a dichotomy arose, between the pragmatic ox-drawn wagon of the farmer and townspeople and the chariot, the possession of successful warriors and kings. As the archaeologist Stuart Piggott once put it, "the ox cart creaks and groans its way into bucolic oblivion."[11] In its place reigned the horse.

CHAPTER 11

The Horse Masters' Legacies

HORSES WERE CREATURES OF the steppes, of the great grasslands far to the north of the lands bordering the Tigris and Euphrates Rivers. The occasional equid traveled southward during the third millennium BCE, but they were never common in a world where communication was, for the most part, by water or donkey caravan. The horse was an exotic beast, known to Mesopotamians as "the ass of foreign mountain countries."[1] They assumed much greater importance as the nomads of the steppes enjoyed thriving economies, settled in every imaginable environment in the north, and developed the war chariot. During the third millennium BCE, gradual, and often sporadic, infiltration of settled lands morphed into much larger incursions that menaced sedentary farmers in new and dramatic ways.

These infiltrations had a grounding in the environmental realities of the steppe. Living as they did on semiarid plains with irregular rainfall, the nomads and their beasts depended on ever-changing patterns of grazing grass and watering. When the rains were good, the people and their herds ranged widely over the steppe, where standing water could be found. In a sense, the plains sucked people in. Most years, there was enough graze and water to supply everyone's needs, although there was often high mortality of cattle during very cold winters. Drought cycles offered the greatest challenges, times when pastures dried up, standing water vanished, and the nomads stayed close to precious permanent water supplies. They also moved to the edge of the steppe, to the better-watered, more fertile land where farmers had lived for centuries. These were settled folk, who lived in the same villages for many generations, anchored to their fields. For centuries, nomad and farmer had developed informal economic links, trading goods and commodities back and forth without undue friction. However, drought combined with growing populations of horses and stock in the north required constant searches for new pasture. The nomads, who are by nature war-like, became aggressive and cast covetous eyes on better-watered, settled lands. Sensing easy prey, the warriors of the north with their chariots invaded lands beyond the steppes in much larger numbers. They were people always on the move, aggressive, accustomed to raiding and spoil, unafraid of traversing previously insurmountable barriers like extensive deserts that had once protected cities and settled farmland from outsiders.

City dwellers and farmers alike lived in dread of nomadic raiders, who brought their herds and flocks with them, annexed farmland, and often showed no signs of leaving. Most nomads had little time for agriculture, or for city life, which depended on a degree of political stability that nurtured the long-distance trade routes that brought wealth and linked them to the wider world. For centuries, raiders from the north preyed on long-established states to the south. Many of them settled permanently in new homelands, while maintaining their dependency on horses. The rulers of cities and states, rightly concerned about political stability, armed themselves with horse-drawn chariots, but they could not stop the constant movements southward. During the second millennium, long after horses were well known, great migrations of horse riders came south, along two major routes. From the western steppes, they penetrated far into Anatolia. Nomads from the heart of Central Asia fought their way deep into India and Iran.[2] Inevitably, descendants of steppe people formed their own empires, the best known that of the Hittites, a major rival to the Egyptian pharaohs to the south and the Assyrians to the west.

Kikkuli Trains the Hittites

THE HITTITES, ORIGINALLY FROM the steppes, founded a state at Hattusa, in north-central Anatolia, during the eighteenth century BCE. At its height under King Suppiluliuma (1344–1333 BCE), the Hittite empire

(Hatti) encompassed much of Southwest Asia, sharing the political limelight with Assyria to the east and Egypt to the south.[3] Hittite armies were efficient war machines, staffed by troops who had a feudal duty to serve, rewarded with booty. Donkeys and heavy bullock carts transported essential supplies, but the vehicle of attack was the light horse-drawn chariot. This was by no means a new weapon. Hatti's enemies, among them the Egyptians, used them as mobile firing platforms, with a driver and archer. Their chariots were medium- or long-distance weapons that fired clouds of arrows into enemy ranks. The Hittites took a different approach, designing vehicles that were longer and deeper, capable of carrying three men: a driver, a warrior, and a shield man to protect the other two. The crew wore armor; so did the horses, their flanks, backs, and necks protected by armor fashioned in scales. The fighter carried a bow and arrow and a short sword, the height of the platform giving him a major strategic advantage at close quarters. Such equipment worked well against other chariot forces and against inexperienced infantry, who could be cut down as they fled.

The Hittites and their enemies spent a great deal of time improving their chariots, but the training of the pairs that hauled them received very close attention indeed. So important were chariot horses that an archive of cuneiform tablets chronicles their training, notably the work of Kikkuli, a horse master for King Suppiluliuma. Not much is known about Kikkuli, except that he was a foreigner from Mitanni, a kingdom that flourished in what is now northern Syria. Judging from his training manual, he advocated rigorous conditioning (see sidebar "Thus Speaks Kikkuli").

"Thus Speaks Kikkuli"

"Thus speaks Kikkuli, horse trainer from the land of Mittani," begins the first of the four cuneiform tablets that comprise Kikkuli's training manual.[4] The manual came to light during excavations by the German archaeologist Hugo Winckler at the Hittite capital, Boghazkoy, in central Turkey, in 1906–7.

Kikkuli was a ruthless taskmaster, whose program started each autumn and lasted 184 days. He rejected horse after horse in the early, rigorous stages of the training, when the beasts were treated harshly and fed inadequately. He was building strength, leading rather than harnessing or riding them. "Pace two leagues, run twenty furlongs out and thirty furlongs home. Put rugs on. After sweating, give one pail of salted water and one pail of malt-water. Take to river and wash down," he prescribes for the fifth day of training. Each day had its prearranged rations of feed, numbers of waterings, workouts, and periods of rest. Once the horses were conditioned, the training became even more rigorous, preparing the beasts for tough conditions. Witness the routine for the fifty-fifth day: "When morning comes he takes them out of the stable and hitches them up. He trots them half a mile and when he trots them back he unhitches them . . . they stand hungry and thirsty. When evening comes he hitches them up and trots them half a mile and over twenty fields and he races them over seven fields . . . He takes them into the stable. All night long they eat hay."[5]

Kikkuli built endurance and stamina while testing the limits of the beasts, covering as much as a hundred fifty kilometers (ninety-three miles) daily for several days. They trained at a gallop, at a slow pace; hauled chariots; maneuvered at close quarters. They were sometimes deprived of water to accustom them to thirst, and regularly crossed rivers, as they would on campaigns. The horses invariably trained in pairs so that they became inseparable. The beasts lived in stables, and were rubbed and washed carefully in a program that resembled the interval training that many modern-day athletes use when training for triathlons. Somewhat similar methods appeal to modern-day equine Three Day Event trainers.

Kikkuli and other Hittite trainers turned out superbly fit, well-trained horses, which is why their king's armies were so successful. So effective were Kikkuli's methods that they are still used by some trainers today. Scholar and trainer Ann Nyland translated the tablets, and then tried them with Arabian horses. The seven-month program is said to work really well, to produce "a superb equine athlete without the use of drugs or expensive feed additives."[6]

Interestingly, none of the surviving archives tell us anything about the chariot drivers. Presumably they trained alongside their pairs, so they became as one with the horses and were able to control them under even the most stressful circumstances.

Hittite military campaigns involved large numbers of horses and chariots. Hittites fought Egyptians in a memorable battle at Kadesh, waged on the banks of the Orontes River in 1274 BCE. The Hittite ruler Muwatalli II deployed at least thirty-five hundred chariots against Egyptian pharaoh Ramesses II's army, which included about the same number of them. The battle was inconclusive, despite heavy casualties on both sides. Ramesses II claimed victory in several grandiloquent murals that adorned temples along the Nile, in which we see him routing the Hittites, but this was mere propaganda. "He betook himself to his horses, and led quickly on, being alone by himself. . . . His majesty was like Sutekh, the great in strength, smiting and slaying among them; his majesty hurled them headlong, one upon another into the water of the Orontes."[7] Chariots also played a significant role in the Trojan wars, perhaps the culmination of centuries of warfare surrounding Troy's control of strategic trade routes along the Dardanelles and to the north. The beasts carried heroes such as like Achilles into single combat.

Chariot warfare waned with the collapse of the Hittite empire during the twelfth century BCE. The implosion of established order coincided with a major shift in local attitudes toward horses. For centuries, elite Mesopotamians considered riding them somewhat undignified. In a famous exchange, King Zimri-Lim of Mari (1779–1761 BCE) planned a tour of Akkadian cities under his rule. "Drive a chariot," he was advised. "Or, if you must ride, ride a mule. For only then will you preserve the dignity of your royal position."[8] History doesn't relate whether Zimri-Lim listened to his advisers, but good horses were rare and expensive, costing in the order of seven bulls, ten donkeys, or thirty slaves, a commentary on the value of human as opposed to animal life in those days. Mounted couriers used them; so did lightly armed horsemen serving as scouts. Guards on horseback herded thousands of conquered people and their animals to sparsely populated, distant lands to minimize chances of rebellion. Large-scale warfare waged by cavalry was unthinkable until Scythian horsemen from the steppes revolutionized military strategy.

"The Tombs of Our Forefathers"

THE SCYTHIANS INHABITED A world of horses and enormous distances, a world where one's steed accompanied one in life and death. Prominent members of the Scythian elite expected to be buried with their mounts and several other horses under burial mounds called kurgans, which were revered for generations. When the Scythian ruler Idanthyrsus refused battle with Persian king Darius, who invaded his lands in about 508 BCE, he made one exception: "One thing there is for which we will fight—the tombs of our forefathers."[9] Kurgans loomed high above the Eurasian steppe. Stone stelae encircled many burial mounds, symbolic trees of life that linked the layered cosmos—the underworld, the steppe, and the heavens. Scythian chiefs went to eternity in splendor, buried with lavish feasts and animal sacrifices. One kurgan near the Dnieper River was twenty meters (sixty-seven feet) high. Fifteen horses adorned with gold and silver ornaments lay under the tumulus, one with its head and neck stretched forward and legs tucked under its body.[10]

The most spectacular kurgans date to the eighth century BCE, notably in the Sayan Mountains, west of Lake Baikal, on the boundaries of Mongolia and Siberia. One huge, drum-shaped cairn, 110 meters (360 feet) in diameter and 4 meters (13 feet) high covered the burial of a ruler and his consort, richly dressed in sable and adorned with gold ornaments. Six elderly men and their harnessed saddle horses surrounded them. Horsetails and manes lay on the floor of the burial chamber. Seven chambers contained 138 burials of elderly stallions, each saddled and bridled, perhaps gifts from subordinate tribes. Three hundred

Figure 11.1 *A horseman depicted on a carpet fragment from one of the Pazyryk burials. Fine Art Images/Shutterstock.*

graves on the periphery held horsehide burials, the remains of a ceremonial feast. The mourners sacrificed four hundred fifty horses.

Two hundred fifty years later, five princely graves at Pazyryk, in the Altai, contained harnessed and caparisoned riding horses, also a team of four horses in one grave that drew a great ceremonial carriage, probably of Chinese origin.[11] The region's severe winters caused the graves to freeze, preserving even fragile silks and other textiles, and carpets. The saddle blankets bore elaborate appliqué designs of stylized deer antlers, symbolizing rebirth. A magnificent felt hanging showed a richly attired rider astride his horse. The chieftains displayed tattoos. They lived violent lives; one of the dead had been scalped.

The kurgans reveal people who were far more than the unsophisticated horsemen beloved of earlier generations of classical historians.

For instance, four long lines of kurgans dating to between about 330 and 270 BCE lie on a natural terrace along the Bukhtarma River, near the village of Berel, in eastern Kazakhstan. Each stands about 4.6 meters (15 feet) high and measures about 30 meters (100 feet) across. At least twenty-four kurgans have been investigated so far, their contents effectively deep-frozen by the permafrost, preserving a jumble of bones, hair, teeth, nails, and flesh. Some of the dead horsemen bore tattoos and had been embalmed, their hair cut short before their heads were covered with wigs.

Several of the excavated mounds commemorated lesser figures, usually just a man and his horse. But Kurgan 11 was another matter. The mound contained a man in his thirties who had met a violent death, a woman who had died later, and thirteen sacrificial horses, killed after being adorned with their full ceremonial regalia. The excavators removed the horse carcasses from the soil in still-frozen earthen blocks, and then excavated them carefully in the laboratory. Bridle tack displayed plaques depicting real and mythical animals like griffins, which have the heads of eagles and the bodies of lions. Decorated wooden bands on the other animals displayed stylized heads of animals and mythic beasts. These were no ordinary horses, for they wore pendants and garlands and red felt saddle blankets that glittered with gold ornaments.

The Berel kurgans preserve the wealth of elites who spent much of the year with their own small tribal groups, moving with the seasons by horse and sometimes camel. In a classic transhumance pattern, they tended flocks of sheep and goats in higher-altitude summer pastures, moving to the lowlands in winter. From late autumn and winter campsites, parties of mounted warriors embarked on raids to acquire not only animals but also the luxury goods cherished by the elite. They, in their turn, used such booty for ceremonial displays and distributed exotic artifacts to key followers as part of an endless process of alliance building, which was the key to power on the open plains.

Warfare from horseback developed out of necessity in a world of enormous distances and chronic mobility. Cavalry horses were something new. They can have become a potent weapon only among people who lived and breathed riding and who developed extremely close relationships with their beasts. Just training a horse for combat, let alone fighting with it, was a challenge, a task achieved in steps. It involved transforming a highly temperamental animal, with an instinct to take flight, into a quite different beast. A cavalry horse had to be unfazed by loud noises, to face acute danger, and to maneuver rapidly, jumping without notice and galloping at human command. Such horses also needed to be higher and larger than the squat beasts, whose ancestors were the tarpan and Przewalski's horse, too small for use in cavalry units. Larger horses were faster, more agile, and had more stamina. Their additional stature made it possible to fight from horseback with lances. Quite when such larger steeds were first bred remains uncertain, but their descendants turned the Scythians into the world's best light cavalry.

Xenophon's Mantras

HARD-LEARNED STRATEGIC LESSONS GRADUALLY passed southward from the steppes into chariotry circles. Centuries passed before the Assyrians learned the art of cavalry fighting from their neighbors the Urartians of present-day eastern Iran, who had ready access to the steppe and fought almost entirely in hilly terrain, where chariots were useless. Once convinced of the value of mounted warfare, the Assyrians learned quickly. They trained drivers to control a pair of horses unencumbered with chariots, the second rider being purely a bowman. The strategy was so successful that, inevitably, nomadic ways of fighting from horseback became deeply embedded in Assyrian and later armies. Metal bits replaced bone ones; single riders rode into battle instead of maneuvering in pairs. The Assyrians acquired ever-larger numbers of horses from the steppes, and then started breeding them themselves on a large scale, as they turned cavalry from a mob of individual riders into a powerful strike force. Chariots became an anachronism, reserved for ceremonial occasions and parades.

A regiment of disciplined horsemen could deliver well-timed hammer blows against the enemy. By now, Assyrian kings had learned the new rules of warfare. Nearly 2,000 of King Shalmaneser III's cavalrymen attacked 3,940 chariots in a battle against Levantine forces at Qarqar in 853 BCE, capturing numerous chariots and their horses. By the reign of King Sargon II in the eighth century, his armies had many more cavalrymen than chariots.

Cyrus the Great (578–530 BCE), the founder of the First Persian (or Achaemenid) Empire, was both a brilliant administrator and an expert strategist who knew well the value of horse-mounted shock troops. Darius I (who reigned 522–486 BCE) was the third Achaemenid monarch, who expanded the empire to encompass twenty provinces between the Aegean and the Indus River, conquered by fast-moving cavalry with superior weapons. He campaigned against the Scythians on the open steppe, but as we have seen, they evaded him, saying that they would attack only if he assaulted their kurgans. By the time of King Xerxes, who tried in vain to conquer the Greek city-states in 480 BCE, the Persian cavalry mustered eighty thousand horses, but equestrian might was powerless in the face of the naval supremacy enjoyed by the Greeks.

Not that the Greeks were unskilled equestrians. The historian, soldier, and philosopher Xenophon achieved historical immortality by helping lead a force of ten thousand Greeks from the heart of Persian territory to the Black Sea. In his seven-book *Anabasis*, describing the journey, Xenophon devoted one volume to the training and owning of horses with a philosophy quite different from that of Kikkuli. He urged trainers to treat horses kindly by touching and caressing them. "As the result of this treatment, necessarily the young horse will acquire—not fondness merely, but an absolute craving for human beings." One aimed to train one's steed to "adopt the very airs and graces which he naturally assumes when showing off to best advantage, you have got what you are aiming at—a horse that delights in being ridden, a splendid and showy animal, the joy of all beholders"[12]—wise words, adopted as gospel by thousands of cavalrymen over the centuries. Alexander the Great is said to have been strongly influenced by the *Anabasis*.

Xenophon's guidelines for horse care and training endured through Roman times and into the Middle Ages. His recommendations persisted in part because they were effective and also because his distinctive methods worked well with beasts ridden bareback, with only a cloth for the rider, and no stirrups. Riders practiced with wooden vaulting horses in a gymnasium. When a rider prepares for the spring onto the horse's back, Xenophon advised, "let him pull up his body with his left hand, and keep his right hand straight to raise himself."[13]

For all the emphasis on charges and killing, the essence of the entire cavalry experience was the close, even emotional partnership between the horse and its rider. The Macedonian general Alexander the Great entered legend when he succeeded in taming the Thessalian horse Bucephalus ("Oxhead") at age twelve, when he noticed that the horse was afraid of its shadow. Bucephalus was his closest companion during years of conquest. The Macedonians were superb horsemen, trained by horse masters to fight in close formation. The eight hundred "King's Companions," armed with thrusting spears, were near-invincible when pitted against Persian cavalry. At the Battle of Issus, on the Syrian Plain in 333 BCE, Alexander and his five thousand horsemen routed King Darius's eleven thousand cavalry by attacking in constricted terrain where the Persians could not deploy their full cavalry forces. By the time of Alexander's death in 323 BCE, cavalry had effectively superseded chariots on the battlefield.

Chariots remained popular for hunting, display, and racing. Assyrian king Ashurbanipal adorned the walls of his palace with masterful bas-reliefs of a royal lion hunt in his game park, now beautifully displayed in London's British Museum. We see the caged lions being released and an enthusiastic crowd cheering on the king as he releases arrows from his chariot. The carefully organized event was a remote ancestor of medieval royal hunts in Europe many centuries later. Chariots evolved into light, strong vehicles, assembled by using bent wood, leather, and metal to produce fast, durable conveyances pulled by trained beasts of a type resembling modern-day Arabians. These were expensive conveyances that required skilled artisans to maintain them and cosseted stabling for the horses. Just obtaining the different kinds of hay for the diet of high-performance steeds required special effort. Such feeding placed heavy demands on local subsistence farmers. Piggott estimates that a single pair of chariot horses in late prehistoric Britain would have required a crop of barley from three to four hectares (eight to ten acres) annually.[14]

Possessing chariots involved far more than buying a vehicle. The wealthy owner had to acquire teams of trained horses, a staff to look after them, and, above all, trained charioteers who had a close working relationship with the horses and who were capable of driving in combat or racing the chariot, caring for the horses, and repairing the vehicle, if need be. It was no coincidence that charioteers were individuals of high status, often equal to that of the passenger. Among the Akkadians, the charioteer was a *mariann*, a member of the nobility. In Egypt, landowning officers fought from chariots. Above all, chariots were vehicles of pleasure and prestige, much used in public displays and processions.

The Noble Animal and Lesser Beasts

FOR THE ROMANS, THE horse was the prestige animal, ridden by emperors, princes, and generals. On campaign, horses were the mounts for the emperor and his entourage when they went in the field, as they were for generals. The horse elevated the leader above his army. It was a symbol of authority, part of the mystique of kingship and leadership. Inevitably, the horse became a noble animal, named and cherished, its hide polished to a gloss. Alexander's was named Bucephalus. The names given chariot racing horses and the tradition of naming noble mounts went back deep into history, for they were really part of the family. Horse breeding became a profitable business in Roman times, in part because of a demand for fine horses and racing animals as well as for strong military beasts.

Roman cavalry engaged in intricate exercises in peacetime, with young riders wheeling, separating, and engaging in mock fights. Those who performed in these games were of noble rank and wore helmets and yellow plumes.[15] They wore tightly fitting trousers, quite unlike the loosely tailored pants used by Persian cavalry. All this lavish display was hardly typical of classic Roman restraint and sobriety. Emperors and high officials were models of public dignity. A surviving equestrian statue of Emperor Marcus Aurelius (who reigned 161–180 CE), in gilded

Figure 11.2 *Emperor Marcus Aurelius as the epitome of public dignity. Ken Durden/Shutterstock.*

bronze, shows him riding without stirrups on a horse whose front right foot is raised, perhaps to rest on a now-vanished figure of a barbarian, someone outside the law.

A noble horse, such as Marcus Aurelius's steed, often called *Magnus equus*, "the great horse," was a larger beast, perhaps standing around 150 centimeters (about 5 feet) and a superior breed in the Roman lexicon. There were pack and military horses as well, often stockier animals used for hauling loads on roads and on the farm. By medieval times, a European packhorse could carry between 99 and 150 kilograms (218 to 330 pounds), probably somewhat similar to Roman loads.

As the Roman Empire grew and consolidated, horses played an increasingly important role in warfare. They were fast, could navigate rough terrain, could be trained for durability, and carried significant loads. They could also forage for themselves on the move, an important strategic advantage. By day, the cavalry formed a protective screen around marching legions and baggage animals. Mounted scouts ranged widely at night. The best cavalry marched at the rear, to guard against surprise attacks. The Romans based their cavalry in what is now Milan. The huge road network that linked all parts of the empire allowed mounted regiments to deploy rapidly when rebellion threatened. At the same time, mounted couriers and official chariots carried mail from one province to another, using changing stations to acquire fresh horses. The couriers rode along the edge of the road, which carried for the most part either regiments or plodding donkey or mule caravans. With frequent changeovers, such riders could cover as much as 385 kilometers (240 miles) in a day.

Roman horses were heavier than Scythian mounts, which made them more susceptible to heat stress. Unlike horsemen from the steppes, the Romans did not have access to unlimited numbers of beasts. They levied horses from Gaul, Thessaly, and elsewhere and raised them on ranches in the most fertile regions of Italy. They pastured them in the mountains in summer, where the rocky terrain toughened their hooves, like those of donkeys. From the outset, military horse trainers conditioned their charges for the clamor and disorder, as well as the violence, of battle, teaching them to jump deep trenches and to swim across rivers, just as the Assyrians had done in earlier centuries. Cavalry maneuver frequently, twisting and turning in such a manner that makes bareback riding ineffective. Inevitably, some form of rigid saddle came into use, perhaps adopted from the steppes to the east.

So successful was Roman breeding of high-quality mounts that export of them to subject peoples was forbidden. Of horses, the scholar and rancher Marcus Terentius Varro remarked, "As some horses are fitted for military service, others for hauling, others for breeding, and others for racing, all are not to be judged and valued by the same standards. Thus the experienced soldier chooses his horses by one standard and feeds and trains them in one way, and the charioteer and circus-rider in another; and the trainer who is breaking horses for riding under the saddle or for the carriage does not use the same system as the man who has military service in view; for as on the one hand, in the army, they want spirited horses, so on the other hand they prefer more docile ones for road service."[16]

As we shall see in chapter 14, the centuries that followed witnessed the increasing influence of Christian doctrine on the ways in which people treated animals. Biblical teachings, with their messages of dominance, replaced Xenophon.

CHAPTER 12

Deposing Sons of Heaven

Northern China, 1200 BCE. The light chariot stands atop a low ridge overlooking a shallow valley near the Huang He River. Flies swarm around the beautifully matched horses. Their tails swish gently in the hot air. Shang Dynasty ruler Wu Ding and the driver stand motionless in the small conveyance, feet slightly astride on the plaited-leather floor. The expressionless leader steadies himself with a hand on the heat-bent wooden rail. Banners flap lazily in the morning air. In the valley itself, his troops are stationary, weapons at the ready, eyes on the massed ranks of their enemies. A raised hand from the chariot, officers shout, the regiment advances. Dense clouds of dust swirl around the conflict, so the driver eases the horses ahead. The spoked wheels of the mobile command post squeak gently over the rutted ground.

WE KNOW OF SUCH chariots only as ghosts. They stand in deep burial pits near the city of Anyang, once capital of Shang Dynasty rulers, surviving as dark casts in the soil excavated by twentieth-century archaeologists.[1] At least eleven beautifully fashioned chariots have been found. Delicate brush strokes have uncovered their wheels, each with between eighteen and twenty-eight spokes, far more than the four to eight of such vehicles in the West. The skeletons of the driver and the matched horses lie in place, ready to carry their master in the next world.

Chinese Chariotry

CHARIOTS APPEARED SUDDENLY IN China, during the reign of the Shang ruler Wu Ding, in about 1180 BCE.[2] By any standards, they were sophisticated wheeled vehicles, constructed with an elaborate technology of bent wood and leather identical to that developed thousands of kilometers away in the West. They came from the steppe—fully refined, horse-drawn weaponry that conquered the vast distances of Mongol country with an effortless panache made possible only by the horse.

Not that the horse was unknown in China at the time the chariot appeared. Domesticated horses had spread rapidly eastward across the steppes, to arrive in eastern China earlier in the second millennium BCE. The first were squat beasts that served as pack animals. They hauled carts and wagons for the privileged nobility. Then came the chariot, the equivalent of a Cadillac or Mercedes in the Shang world. The nobility embraced the new conveyances with enthusiasm. Important leaders used them as mobile command posts on the outskirts of a conflict. Brilliantly caparisoned with banners and harness bells, Shang chariots were prestigious transportation on public occasions and for battle command, not necessarily for actual fighting. When a ruler died, his chariot accompanied him, as did dozens of sacrificial victims, many of them prisoners bound and buried alive, decapitated, or just plain butchered.

The Shang fought numerous wars on the northwestern steppes, which yielded not only prisoners, but rich hauls of horses and weaponry. In time, they found at least some allies among the frontier tribes, from whom they acquired horse trainers, wheelwrights, veterinarians, and other experts to maintain and drive what was a revolutionary technology to people who had been farmers for millennia. Just managing the horses demanded unfamiliar skills from people who dealt habitually with farm animals.

The Zhou, who overthrew the Shang in 1045 BCE, were the first Chinese to use light chariots in combat on the battlefield.[3] They deployed three hundred chariots and archers with composite bows against their Shang foes at the Battle of Muye, despite being outnumbered, and trounced them. The ruler Wen, who founded the Zhou Dynasty, is said to have been a "barbarian," a man from the steppes, which probably accounts for his mobile strategy. Massed regiments of chariots, many of them with four-horse teams, became popular throughout northern China within a few centuries. Competing rulers fought constantly from the fifth to third centuries in a bewildering morass of violence, this apart from Mongol raids from the north. War brought technological innovation. Iron metallurgy arrived from the steppes by 800 BCE. Chariots became ever more elaborate. Lustrous metals provided ornamentation that turned the conveyances into status symbols, often awarded by rulers as rewards for meritorious service on or off the battlefield.

Barbarian Horseman

THE NORTHERN BORDERLANDS SUFFERED under a classic regime of nomads encroaching on settled lands along a porous frontier where people traded horses and cattle for grain and other agricultural products. The climax of the trade came in the fall, when steppe animals were fat and the harvest was over. In some years, the Chinese failed to open their markets. Invariably, nomadic horsemen descended to raid grain stores. More organized warriors on horseback first appeared on the steppes north of the frontier by 484 BCE. They advanced and retreated with bewildering rapidity, never striking at the same location, and almost invariably in larger numbers than the defenders. Defense was a nightmare for a much-slower-moving soldiery scattered along a long frontier. Accurate bowmanship and complete mobility proved so effective that three northern states built walls to deter the invaders as they penetrated ever deeper into China's heartlands.

With their deadly bows and efficient riding attire, the nomads had become a frightening menace to conservative states where bureaucracy and precedent reigned. Their effectiveness depended in considerable part on their clothing in the saddle. The nomads wore several upper layers of tuniclike garments fastened with a belt, and a pair of trousers, a garment that was invented on the steppes, probably soon after people started riding horses. Tucked into boots, the durable and flexible trousers made it possible for a rider to swivel and move around on horseback, and allowed him effective control of the beast with his knees. Archery from horseback when attacking at speed became highly effective, especially when shooting to the side and rear, a devastating advantage when combined with high mobility.

A few desperate leaders responded boldly. The ruler Wu-ling (who reigned 325–299 BCE) of Zhao was among the leaders harassed by nomad raids. He ordered his court and military to wear what was termed "barbarian uniform." He himself donned nomad pants, boots, and fur garments, this in the face of obstinate resistance from his conservative officials.[4] Almost immediately, the fighting capability of the Zhao army improved dramatically. Wu-ling expanded his territory while securing his frontiers. A similar move toward mounted warfare must have taken hold across broad areas of China at about this time— strategically it could have been no other way, so powerful was the impact of the horse.

At the time, China was a patchwork of feudal states, constantly at war with one another as well as espousing competing political philosophies. The Qin state in the Wei Valley of the northwest enjoyed a geography of mountains and rivers well suited to defense. Its rulers turned from feudalism to legalism, a doctrine that advocated control and discipline under a strict rule of law. A dynamic ruler, Qin Shihuangdi (260–210 BCE), used his strategic base, and unbridled severity, to embark on a series of military campaigns using chariots, cavalry, and metal weapons. He forged China's warring states into a single imperial state.[5] Just like King Darius of Persia three centuries earlier, Qin Shihuangdi then embarked on an ambitious program of road construction that allowed him to move people and cargo as well as armies rapidly from place to place. Donkeys, horses, and mules became important vehicles of government and commerce. Horse-drawn carriages carried important officials. Horses served as "moving seats," ridden gently while traveling. More efficient communication meant that the emperor could exercise efficient control over his domains. He used horses and guards to move people to underpopulated territory, where iron plows opened up new agricultural land. In the north, one of his generals, Meng Tian, used half a million convicts to build a wall that expanded previous defenses against nomad incursions—the first Great Wall.

Shihuangdi may have been a remarkable leader, but he was a cruel and despotic ruler with a paranoid fear of death. He gathered more than seven hundred thousand prisoners and slaves to construct a vast necropolis near the modern city of Xi'an. Here, a serried regiment of more than seven thousand life-size terra-cotta soldiers guard his enormous burial mound, which is said to contain a map of China with its rivers delineated in mercury and a model of the cosmos. (It remains unexcavated.) The terra-cotta soldiery stand in strict order, bearing their weapons. Five hundred cavalry and chariot horses and more than a hundred thirty chariots accompany them, all modeled in brightly painted clay. The cavalry horses are squat Mongolian beasts, wearing bridles identical to those developed by the Scythians near the Black Sea during the sixth century BCE. Two of them haul a magnificent bronze carriage, virtually a house on wheels fitted with an eaved canopy, testimony to the luxurious travel that China's nobility enjoyed. Shihuangdi's cavalrymen wear the trousers and short boots favored by nomad riders in the north. It is no coincidence that Shihuangdi, like the innovative Zhou ruler Wen, was probably of steppe ancestry.

Figure 12.1 *Chariots and horsemen in Emperor Qin Shihuangdi's terracotta regiment. Totophoits/Fotolia.*

Xiongnu's Horses

THE HORSE PLAYED A decisive role in the unification of China, but it developed into a serious source of weakness for later emperors. Four years of civil war followed Shihuangdi's passing, which ended in the establishment of Han rule under Emperor Gaozu in 202 BCE.[6] Then fighting broke out in earnest. Gaozu's successors faced menacing aggression from the steppes, notably from the Xiongnu nomads, said to be capable of deploying three hundred thousand horse archers for battle. Their leader was Modu, a decisive, charismatic khan who rose from relative obscurity to unify the tribes of the East Asian steppe into a formidable confederacy. Sent by his father as a hostage to a neighboring group, the Yuezhi, Modu escaped on horseback and received ten thousand mounted archers as a reward. He trained them with such discipline that he is said to have ordered them to shoot his favorite horse and wife. Those who failed to fire were executed immediately. He succeeded in eliminating all his rivals, defeated the Yuezhi, and drove them west. His son completed the task and fashioned a gilded drinking vessel from the skull of the defeated ruler.

The Xiongnu were now such a powerful force along the frontier that numerous Chinese officials with political ambitions defected to the nomads. So did merchants, for Xiongnu horses were vastly superior to any bred in China. A Chinese official, Zhao Zu, remarked, "In climbing up and down mountains and crossing ravines and mountain torrents, the horses of China cannot compare with those of the Xiongnu."[7]

Gaozu opened negotiations with the nomads. Modu was eager for greater stability, for he was well aware that the nomadic economy, with its heavy emphasis on grazing, was potentially vulnerable to animal diseases, drought, extreme cold, and other climatic fluctuations, also chronic raiding and theft. The Chinese agreed to make fixed annual payments of foodstuffs, including grain, silk, and wine, to what was recognized as an equal state, recognition reinforced by the marriage of a Chinese princess to the khan. The Great Wall became the official boundary between the two states. Modu benefitted enormously from the agreement, using wine and exotic goods to cement relationships with other rulers and trading silk far to the west. But it was never an easy relationship. The Xiongnu alternated raids with peaceful coexistence, being well aware that the Chinese moved slowly, and that they were short of horses of high quality.

Heavenly Horses

FIGHTING ON HORSEBACK HAD obvious advantages, but the Chinese lacked reliable supplies of the larger horses that made for effective, disciplined cavalry. Such mounts were difficult to obtain, for they came from distant parts of Central Asia. They may have originated in a large area of western Asia north of Iran. We know of these beasts from the spectacular horse burials from Pazyryk in the Altai, described earlier. These were strong, nimble animals of golden-brown color, which contrasted dramatically with the squat equines widespread across the steppe. Their larger size and strength came from better feeding, selective breeding, and systematic castration to maintain high-quality breeding stock.

While the Chinese improved somewhat on squat Mongolian horses by careful breeding, to the point that those of specific color and characteristics were much prized, beasts suitable for the battlefield appear to have been rare, so much so that the government banned the export of horses of more than thirteen hands high from imperial domains. This edict was probably an attempt to address a chronic shortage of war horses, a constant in Chinese history. Fierce struggles erupted over control of horse supplies in the north and flared up over many centuries.

The Han emperor Wudi (who reigned 140–87 BCE) placed such importance on good cavalry horses that he organized a series of expensive campaigns to expand the boundaries of China far to the west.[8] His deep thrusts into Central Asia resulted in numerous equine and human casualties. Wudi's armies fought savage engagements with a confederation of Xiongnu nomads that extended across a huge area from Mongolia to eastern Kyrgyzstan. Even when not at war, the Chinese were desperate for good cavalry horses. They bought them, sometimes with silk, fought for them, seized them in raids, and bred their own war-horses from imported stock.

Wudi's desire for good horses led to the opening of part of the Silk Road that was to link China and the West. In the second year of his reign, he sent a delegation of about a hundred people under Zhang Qian to contact the Yuezhi, now living far to the west, outside Xiongnu clutches. Zhang Qian had an adventurous journey. The Xiongnu held him for twenty years. He escaped, traveled far west, and observed superb horseflesh. When he reached the Ferghana Valley, in what is now Uzbekistan, he found magnificent horses that appeared to sweat blood. (We now know this resulted from a parasitic condition.) Ferghana horses were powerful, short-legged beasts, superior to mounts from Wusan and other locations to the east. The emperor was so impressed that he named them "Heavenly Horses." The Han authorities started importing so many Ferghana beasts that local rulers closed their borders for horse trading.

Shortages, Shortages

"Horses are the foundation of military might, the greatest resource of the state," wrote Ma Yuan, a brilliant Han general and stockman from northern China of the first century CE.[9] He knew full well that mounted nomads were the greatest military adversaries for China, especially when fractured steppe groups unified under powerful leaders. Small wonder the emperor went to war with Ferghana. In 104 BCE, an expedition of forty thousand men trekked there but was defeated. A year later, Wudi sent sixty thousand men westward. This time they prevailed and managed to acquire three thousand horses, but most of them of ordinary quality. Only a thousand arrived safely in China. The negotiated agreement specified that the Ferghana supply two Heavenly Horses annually to the emperor. The troops also brought back lucerne seed, which provided high-quality pasturage for raising cavalry horses. But despite Wu's campaigns, the Chinese were always short of horseflesh, even after prolonged thrusts into the steppes.

The Tang Dynasty emperors (618–907 CE) began their rule with five thousand horses. Within a few decades they had increased the number to seven hundred thousand head by aggressive breeding.[10] But they still needed foreign mounts, and obtained many of them from nomads to the north. This was always an expensive enterprise. In 773, Uighurs from the north sent an agent with ten thousand horses for sale. They cost more than the government's entire annual income. Fine silk was the major currency, especially when trading with the Xiongnu. A simple principle of the law of supply and demand was in play. The Chinese had fine silk; the Xiongnu had plenty of horses and craved delicate fabrics. By the ninth century, the demand for fabric in exchange for horses was so intense that shortages developed, the quality dropped, and weavers had trouble meeting demand. The Uighurs and others complained, and with good reason. Much of the silk they received promptly traveled to the West, where the profits were enormous.

For all the breeding and bartering, horse shortages were a perennial challenge. There were times when there were plenty of cavalrymen but only one or two out of ten had a steed to ride in a military world where large numbers of horsemen were the currency of battle. Generations of Chinese officials worried over the issue of horse procurement without success. Eventually, tea became another commodity exchanged for horses, it being so much in demand by the nomads that it tended to supersede silk. The Song government (960–1279 CE) set up "Tea and Horse Offices" near the border, to control tea exports and maintain artificially high prices, so they could obtain more beasts. Inevitably, smuggling became endemic, discouraged unsuccessfully by death sentences for offenders. Successive dynasties created elaborate bureaucracies to breed and acquire horses. The Han emperors placed such importance on the horse trade that the official in charge of the program ranked eighth among the highest ministers of state. Despite careful attention to both breeding and grading of horses, the quality of cavalry mounts was a constant problem. Inevitably, the chronic shortage of horses led to catastrophe, triggered by the conquests of Genghis Khan.

The Flail of God

"I'M A FLAIL OF God," proclaimed the Mongol ruler Genghis Khan from the pulpit of the central mosque at Bokhara in 1220. "If you had not committed great sins, God would not have sent a punishment like me upon you."[11] A flail he truly was, one that descended on great cities and settled lands like a whirlwind. The Mongols had elected Genghis Khan as their great khan in 1206 CE. Not only a brilliant strategist and conqueror, but also a superb administrator, he quickly broke up the ancient tribal structure and organized his ferocious armies into tightly controlled, standardized units in multiples of ten. The troops fought as small teams so that orders never had to be given to more than ten men. Over just twenty years, Genghis Khan's armies swept westward and southward across the steppes with breathtaking rapidity and ruthless efficiency. Merely the threat of attack caused cities to fall before the Flail of God. Genghis Khan was forging a huge empire that extended over Eurasia, held together by efficient horse-based communication and threats of violence.

Genghis Khan's ancestry lay among people whose lives revolved around horses and supreme horsemanship. He was certainly bloodthirsty and ruthless, but his legacy was far more than conquest. He embraced religious freedom, united complex patchworks of warring tribes, rewarded merit, encouraged education, and advanced the rights of women in Mongolian society.

There was no one epiphanic moment when Genghis Khan acquired his genius for warfare, his extraordinary ability to attract the loyalty of his followers. This was a man who learned from hard experience, who adapted effortlessly to ever-changing circumstances across an unforgiving landscape. Genghis Khan was an utterly pragmatic leader whose skills developed, ultimately, out of his mastery of the horse. He was the greatest conqueror in history, a warrior of remarkable ability, but he ultimately owed a great deal of his success to the horse and to the mounted warfare it enabled (see sidebar "Archers and Horses on the Move").

Archers and Horses on the Move

The entire Mongol military system, developed in large part by Genghis Khan, depended on obedience, strict discipline, and the horse. Mongol armies combined their brilliant skill on horseback with firepower, shock tactics, and superior mobility. Their ways of waging war were sophisticated by the standards of the day, relying on not only aggression on the battlefield, but also what today we would call psychological warfare. Their ability to cover ground fast enabled them to gather intelligence over wide areas, which they combined with the masterly use of false rumors about impending attacks or raids. Genghis Khan and his generals relied on fear as a powerful strategic weapon. In this they were very successful. The mere word *Mongol* was enough to conjure up visions of charging horsemen and brutal killing. Cities surrendered and paid tribute rather than suffer a Mongol attack. A carefully cultivated reputation for terror combined with an aura of invincibility lay behind many of the Mongol conquests.

Figure 12.2 *Modern-day Mongolian horsemen reenacting a calvary charge.* © *Rick Sammon.*

A warrior stayed with the same unit permanently, but the leaders were given considerable latitude in the field. This highly flexible command structure allowed the Mongols to attack as a large group or, at a moment's notice, divide into units as small as ten men, in order to encircle an enemy or hunt down fugitives. Each Mongol soldier maintained between three and five horses, which allowed him to change mounts and travel at high speed for long periods without exhausting his animals. When invading Hungary in 1241, the Mongols, led by grandsons of Genghis Khan, covered as much as 160 kilometers (100 miles) a day, an unheard-of mobility for a Western army. Both horses and warriors lived off the land, the latter often off mare's milk, which added to the flexibility and effectiveness of units large and small.

Consummate horsemanship and close relationships between horse and rider came from lifetimes spent on horseback, and from constant practice. Every warrior wore a long, heavy coat under lamellar armor made up of dozens of small, hardened leather-and-iron plates sewn to a fur lining and attached at the waist with a leather belt. A sword, dagger, and sometimes an axe hung from the belt. Underneath was a heavy silk undergarment. Everyone wore trousers on horseback, and a steel or leather helmet. The primary weapon was a recurved bow made from wood, horn, and sinew that was relatively small but extremely powerful. Each archer typically carried two or three bows, each with a range of more than 2,000 meters (6,600 feet). The archers could routinely hit a target at a range of 1,500 meters (4,920 feet). Combine powerful bows, expert archery, and the speed and mobility of horses ridden by men who could shoot multiple arrows at a gallop, and you had one of the most successful animal-human relationships in history.

The close ties between warrior and steed were an integral part of battlefield tactics. Mongol leaders never engaged in the wasteful mass frontal assaults commonplace in the European and Near Eastern worlds. Instead, they used diversionary attacks to encourage the enemy to stay in place, and then sought to outflank and encircle them. The archers would lay down withering barrages of arrows, rearming themselves from baggage camels that followed them into battle. If an attack was unsuccessful, the Mongols would withdraw, quietly study the enemy's tactics, and then attack later. Sometimes they would rely on a feigned retreat, appearing to withdraw in confusion, and then wheeling around to the attack without notice. Once again, expert horsemanship and complete trust between human and beast were essential. Horses and archers forged empires, conquered established civilizations, and toppled emperors.

The Mongol empire depended heavily on horses. Every tribe, every army, engaged in a constant gavotte between people, their animals, and droughts or cold snaps that could kill hundreds of animals in a few months. Horses cut travel times across the harsh steppe, expanded territorial boundaries by a factor of five, and allowed people to exploit widely distributed raw materials and grazing grounds. But every temperature change and rainfall shift altered the relationship. Drier periods brought stunted pasture, decimated herds, and led to extended searches for grass and water. Inevitably, warfare increased as tribes encroached on one another's territories. In milder, better-watered years, territories became smaller, the carrying capacity of grazing land improved dramatically, and fighting died down. Those who lived on the fringes of the steppe lived in constant fear of drought years, when fierce nomads driving animals would arrive without warning, creating mayhem from horseback as they sought better pasture.

The endless rhythms of warm and cold, plentiful rain and drought, ample grass and no forage, were a major engine of history in Eurasia, dictated in large part by a close relationship with the horse. When drought on the plains coincided with unrest and brilliant generalship by the likes of Genghis Khan, the foundations of history shook—all because, thousands of years in the past, some bold young men dared jump on the back of recently tamed horses and ride them. Genghis Khan was well aware of the vulnerability of his domains. He tried to move his empire away from its dependence on the horse and the irregular cycles of drought and rainfall that governed life on the steppe. In this, he and his successors were at least partially successful.

Toppling an Emperor

GENGHIS KHAN STARTED HIS conquest of China with small-scale raids across the Huang He River. In 1209 he accepted the surrender of Emperor Li Anquan of Western Xia. Two years later, he declared war on China's Jin Dynasty, crossed the Great Wall, and ravaged northern China. He captured Beijing in 1215. A grandson, Kublai Khan (who reigned 1260–1294), completed his conquest. Born the year Genghis captured Beijing, he was largely brought up by his mother, the remarkable Sorghaghtani Beki, who "trained all her sons so well that they marveled at her powers of administration."[12] Genghis Khan's eldest son, Mongke, became great khan, and gave his brother responsibility for China. Sorghaghtani Beki made sure that Kublai understood that the best way to govern the Chinese was by enlisting their support, thereby acquiring revenue from their rich farmlands. The Mongols already controlled northern China, so her son's first task was to conquer Sung-controlled, densely forested southern China. There was a stalemate until 1253, when Kublai captured Dali and outflanked the Sung army.

Kublai was elected great khan in 1260, at a time when disunity had descended on the Mongol Empire. He promptly moved his capital to Beijing and declared himself emperor of China, despite competition from the southern Sung, who were not finally defeated until 1279. There was no way the Mongols could govern China, so he allowed the Chinese to administer themselves under Mongol supervision. There was a huge cultural gap between Mongol and Chinese, so Kublai and his successors maintained strong ties with the steppe and also relied on foreigners to control the bureaucracy. He also strove to improve communications. Fifty thousand horses, thousands of oxen and mules, four thousand carts, and six thousand boats connected fourteen hundred postal stations. Couriers on horseback wore bells that warned of their approach and the need for a replacement mount. Such men could cover 400 kilometers (250 miles) in a day.

Mongol rule deteriorated rapidly after Kublai Khan's death in 1294, a victim of perennial clashes between pro-Chinese and steppe-oriented factions. The Ming emperors, who restored the Chinese imperial tradition in 1368, suffered from just as many equine shortages as their predecessors. By the fifteenth century, they were importing ten thousand head annually and continued to do so for over a hundred years. Their trading partners were usually uncooperative. The Mongols often sent only gelded and well-used ponies between four and eight years of age, preferring to keep the mares for themselves. The few females that did come south were apparently crossed with donkeys to produce mules for pack and draft purposes, a telling commentary on Chinese priorities. They were, after all, predominantly farmers, who left little space for pasture. Even when the military reserved areas for grazing horses, the people complained that the reserves were depriving farmers of their livelihood. Inevitably, the largest grazing areas were close to the northern borders, where raids were a constant problem.

A profound ambivalence surrounded Chinese attitudes toward horses. They became a military essential, but many authorities assumed that soldiers were unaccustomed to riding.[13] Some of them were indeed superb horsemen, but one gets the impression that riding horses was considered a foreign practice, except along the northern and western borders. Chinese art is revealing, for many of those who handled and tended horses appear to be non-Chinese. There was bureaucratic attention certainly, an organization set up to acquire horses, but the entire operation over many centuries appears to have lacked true passion. Many Chinese cavalrymen never seem to have acquired a close relationship with their beasts either in the face of Mongol invasions or in later centuries. Apparently, they never mastered the true art of managing and riding horses, or of fighting with them; so, inevitably, the nomads of the north conquered them. Never did the importance of a close partnership between human and beast have greater significance.

Ships of the Desert

CHAPTER 13

"Animals Designed by God"

SOMEONE ONCE DESCRIBED CAMELS as horses created by committee. They had a point, for they can carry double the load of an ox at twice the speed and cover much greater distances. They are faster than donkeys and can travel for long distances without water across searing hot terrain. Few animals had a more profound effect on history.

Ultimate Desert Pack Animals

CAMELS HAVE A SERIES of physiological adaptations that allow them to survive for long periods without water. Their humps are reservoirs of fatty tissue that minimize the insulating effect of fat that would otherwise be distributed all over their bodies. Their red blood cells are oval rather than circular, allowing better cell flow during dehydration. The same cells also allow the beasts to ingest large quantities of water in remarkably short periods of time. A six-hundred-kilogram (thirteen-hundred-pound) camel can drink two hundred liters (fifty-three gallons) of water in three minutes. Thanks to a complex of arteries and veins lying close to one another, camels are also able to withstand the major swings in desert temperatures. They can lose a quarter of their body weight to dehydration, compared to the 12 to 14 percent of most mammals. Thick coats and long legs insulate them from intense heat radiating from the ground; their leathery mouths enable them to feed off thorny desert plants. A camel's gait prevents it from sinking into sand; a third eyelid enables it to dislodge dust from its eyes. Never was an animal better adapted to life in arid and semiarid lands or to life carrying loads.

Domestication

By ABOUT 3000 BCE, human predation had driven wild camels to near extinction in Africa, Southwest Asia, and Central Asia.[1] Who first domesticated them is a mystery. The historian Richard Bulliet believes it was hunting groups living in enclaves along the Southern Arabian coast. There they subsisted off seafood and occasionally hunted camels that had adapted to a predator-free regime of extreme heat. A classic scenario developed: isolated camel populations unafraid of humans living nearby, ever-closer familiarity with small herds and individual animals, then the corralling of more docile females and their young. Why tame camels at all? Given the arid environment, Bulliet makes a case not for their meat, but for their milk, commonly drunk by Somalis and others to this day. Quite when the changeover occurred is a matter of guesswork—perhaps between 3000 and 2500 BCE.

With milk in high demand, there may have been no need to load or ride camels until the hunters became full-time herders attuned to the realities of finding graze. It was then, perhaps, that they turned to their now-tamed beasts as at least part-time pack animals. Their camels provided milk and carried baggage from camp to camp in landscapes far from the cities of Mesopotamia and the Nile. Centuries passed before the camel came into more general use, although people were certainly aware of it. Crude depictions appear in the Nile Valley and farther afield in the Levant between about 2500 and 1400 BCE. A fragment of camel hair rope came from a gypsum works in Egypt dated to about 2500 BCE, although this could, of course, be an import from elsewhere across the Red Sea.[2] Most likely, a few camels brought occasional loads of goods from southern Arabia, but were never bred farther north. Camel bones from the ninth century have also come from a copper mining site in southern Israel's Aravah Valley. The ultimate catalyst for the camel revolution—in the end it was nothing less—was the Arabian incense trade.

The Lure of Frankincense and a Matter of Saddles

FRANKINCENSE IS A HIGHLY prized aromatic resin obtained from the hardy *Boswellia* trees that thrive in Southern Arabia and on Socotra, off the Horn of Africa. Insatiable demand in Egypt, Mesopotamia, and throughout Southwest Asia supported a lucrative international marketplace supplied by ships and camels. The Egyptians used frankincense for eye liner and temple incense for thousands of years. A famous mural in Queen Hatshepsut's temple at Luxor in Upper Egypt commemorates a maritime trading venture down the Red Sea to the Land of Punt (probably Somalia) in about 1458 BCE. In it, sailors are depicted loading sacks of frankincense aboard a ship. The Red Sea is dangerous for sailing vessels both on account of strong headwinds and the same piracy that plagues its waters to this day, so an arduous overland coastal route may also have extended up the sea's eastern shore. The lucrative incense trade expanded rapidly in the hands of Semitic merchants. By 1200 BCE, camel breeding had taken hold outside Arabia. The trade was held back by the lack of a load-carrying saddle that really worked.

For centuries, the only camel saddles were mats tied on with ropes. Now incense traders had to confront the issue of the hump.[3] Theoretically one could put a load atop it, but the hump shrinks during a desert journey. The first pack saddles were cushions placed over the hindquarters, held there by a girth extending forward. These enabled the driver to ride the camel on long journeys. The experiment worked. By Assyrian times, in the first millennium BCE, camels had become commonplace in Mesopotamia, figuring largely in both the incense trade and, increasingly, the battlefield. During the reign of Assyrian king Tiglath-Pileser III (745–727 BCE), booty from Arabian rulers such as Queen Samsi allegedly included thirty thousand camels, twenty thousand head of cattle, and five thousand spice bundles—a rich haul indeed.

Another saddle also came into use, a horseshoelike cushion surrounding the hump, with a saddlebow and horizontal wooden struts, which provided a means for tying on loads. This saddle may have originated from strategic needs, for riders who fought from the saddle. The hump-based design was closer to the neck, offering better control of the beast. A fighting rider was also much higher from the ground. Why two saddle types? Perhaps the rear one was for load carrying, the hump-based form for military purposes. No artist has left us a record. In practice, the camel was too insecure a platform for either a lancer or an archer, so the animal was used mainly for carrying military baggage.

Figure 13.1 *A Tuareg nomad with his camel, wearing a North Arabian pack saddle. Trevor Kittelty/Superstock.*

The revolution came between 500 and 100 BCE, when a new camel saddle transformed the course of desert history. Richard Bulliet calls this the North Arabian pack saddle, after the place where it was invented.[4] Two large arches like inverted Vs lie atop two pads, the one in front of the hump, the other behind it, connected by sticks forming a rigid framework converging at the top with the hump in the middle. The rider sits on a pad set above the frame, his weight distributed evenly not on the hump but on the beast's rib cage. If you want to carry a load instead of a person, you simply suspend two packs on either side of the frame.

It's very easy to claim that ancient inventions revolutionized history in a simple cause-and-effect relationship, but the North Arabian saddle's full impact on history came only when camel breeders became fully integrated into wider society. This was not easy, on account of long-held prejudices against desert nomads among both farmers and city dwellers.

Blurring the Desert and the Sown

EVEN WITH SADDLES, DESERT raiders with bows and arrows were no match for caravan guards armed with iron weapons. The profits from the trade stayed with the merchants, not with the nomads who sold and rented beasts to them. During the second century BCE, the military balance changed when the attackers acquired long stabbing spears and moved in atop their beasts, mounted on North Arabian saddles. Soon people such as the Nabataeans, living on the northern fringes of the desert, gained the ability to control desert trade. They built a caravan city at Petra, in what is now southern Jordan, as early as 332 BCE. The Greek geographer Strabo described the Nabataeans as "not very good warriors, rather being hucksters and merchants."[5] Petra probably controlled the northern part of the Arabian route.[6]

In 105 CE, Emperor Trajan absorbed Petra into the Roman Empire, much of the trade being diverted farther north, to Bosra, in what is now southern Syria, which flourished as a Roman caravan city.[7] By the second century CE, other cities such as Palmyra became prosperous as waypoints on the caravan trade between the Mediterranean and the Euphrates River. The incense trade declined with the rise of Christianity during the second century, in a world where there were now four kinds of commercial locations: production centers, places that consumed product, transshipment points that often served as crossroads, and dues-collecting stations such as customs posts. Mecca became the most famous organizing center. Its rulers forced local tribes to cooperate with caravans rather than raiding. A location with an important shrine, Mecca was far from major imperial powers and achieved considerable prosperity long before the rise of Islam in the eighth century.

By the fourth century CE, Arab merchants used their camels not only to equip caravans—there were, after all, limits to the scale of such operations—but also to compete in the transport business in an eastern Roman Empire that was much more closely integrated into the desert. Camels could heft quarry stone, transport grain from the fields, and carry goods to market much more reliably and across more difficult terrain than the wheeled cart. By late Roman times, camel transport was 20 percent cheaper than that by wagon, taking into account the cost of fodder and of building the vehicle. A shift in military power and the breaking down of ancient cultural barriers between desert and sown land, and the existence of the North Arabian saddle, meant that the camel replaced wheeled transport across a huge swathe of the eastern Mediterranean world. Long before the rise of Islam, the camel, the donkey, and the mule were the load carriers of city dwellers, farmers, desert nomads, and armies.

Into the Sahara

THE ANCIENT EGYPTIANS INHABITED a linear kingdom, where the transport of goods and people proceeded by water. As we have seen, the donkey also played an important role in Egyptian trade, carrying incense and other commodities from ports on the Red Sea to the Nile and to oases west of the river, perhaps even as far as the Lake Chad region. Both camels and the experience to breed and operate them crossed the Red Sea, perhaps from the port of Leuce Come, which lay opposite the Egyptian harbor of Myos Hormos that was operated by the Ptolemies. Camel breeding in Africa probably began in the hinterland between the Red Sea and the Nile, and then spread southward into the Sudan. By the first and second centuries BCE, camel caravans operated along desert routes east of the valley, but it was not until Roman times that indigenous rather than Arab camel nomads, such as the Beja of the northeastern Sudan, assumed greater military and political power. Camels became increasingly important components of the transportation economy of the settled lands.

Here again, new saddle designs came into play. Unlike the North Arabian saddle, which developed in response to military needs, the Saharan saddles were for long-distance riding. A rider atop such a device could use his feet to control his beast by putting pressure on the neck. Such saddles developed from North Arabian designs as camel nomads penetrated the southern Sahara, all the way from the Nile to as far west as Mauritania, a desert route without major obstacles.

Exactly when the camel came to North Africa is a matter of controversy, but there was little or no caravan traffic along the coast, as travelers usually preferred to go by sea. Most likely, camels reached the north from the desert and ultimately from the Sudanese region. At first the number of beasts was small, obtained by sporadic contacts between Romans and desert nomads. It was not until the first or second centuries CE that the Romans gained access to large numbers of camels. Not being enamored of caravans and not being drinkers of camel's milk, they used the animals for other purposes. They needed draft animals to haul carts and to turn the tough soils of Tripolitania and southern Tunisia, and for use in battle. A circle of crouched camels makes for an effective laager for infantry. To the Romans, the camel was a pack animal, a commodity, not a ridden beast like those prized by its nomadic Berber owner.[8]

The Golden Trade of the Moors

NO ONE KNOWS WHEN the first camel caravans traversed the central and western Sahara, but it must have been before Islamic armies conquered North Africa during the seventh century CE. What had once been obscure tracks now became well-trodden caravan routes controlled by Muslim traders with a far wider outlook than that of their predecessors. Thus was born what has been called the "Golden Trade of the Moors."[9] Each fall, camel caravans plodded southward from Sijilmassa in Morocco to Taghaza in northern Mali, where they picked up cake salt from nearby mines. Salt was, and still is, a precious commodity for West African farmers, who lack local supplies of it. From Taghaza, the caravans followed familiar paths to Walata, Ghana, and Jenne, on the Middle Niger River. There they picked up gold dust, mined from auriferous gravels in the Bambuk region of the Senegal River.[10]

Caravans (*qualafil* in Arabic) large and small traversed the Sahara for many centuries. Larger ones comprised thousands of beasts traveling in lines that extended several kilometers.[11] One has an image of unchanging desert tracks, of camels moving steadily across utterly arid landscapes looking neither left nor right. Nothing could be further from the truth. Reality was harsh in the extreme. The caravaner was at the mercy of a constantly changing desert, where environmental and weather conditions differed from month to month, year to year. The agricultural calendar and heat determined the start of the caravan season, which typically lasted from October to March. Most caravans traveled from dawn until just after noon, the time of the afternoon prayer. Many journeyed at night. An average day covered about 34 kilometers (21.7 miles),

Figure 13.2 *A Saharan camel caravan led by a puller. Anna Gibiskys/
Shutterstock.*

but there was no such thing as an average day, thanks to strong winds,
rough terrain, and the varying number of beasts.

The caravaners walked alongside their beasts through featureless
landscapes where mirages were commonplace, the horizon masked by
haze. The caravaners' minds were beset by boredom, their bodies by
dehydration and exhaustion. In 1858 the traveler Mardochée Aby Serour
complained that the "ground is as uniform as paper and reverberates in
your eyes like crystal."[12] He remarked that camel droppings appeared to
be human riders at a distance. There were, of course, relatively predictable areas where water and grazing could be found, but the sparse rainfall and pasture varied from year to year, so routes changed constantly.
Every caravan depended on intelligence about watering holes and graze.
A high level of trust existed between different leaders, merchants, and
agents, some of whom formed collectives to organize larger, safer caravans. Caravaners shared route planning, information on potential markets, and insights about volatile political conditions along the way.

Caravan guides provided expert advice from their encyclopedic
knowledge of landscape, water supplies, and the latest environmental
conditions. Many were expert trackers of animals and of potentially
hostile nomads, and knew the most insignificant of landmarks. The
fourteenth-century Arab traveler Ibn Battuta marveled at the skill of

his guide, who was "blind in one eye and diseased in the other and yet knew the way better than anyone."[13] Every guide had to be able to navigate with the aid of the heavens. The polestar, *bilhady* in Arabic, did not move, and guided the traveler toward north. Saharan navigators knew the constellations that traveled across the heavens and used them to establish their position, to calculate the distance traveled. Skies were generally clear, but when a sandstorm blew, the caravan was as lost as a mariner in the midst of the Pacific Ocean.

Extreme heat, mirages, thirst, raiders, and sandstorms—the caravaner learned the realities of a tough trade at an early age and was literally born to the job. There was, of course, far more to the plodding caravan than the camel and its rider. Families, entire communities, wealthy merchants, and breeders all played important parts in a trade that has now all but vanished in the face of the truck and the diesel engine. Only a few caravans and a will-o'-the-wisp of vivid recollections survive.

The journey was never easy, with the attendant hazards of heat and dehydration, quite apart from desert nomads, clad in blue burnooses, who would attack without warning. Safety lay in numbers and in carefully thought-out logistics, for the larger the loads the greater the profits. As early as the eighth century, West African gold was well known in the Islamic world, financing wars of conquest and bringing immense wealth to Islam. By the twelfth century, some caravans numbered as many as twelve hundred to two thousand beasts. In July 1324, the sultan of Egypt welcomed a truly exotic visitor, Mansa Musa, ruler of the West African kingdom of Mali. He traveled in style, with hundreds of camels and numerous slaves. The Malians injected so much gold into the Egyptian economy that the value of this most precious metal dropped as much as 25 percent for some years. Before Columbus sailed west, Mansa Musa and his successors supplied two-thirds of Europe's gold. Such was the demand for gold and salt that caravans traversed the Sahara long after Portuguese ships landed in West Africa and gold flowed from American mines.

Even in the twenty-first century, the last remnants of the trade survive. Camel caravans connect the salt mines at Taoudenni, deep in the Sahara, and Timbuktu, near the Niger River on the southern fringes of the desert (see sidebar "The Salt Carriers").[14]

The Salt Carriers

The four-wheel-drive diesel truck is today's Saharan camel, but a few remnants of the ancient caravan trade linger on. Camels still transport cake salt slabs in Mali, four slabs per beast, the driver keeping one at journey's end. How much longer the caravans will continue is an open question, for the truck drivers pay cash up front for their loads, and prices have fallen. At least camels do not require diesel fuel or expensive maintenance.

Salt has been Saharan gold for many centuries, since at least the twelfth century when Islamic merchants discovered the rich deposits deep in the remotest parts of the desert. This most commonplace of substances may not seem like gold to you and me, but even small bags of it were critically important to tropical farmers, who lived off predominantly carbohydrate diets. Each winter, large slabs of Saharan salt reached Timbuktu, at the southern edge of the desert, on the backs of thousands of camels. Once in Timbuktu, the salt traveled by boat downstream to the riverside town of Mopti, where it was broken into smaller packages for sale in other markets in the Sahel.

The Tuareg call these seasonal caravans the *Azalai*. Traditionally, they were journeys from Timbuktu to the salt mines at Taoudenni, eight hundred kilometers (five hundred miles) to the north in northern Mali. At one time, the *Azalai* extended from Timbuktu to Taoudenni, then northward onto Taghaza, another salt mining location, then to the Mediterranean. North-traveling caravans of as many as ten thousand camels carried gold and slaves. The beasts returned laden with salt. Enormous caravans traveled back and forth through remote, featureless desert. The winter caravan of 1939–40 involved more than four thousand camels and thirty-five thousand slabs of salt. Current production has declined, but remarkably, the camel caravans persist to this day. The numbers are much smaller, each weekly caravan involving perhaps fifty beasts, but the routine never varies, with much of the travel at night. The eight-hundred-kilometer (five-hundred-mile) trek takes about fourteen days through some of the hottest and most featureless dune terrain on earth.

Taoudenni is an unpleasant place by any standards. For some decades a penal settlement, the tiny village occupies an ancient lake bed in one of the hottest regions on earth. Here, summer temperatures reach 40 degrees Celsius (120 degrees Fahrenheit), with average winter highs around 27 degrees Celsius (81 degrees Fahrenheit). Over one hundred sixty kilometers (a hundred miles) of unrelenting Saharan landscape isolate the inhabitants from any popular center of any size. Arid, windy, and blessed with a mere four days of rainfall a year, Taoudenni has only one asset: cake salt. Thousands of cavelike pits from centuries of mining litter the salt lake bed, each about four meters (thirteen feet) deep, dug by teams of three miners, who are usually indentured servants. Three layers of high-quality salt lie under poorer-quality material and red-clay overburden. Using crude axes, the men cut rectangular slabs of salt weighing about thirty kilograms (sixty-six pounds), each about five centimeters (two inches) thick. These the camels carry to Timbuktu four slabs per beast, stacked from the saddle, one going to the owner. Everyone takes care not to break the slabs, for their value would then plummet. The mining takes place during the cooler winter months, with the miners living in crude huts made of poor-quality salt blocks.

The caravan journey is almost mystical in its isolation, traversing featureless dunes across a landscape that warps one's sense of distance. Nothing grows for thousands of square kilometers. Water is measured in drops rather than liters. The camels walk from watering hole to watering hole, led by a human guide, who has only the wind, the stars above, and the subtle changes in the color of the sand to help him. He knows the route like the back of his hand, his knowledge of desert pilotage a legacy going back centuries. Each guide operates by dead reckoning, keeping careful track of days and distances. To miss a watering hole means almost certain death. The young drivers, sometimes mere boys, act as "pullers." They head each column of beasts under the charge of the guide. However young, they are well aware of the hazards of the featureless landscape with its ever-shifting horizons and dunes. The big problems are forage and water, so each caravan drops loads of hay every few days, to be used on the return trip. They also tend to travel in the early morning; later in the day, to avoid the midday heat; and quite often, at night. This journey of great isolation is far more than a journey back to a medieval world of camel caravans. For the young pullers, it's a spiritual journey, a kind of pilgrimage that takes them closer to Allah. Their suffering and fear give them a powerful spiritual awakening, a chance to see themselves in a landscape that some Islamic sages call a mirror of the soul.

Camels on the Silk Road

AROUND 2500 BCE, NOMADS living in the mountains and plateau regions between Iran and Turkmenistan domesticated the two-humped Bactrian camel.[15] The art of breeding this animal spread across the Iranian Plateau, into Central Asia, and into Mesopotamia, where the Assyrians depicted it on bas-reliefs as war booty. Many of these camels hauled carts.

Bactrians are better adapted to colder landscapes and became a staple of the Eurasian Silk Road, especially during the first century CE, when trade between the Han Dynasty and the Parthians of northeastern Iran expanded dramatically. Somewhere in the breeding ranges of southern Mesopotamia, some herders interbred one- and two-humped beasts. The resulting hybrids were powerful single-humped camels that were formidable load carriers. According to the Greek author Diodorus, some of them could heft loads weighing nearly 410 kilograms (900 pounds). The Silk Road caravans ultimately depended for the most part on hybrids in warmer landscapes and on hardier two-humped Bactrians in cold regions such as the Altai and the Hindu Kush.

What Was Eurasian Caravan Travel Like?

THE TRAVELER AND WRITER Owen Lattimore gives us one of the few firsthand accounts of what it was like to travel in a Eurasian camel caravan before motor vehicles diluted the experience.[16] In the 1920s, he joined caravans traveling from eastern China through the Gobi Desert to Mongolia. The Bactrian camels traveled in rows of about eighteen beasts, with a puller for each file. A caravan master led the way, the equivalent of a ship's captain, whose word was law. On the march, the puller led the first camel in his row with a guide rope attached to a wooden peg in the lead beast's nose. Similar ropes linked the lead camel to the ones behind it.

Being a puller was not an easy job. He was responsible for the health of his beasts, which required keeping them away from poisonous plants and finding the best grazing for them. Pullers coped with camels' pack sores and minor injuries, ensured the loads were distributed properly, and prevented the camels from drinking too much water. They also secured their beasts for the night and checked they had adequate protection from wind-blown snow in winter. Loading a camel was an art unto itself, well described by missionaries Mildred Cable and Francesca French, who traveled widely in the region during the 1920s: "In the loading of a camel its grumblings commence as the first bale is placed on its back, and continues uninterruptedly until the load is equal to its strength, but as soon as it shows signs of being in excess, the grumbling ceases suddenly."[17]

The caravans carried food and tea for the drivers and any passengers, also dried peas or barley, the cheapest camel feed available. Lattimore heard estimates of thirty loads of fodder for every one hundred of merchandise. The paid cargoes were commodities such as cotton, wool, and tea, and manufactured goods for sale. There were exotica, too: jade from Khotan, elk antlers that were prized in Chinese medicine, and even the remains of dead caravaners and merchants, which traveled in special caravans—or at least their bones did, for the bodies were temporarily buried until the flesh had fallen off the bones. There was opium, too, carried surreptitiously at night. During the summer, when camels molt, their owners would pick up extra profit by selling the wool. In Lattimore's day, the pullers had learned to knit from White Russians in exile after the Russian Civil War. When they needed wool while knitting on the march, they would simply pluck some from the nearest beast, turn it into thread, and continue knitting.

Lattimore found that the caravans traveled between sixteen and forty kilometers (ten and twenty-five miles) a day, moving at the walking speed of the pullers. The distance depended on the topography, weather, and availability of water supplies. Chinese caravans were slower than Mongol ones, who had the advantage of being able to draw on fresh camels from their herds close at hand. Lattimore reveled in the life: "I had been getting used to breaking camp at anytime of the night, eating anything that came handy, and sleeping where I could lie down." He also had the priceless gift of sensing landscapes in all their subtlety. "A good Mongol can tell at once whether a camel comes from a *nutak*, a homeland or orbit of migration, that is a little too hot in summer for the preference of a camel, or whether a cow was bred in high alpine pastures, on a wide, rather sandy plain or in the deep green pasture of a well-watered valley."[18]

Over many centuries, camel nomads acquired subtle ecological knowledge about their environment and the animals they managed. Lattimore learned of this from older men, who could recognize "the smell" of the earth of a road or region when traveling at night. They could dismount, take up a handful of earth, sniff it, and say, "No, this is not our road, which should go in that other direction."[19] They knew their roads, even at night, and their relationships to patches of soil and vegetation.

The caravan masters and their pullers used a rich vocabulary to describe their landscapes and the animals they used. The age, color, and individual characteristics of a camel or, for that matter, a horse could be recited by Mongols with uncanny precision. There was, and still is, a lexicon for different kinds of hills, for ridges, plains, bodies of water, streams and springs. Oral directions guide travelers from one of these often-inconspicuous landmarks to the next, across landscapes that have few obvious features. The same landmarks had sacred geography, marked by stone cairns known as *obas*, landscapes defined by watersheds and not valleys, because grazing grounds are defined that way.

Thus it was that desert caravans, wherever their locations, used subtle indicators to make their way across barren landscapes. Those who handled the caravans read the heavenly bodies to navigate their way, just as Pacific canoe skippers used the same kind of knowledge when out of sight of land. The comparisons with traditional sailors are irresistible: a deep conservatism in behavior, an intimate knowledge of the environment and its moods, encyclopedic knowledge of grazing and water supplies in remote, little-traveled terrain. Camels truly were the ships of the desert, but instead of wind and current, they responded to their human guides. The beasts carried the loads; the humans led them to graze and water. This simple partnership, born of a pragmatic need for survival, has endured for at least two thousand years.

If the donkey began the globalizing caravan trade on a large scale, the camel extended it, helping to bring the riches of Africa and Asia to Europe and beyond. That the camel trade survives today, even in the age of automobiles and cargo planes, shows how well adapted this partnership is to the extreme conditions of remote desert transport.

"Mild, Patient, Enduring"

CHAPTER 14

Dominion over Beasts?

Western England, late winter 1380. The file of packhorses plods steadily through the endless rain, heads down, hooves splashing in the mud of the narrow trackway. Stout ropes hold large bundles of grain on their backs, and laden panniers hang from their flanks. The packers walk ahead along the meandering lane, saying little, huddled in their leather cloaks in the wet. Dripping trees press on the defile that leads to a constricted masonry bridge across a fast-moving stream. A young man leads the way. The patient animals follow in single file between the low parapets that stand clear of their loads. This is an easy crossing compared with the more common timber bridges that would be lethally slippery on this dank, wintery day. The smell of wood smoke, barking dogs, a church bell tolling for a dead woman. The packers turn their beasts into a courtyard and unload them. They pile the bundles of grain in a nearby barn, ready for market day on the morrow.

NO ONE LIVING IN the small market town would have looked twice at the weary pony train. Like everyone else, whether artisan, farmer, or merchant, its inhabitants depended heavily on animals for food, clothing, and transportation, especially on the ox, the sheep, and the horse. One estimate has it that, with their animals, medieval Europeans had five times the motor power of Chinese civilization of the day.*

---

* In this chapter, also chapters 15–18, my narrative focuses mainly on Britain, seemingly at the expense of other parts of the world. This was a conscious decision on my part, based on the literature available to me, on space, and on my linguistic skills. There is, of course, an abundant literature on animals from other parts of the world, much, but not all, of which mirrors the developments described in these pages.

Figure 14.1 *Pack horses transporting timber in Northumberland, northern England, c. 1812. SSPL/Getty Images.*

Warhorses were the most valuable animals in medieval Europe, a society where agriculture and feudalism supported mounted warriors. The owner of a trained warhorse was an individual of status, defined by myths of chivalrous warfare, of devotion shared by knight and steed. Theirs was a very different world from that of the working horse, which, by the twelfth century, had taken over most plowing in France from the much slower oxen. The shift occurred later in England, where plowmen deliberately went slowly while plowing under feudal obligation to land-owners.[1] The changeover involved significant innovations in nonchoking collar harnesses and nailed horseshoes, essential in the damp climate of Northern Europe. The adoption of the three-field rotation system also made the changeover easier. This allowed farmers to produce oats and other forage for their animals as well as rye. Horses worked faster than oxen; moved well on steeper, stonier ground; and could handle all manner of tasks, from plowing and harrowing to hauling loads. But they were more expensive to feed and maintain and had no value at the end of their working lives, unlike oxen, which could be fattened and sold for food. At first, oxen pulled the heavier loads, but over time, horse breeders developed bigger, stronger creatures, capable of handling greater weights. Equines were especially useful on larger farms and on the lighter chalk soils of southern England. Where there was plenty of lush pasture and heavier soils, oxen prevailed, while horses merely hauled carts and did the harrowing. Meanwhile, cattle and sheep provided flesh, leather, and wool. The insatiable demand for fine English wool in Europe led to meadows replacing plowed land in many places. This made economic sense. A few herdsmen could manage large numbers of sheep at a fraction of the labor involved in cereal cultivation. Wool provided no less than 5 percent of the English Crown's revenue by the mid-fourteenth century. Everyone in England ate mutton, but not horse meat, especially as influential people considered horses they had ridden both noble and too close to humans for either clerics or lords to consume. It was almost as if their prized mounts were human.

Compact Packers

FARMERS AND WORKING COUNTRY people owned relatively few riding horses, given the expense involved. Some kept a solitary beast that carried the farmer's wife to market or hefted packs and panniers with everything from corn to firewood. Owning one widened one's horizons beyond the narrow compass of village homestead. An owner could ride more than forty-eight to sixty-four kilometers (thirty to forty miles) a day, and merchants served customers over a wider area. Most farm horses hauled loads, towed plows, and worked the harvest. They also drove machinery that drained mines, operated mills, and hauled goods from ports and rivers to landlocked towns and villages. The numbers of riding horses rose irregularly until the eighteenth century, when 86 percent of one parish at the edge of eastern England's Fens owned horses and rode them regularly. This reflected a rising standard of living among rural householders.

By the sixteenth century, English horses were, for the most part, smaller beasts, with Irish and Scottish mounts being much preferred, the latter being "fast knit and strongly made for to endure travaile."[2] Most working horses were compact and well proportioned, used for long journeys such as those of the seventeenth-century antiquarian William Camden, who surveyed Britain's past from horseback. From Camden's day up to the 1700s, Britain ran on small pack ponies.

Small, compact packhorses carried relatively small loads, but they were ideal for rough terrain, on hills, and under the muddy conditions that bedeviled every highway. They cost less to feed and were cheaper than larger beasts. As with donkey caravans, individual animals could be added or subtracted on the road. They were also faster than larger draft horses hauling carts, but were more expensive per kilometer in cargo cost than the larger animals and their wagons. Packhorse trains carried all manner of goods to London and were commonplace until the eighteenth century, when toll roads led to highway improvements and better conditions for draft horses. The transportation method of choice was still, of course, water, where bulk loads could be floated long distances. Land carriage was much more expensive. The price of coal, for example, doubled every sixteen kilometers (ten miles) overland, so there were obvious commercial advantages to mines operating close to waterways. Much coal traveled in small two-wheeled carts or in horse panniers.

Small towns with strategic positions on major rivers became important commercial hubs. Lechlade, on the Upper Thames, handled cloth and cheese from Gloucester and other towns. A major cheese market in the town attracted as many as 140 to 200 wagons, and numerous loads carried in on horseback. Horses also towed barges from riverbanks against current and prevailing winds, precursors to the horse-hauled canal barges that proliferated during the Industrial Revolution. Some coalfields constructed wooden wagon ways that allowed operators to move much larger tonnages to distribution points, ports, and riverbanks some kilometers from the pithead.

By the seventeenth and eighteenth centuries, an ever-broadening range of commodities and goods traveled by road, among them cartloads of corn for town markets. More than a century earlier, William Camden had observed of the corn market at Warminster, in southern England, that "it is scarce credible what quantities of corn are each week carried hither and presently sold."[3] Textiles were also a major overland cargo, both as finished cloth and unfinished material. The volume of carrier traffic was such that, as early as 1600, there were regular services from London to York and other northern cities. Road hauling became a major, if hazardous, business, especially because of highwaymen. Long-distance carriers responded by traveling in convoys.

Packhorses were small but strong, usually geldings, which were easier to control. In the final analysis, they were, in economic terms, a more refined version of the donkey and mule, rare in England until the eighteenth century. Two-wheeled carts were the vehicle of choice for carriers with much scarcer, large draft horses, although four-wheeled wagons spread gradually through England after the mid-sixteenth century. Four-wheelers required larger beasts, also used for plowing. An ideal animal "wyll stoupe to his worke, and lay sure holde of the grounde with his feet and stoutelye pull at a pinch."[4]

Meanwhile, Monarchs and the Nobility . . .

THE COURT, WEALTHY ARISTOCRACY, and the upper classes lived in another equine world. They routinely traveled from place to place on fine steeds. Unlike working people, who worked with animals for a livelihood, the nobility regarded good horsemanship as the attribute of a gentleman, ownership as a mark of social status. Such owners admired and cherished their mounts.

The elite often owned dozens of horses. When King Henry VIII died in 1547, he maintained more than a thousand horses at vast expense, in stables around his domains, looked after by a small army of grooms, blacksmiths, and horse masters. He encouraged the breeding of larger animals on big estates. The nobility followed his example. Books on horsemanship proliferated. Groups of landowners used one another's stallions to inseminate their mares. Practical breeding experience passed from owner to owner and became more selective. "Breed few but choice," adjured a Warwickshire horse breeder. Henry VIII had encouraged the practice of importing foreign stock for cross-breeding purposes. Strong Flemish mares enhanced English draft horses. (Draft horses pulled loads and plowed.) In 1572 alone, English owners imported more than four hundred brood mares from the Dutch. Coursers (fast horses, often war horses) from the Kingdom of Naples made excellent parade horses. Light Andalusian Ginetes (light Arabians), with ancestry in Moorish and Berber beasts, made ideal general riding horses and were widely used by cavalry.

Fine horses were powerful statements. King James I told his son Prince Henry, "It becometh a Prince better than any other man to be a fair and good horseman." A rider who handled a "great horse" effortlessly and gracefully "importeth a majestie and drede to inferior persons beholding him aboue the common course of other men."[5] Powerful horses were an integral part of carefully stage-managed appearances by monarchs and important nobles. When Henry VIII rode to greet Francis I of France at the Field of the Cloth of Gold in 1520, he headed a procession of 5,704 people and 3,224 horses. The flaunted power and wealth failed to outdo Francis I, who rode a magnificent bay at the head of his similarly impressive retinue. Portraits of monarchs and nobles depicted them astride great horses, dressed for war. In 1633, Van Dyck painted King Charles I astride a Spanish Ginete, in full armor. His old riding master by his side gazes at him in awe.

Horses served as diplomatic currency as well. King Henry VIII, while allied to France, obtained draft animals from Flanders in the Low Countries, a region controlled by Spain. The king delighted in gifts of fine horses, especially from Italian princes, whose studs used high-quality brood mares and stallions from North Africa and the eastern Mediterranean. Diplomatic gifts between monarchs continued, always for the benefit of only a few. Landowners, who used foreign horses for breeding purposes, paid big money for them. The quality of native English horses improved markedly as a result. Most people purchased their mounts at horse fairs, while the gentry tended to buy much more expensive horses from one another, from people who were friends of equivalent social status, or through agents.

By the seventeenth century, imposing stables served as wings to large country houses, said to look "like so many gentlemen's seats."[6] Just the cost of feeding pampered beasts was enormous, preferably with some upland pasture close at hand. The ultimate prestige mounts were Eastern horses, widely admired for their strength and beauty. Increasing numbers of them arrived in England during the early seventeenth century. The diarist John Evelyn admired three Oriental horses in London's Hyde Park in December 1784. One bay, valued at five hundred guineas, was "in all regards beautifull and proportion'd to admiration." The three horses "trotted like does, as if they did not feele the Ground."[7] Prominent artists painted the beautiful Arabian, which became an equine icon. Arabians were lively yet gentle beasts that responded well to kindness. So they received the best of quarters. The progeny of such imported horses and local stock gave rise to the thoroughbreds that defined English horseracing, where humans and equines worked together in perfect harmony. The aristocracy spent enormous sums of money on their cherished racehorses, while millions of commoners lived in grinding poverty.

But horses, however valuable, were a depreciating asset. When once-cherished mounts grew old and infirm, few wealthy owners put them out to grass to end their days in comfort. They usually discarded them when they could no longer fulfill their role in life. By the end of their often-long lives, they were worthless in a country that abhorred horse meat on the dinner table. Old or worn-out beasts were worth a few shillings for their hides and as dog meat. Many became meat for foxhounds. Wrote John Flavel, a preacher, in 1669, "By such cruel usage, they have been destroyed and cast into a ditch for dog's meat."[8] Perhaps this sentiment is the origin of the common expression "going to the dogs." In a moment, at the whim of its master, a cherished mount became disposable, impersonal flesh for other beasts.

Have We Dominion over Beasts?

ONE SHOULD NOT BE surprised at this in a devout age when Christian doctrine governed the ways people treated animals. The Scriptures gave humans the right to rule over animals that were made by God for humans. The Bible's teachings were set down long before the Romans relied heavily on working animals for food and transporting loads. People may have liked individual animals in their possession, but they were considered, ultimately, either food or unpaid labor. The abundance of working animals seemed to strengthen assumptions that beasts served people. Many believed there was a natural instinct in some animals to obey humanity. Wrote the Puritan pastor Jeremiah Burroughes in 1643, "Sometimes you may see a little child driving before him a hundred oxen . . . as he pleaseth; it showeth that God hath preserved somewhat of man's dominion over the creatures."⁹ A physician, George Cheyne, even proclaimed in 1705 that God had made horse manure smell sweet knowing that people would spend much time among their steeds. Every animal had its purpose, Cheyne wrote—fearsome beasts to serve as "our schoolmasters," apes and parrots to entertain. Even horseflies were God's way of taxing human ingenuity in dealing with them. The Creator's design was utter perfection; the animal kingdom was part of his grand blueprint.

Nevertheless, established doctrine changed perceptibly over the centuries. By the eighteenth century, many thinkers argued that domestication was good for animals: Cattle and sheep were better off because they were protected from predators. Butchering animals was an act of kindness that prevented beasts from suffering in old age and provided food for "a more noble animal." Beasts had no reason, no divine authority, and thus had no rights. The Sixth Commandment, which forbade murder, applied, of course, to humans alone, not to animals. Traditional Christian theological opinion had no truck with the gentler attitudes toward animals and nature associated with Eastern religions such as Buddhism and Hinduism. Christianity was an anthropocentric faith that tended to ignore those parts of the Gospel that spoke of human responsibilities to care for animals, implying that they were part of God's covenant. Thus, an unbridgeable gap separated animals and humans.

Were Animals Rational Beings?

ONLY A FEW VOICES defended animals, the most prominent among them being French statesman and writer Michel de Montaigne (1533–1592), who wrote of animals, "It is no great marvell if we understand them not: no more doe we the Cornish, the Welsh, or Irish."¹⁰ They have a "full and perfect communication" and were no more "brutish" than humans. A flood of discussion about animals during the seventeenth and eighteenth centuries revolved around three emerging trends; new generations of experimental science that involved vivisection, the increasing commodification of animals for food, especially for growing urban populations, and more widely available printed media.

Montaigne's claim that animals were more rational than people contrasted with the views of the French philosopher René Descartes (1596–1660).[11] This learned gentleman developed a doctrine, later called Cartesianism, with Spanish antecedents that proclaimed animals to be mere equipment, just like clocks, incapable of speech and reasoning, without minds or souls. Some of his followers even argued that animals did not feel pain. The howls of a beaten dog were merely external reflexes totally unconnected to any inner sensations. Cartesianism became a way of rationalizing how humans treated animals, especially the heinous practice of live vivisection, a regular event at London's Royal Society during the 1660s. The watching fellows enjoyed the gruesome spectacle and verified the results. Such cruelty was entirely justified, in their minds, for humans were unique, separated from animals as heaven was distinct from earth. Wrote the eighteenth-century novelist and poet Oliver Goldsmith, "In the ascent from brutes to man, the line is strongly drawn, well marked, and impassable."[12]

Even some human beings were considered beasts or near-beasts in an era when the exploration of distant lands was much in the news. The Tahitians of the South Pacific enjoyed brief popularity as noble savages living in a tropical paradise. Others, such as the Hottentots of the Cape of Good Hope, became the epitome of animal-like humans with "piggish" habits and an odor so powerful that one was said to be able to smell them from thirty paces—upwind. Closer to home, the insane seemed like people whose inner beast was emerging, while the treatment of the poor, of slaves, often resembled that accorded sheep. Only spurs and whips could restrain the common people, such as farmworkers or the urban poor. Breaking in a horse often seemed an appropriate analogy for educating the young. For people accustomed to the management of cattle, leadership appeared to resemble the task of a shepherd. Even

the poorest farm laborers believed in the general principle of domination, for they could kick and curse their animals when insulted by their
superiors.

Cruelty at Close Quarters

DOMINATION AND BRUTALITY WENT hand in hand in a world where
everyone depended on animals for food, all manner of products, and
for work. Subsistence farmers rarely kept their stock for sentimental
reasons; cruelty was commonplace.[13] Castration was routine, as it had
been for thousands of years, making beasts easier to handle and reducing the amount of energy spent on sexual activity; it was also thought
to make their meat fattier, healthier, and better tasting. There were even
special measures for fattening beasts: shutting pigs in close quarters
with one another and keeping cattle, lambs, and poultry in special dark
houses for fattening. Some farmers even nailed the feet of geese to the
floor, which was said to help them put on weight. Dogs often baited
gelded cattle before slaughter, an ordeal said to thin the cattle's blood
and make their flesh tastier. Many towns even had ordinances making
it compulsory to bait a bull before it was butchered. The slaughtering
itself was inhumane. Butchers poleaxed cattle, and then killed them
with a knife. Calves and many lambs died more slowly. First their necks
were slit with a knife so that they bled copiously, which made their flesh
white. The bleeding was then stopped, and the animal allowed to linger
alive for a day or so. Farmers habitually bled pigs to death.

Ceremonies and rituals of all kinds were integral to the lives of hardworking commoners, an escape from the arduous routines and suffering
of daily life.[14] Many of these involved cruelty to animals and the use of
animal imagery, including horns, which symbolized masculine virility.
People whipped dogs on St. Luke's Day and drowned strays purely for
sport. In 1232, Pope Gregory IX proclaimed that the cat was a "diaboli-
cal creature." Felines were suspect because many pagans cherished them,
which meant that they were evil in the eyes of the Lord. Furthermore,
they were seminocturnal, and somewhat mysterious. In low light, the
reflective layer of cells behind their retinas made their eyes glow, so

perhaps, inevitably, they became seen as demons. An association with witches soon followed: people who sold their souls to the devil, who gave them a feline familiar (demon), perhaps the source of their power. Many people believed this, so much so that many families gave up having cats for fear of being burned at the stake. Cats were stoned to death as demonic minions in league with heretics, pinned to posts at village festivals on saints' days, and then killed. In France, the monarch ordered sacks of live cats burned publically. An early Tudor school textbook bears a sentence for translation into Latin: "I hate cats." Nevertheless, some people kept cats to keep down rodents, among them millers, fisherfolk, and merchants (see sidebar "The Cat That Urinated"). Many villagers raised young cats for their flesh and fur. An abandoned well excavated in Cambridge yielded the remains of seventy cats that had been killed and then skinned, apparently for their meat.

The Cat That Urinated

My cats walk over my computer keyboard with promiscuous impunity, usually when I'm editing an intricate sentence. They protest indignantly when I tactfully suggest they move off, but at least they don't stroll through with inky paws. No such luck in medieval times, when monasteries kept cats around libraries to hunt the mice and rats that feasted off manuscripts. A monk working at the Deventer monastery in the Netherlands in about 1420 made the mistake of leaving his manuscript out overnight. A library feline decided this was an ideal place to urinate. Next morning, the scribe found his precious manuscript ruined by a urine stain. He cursed, drew hands pointing to the stain and a sketch of the beast, and then wrote (in Latin): "There is nothing missing, but a cat urinated on this during a certain night. Cursed be the pesky cat that urinated over this book during the night in Deventer and because of it many others [other cats], too. And beware well not to leave open books at night where cats can come."[15] The monk appears to have shrugged, drawn his arrows and cursed the cat, and then turned the page and continued writing, presumably inhaling the scent of cat urine for some hours.

Mice were also pests, even when the scribes were at work. The twelfth-century Bohemian scribe and artist Hildebert found a mouse on his tabletop consuming his cheese. Apparently, this was not the first time. A picture in a manuscript shows the monk with a raised stone trying to kill the creature. He wrote in the book, "Most wretched mouse, often you provoke me to anger. May God destroy you!"[16]

For all their paw marks and defiling of precious manuscripts, cats were apparently valued by monastic communities for their hunting prowess, as they had been by the Ancient Egyptians and others. A ninth-century Irish monk wrote a poem about his white cat Pangur Bán, which begins:

> I and my Pangur Bán my cat,
> 'Tis a like task we are at:
> Hunting mice is his delight,
> Hunting words I sit all night.[17]

For all the brutality and hard work, the relationships between medieval owners and their beasts were much more intimate than those today. Closer relationships with animals were commonplace during centuries when herds were still small. Shepherds knew the faces of their sheep and those of their neighbors', even the footprints of their charges. Almost invariably, cattle received names, and were often decorated with bells and ribbons, just as the Nuer adorned their beasts. A rich vocabulary of calls and words summoned animals, or encouraged them while plowing, a practice with deep roots in the remote past. Farm animals were really part of the human family. As the natural philosopher Sir Kenelm Digby wrote in 1658, "There's not the meanest cottager but hath a cow to furnish his family with milk; 'tis the principal sustenance of the poorer sort of people . . . which makes them very careful of the good keeping and health of their cows."[18]

For centuries, too, humans and animals lived under the same roof, often in long houses that were combination dwellings and animal byres, accessible one from the other. One writer of 1682 described "every edifice" as a "Noah's Ark," where cows, pigs, chickens, and the human family all slept together under the same roof. Farmers finally began moving animals out of their homes during the seventeenth and eighteenth centuries, but such cohabitation persisted in some parts of the Britain and Ireland, and in Europe, into the nineteenth and twentieth centuries. The affectionate naming of farm animals was commonplace in many rural European communities continuing into modern times, a custom known from Greece as early as Mycenaean times, some three thousand years ago. The Victorian poet Jane Ingelow waxed lyrical about cows in a medieval meadow as if they were familiar parts of a family linked by simple verbal bonds, using what she thought was spelling of the time:

"Come uppe Whitefoot, come uppe Lightfoot,
Come uppe Jetty, rise and follow
Jerry to the milking shed."[19]

In cities and over much of the countryside, this was already changing.

CHAPTER 15

"The Hell for Dumb Animals"

IN AN ERA OF luxury sedans and SUVs, of freeways, car parks, and airlines, it's hard for us to imagine what it must have been like living in a world utterly dependent on animals for farm work, load carrying, and transportation. Our perspectives extend over thousands of kilometers, around the world. Automobile journeys of five hundred kilometers (about three hundred miles) are routine. The viewpoints of people dependent on donkeys, horses, and mules were far narrower, except for the privileged few, who traveled laboriously and regularly over long distances, usually on horseback. But by the late eighteenth century, what is commonly known as the Industrial Revolution was changing the relationship between animals and people profoundly. The growth of cities in particular worsened the plight of beasts of all kinds.

In cities and towns, animals were everywhere, crowded into houses and small yards; cows were even being milked in the streets. London poulterers kept hundreds of chickens in cellars and attics. As late as the nineteenth century, some people still reared chickens in their bedrooms and kept horses inside urban residences. Pigs were a public nuisance, wandering the streets and starting fires by brushing straw into embers. They often bit, or even killed, young children. By the eighteenth century, England had a higher number of domesticated beasts per cultivated hectare than any other country except the Netherlands.[1] Few people walked in the British countryside if they could avoid it. Horses were like servants: they served their masters and mistresses. They were also the preferred draft animals, while oxen became a dietary staple, especially in growing towns and cities.

Turning Meat into Money

BY THE TIME OF the Industrial Revolution, the English had developed an insatiable appetite for beef. As early as 1624, the writer Henry Peacham declared that London "eateth more good beef and mutton in one month than all Spain, Italy, and a part of France in a whole year."[2] Just under a century later, in 1748, the Swedish-Finnish explorer Pehr Kalm visited England. He remarked that "I do not believe that any Englishman who is his own master has ever eaten dinner without meat."[3] Beef, mutton, and pork had become serious business. By 1726, London butchers alone slaughtered a hundred thousand beeves (fattened cattle), a hundred thousand calves, and six hundred thousand sheep annually. Roast beef became a national symbol in a country where sailors in the Royal Navy received 94 kilograms (208 pounds) of beef and 47 kilograms (104 pounds) of pork a year, even if only a quarter of the population could afford to eat meat once a week. The scientific establishment in the form of the Royal Society encouraged the study of animals, an exploration of their advantages to humanity "as food or physic."

The selective breeding of domestic animals had a long history, notably that of horses for farming, industry, and war. Now the scale of breeding experiments reached new levels. Some innovative farmers turned their attention to systematic breeding of cattle, dogs, and sheep, to the point that a kind of social hierarchy among beasts developed, with the equine thoroughbred at the pinnacle. Until the late seventeenth century, farmers kept cows in small numbers as part of a menagerie that supported the household. As the productivity of crops improved, and more fodder was available for animals, herds became larger, albeit inefficiently managed ones. Meat consumption was soaring in cities and towns, so larger farms now fattened beasts for sale to urban markets, and ways of moving them for sale improved. Subsistence animal husbandry was on the way out.

The size of animals slowly increased, too, especially after the late 1700s, as attitudes toward cattle changed profoundly. Once like individual members of the household, they now became meat on the hoof, to the point that land was thought of in terms of pounds per acre. One observer remarked of Leicester and Northampton that "from 128 to 160 lb. [58 to 72.5 kilograms] per acre, of beef or mutton, is as much as can be bred and fatted on good pasture land." The cattle themselves were fattened for meat, especially when old and worn out. Then there were the by-products: "His skin and his suet sell for a good price. Even his horn and his gall fetch somewhat."[4] However, stockbreeding was still a haphazard business, where size was the primary interest, and strong legs for plowing—until Robert Bakewell came along.

Bakewell's Beasts

IF ONE PERSON CAN be said to have transformed stock husbandry, it was the Leicestershire farmer Robert Bakewell (1726–1795), who lived at Dishley, near Loughborough, in central England.[5] A visitor described him as "a tall, broad-shouldered, stout man of brown-red complexion, clad in a loose brown coat, scarlet waistcoat, leather breeches, and top-boots."[6] Bakewell was a professional farmer, not landed gentry, who inherited his farm from his father. His hands-on approach to animals led him to breeding experiments, first with carthorses, which he sought to improve for better load hauling. He developed a thick, short-bodied animal with short legs. Such beasts looked like medieval warhorses. They were highly prized for plowing light soils and by urban draymen.

Bakewell treated his animals kindly and guarded his secrets jealously, so much so that he is said to have infected the sheep he sold to market with the rot (a wasting disease), so they couldn't be used for breeding. He also bred cattle for the butcher—heaviest in the joints that yielded the most meat. "Small in size and great in value" was the motto of this eccentric gentleman, who displayed the skeletons of his most famous animals on his walls, and joints that showed off their best features. His hospitality was so lavish to one and all that he is said to have died bankrupt.

With ruthless intensity, Bakewell dismissed as irrelevant all such traditional points of admiration as head shape, legs, horns, or color. He raised animals of the same form and family. He bred what he considered the finest specimens of the breed, selected for quality of flesh and fatness. Bakewell's cattle were machines for turning meat into money. They produced meat and fat, not milk. Others focused on milk to make cheese. Leicestershire, for example, became famous for its cheese, including the famous Stilton, still the prince of blue cheeses, first produced by a Mrs. Paulet of that county in the 1760s.

Bakewell's greatest success was with sheep; he bred long-wool animals from Leicestershire and Worcestershire and created the "new Leicester," a hardy, small-boned sheep that matured so rapidly that he was able to bring new sheep to market in two years. New Leicesters were a highly profitable sheep for those who raised them. Bakewell made more than three thousand guineas (about five thousand dollars today) by renting out his prize rams. The success of the New Leicester led to experiments with other breeds, such as the Lincolnshire beasts, with their heavier fleeces. In time, focused breeding led to native sheep dying out in the face of improved animals, adapted to a variety of different environments. Bakewell's objective was always meat and wool yield, to make money in the marketplace.

Figure 15.1 *A New Leicester (Dishley) sheep, created by Robert Bakewell. Superstock.*

Cattle breeding became quite fashionable, especially among wealthy landowners. Hubback, a prize shorthorn bull owned by Charles Collet of Lincolnshire, who had learned from Bakewell, traveled throughout England between 1801 and 1810 in a specially constructed carriage. Thousands of farmers admired Hubback as an example of an ideal ox. As Bakewell's standards of excellence became widely recognized, the size and weight of animals sold at market rose dramatically, with the weight of sheep alone rising from 13 to 36 kilograms (28.6 to 79.0 pounds) between 1710 and 1795. Careful breeding had much to do with this increase. So did the policy of enclosing land and reducing open fields and the commons, at the time a highly controversial move. However, it had the effect of allowing the cultivation of such crops as turnips and clover, which doubled the carrying capacity of the land. At the same time, earlier maturation meant that animals could be fattened much faster, although the quality of the lighter wool from free-ranging sheep that matured more slowly was much better. This would eventually trigger a lengthy dispute between clothing manufacturers and farmers.

Population Growth Depersonalizes Animals

OLD SUBSISTENCE-FARMING PRACTICES THAT basically fed families for minimal outlay gradually yielded to new strategies that involved the much-larger-scale use of fertilizers such as cattle manure and a curious clay-and-phosphate-rich shell mixture from the Norfolk coast known as crag. Farmers grew not only cereals, but also animal feed: clover, beans, barley meal, and hay. Instead of cattle and sheep becoming mere bags of skin and bones by the end of winter, the herds survived the winter comfortably. The owner doubled his return on his money, bringing his beasts to market in half the time. The feed and fertilizer became meat; the manure supply improved in both quantity and quality, with the aid of advances in chemical research.

These developments changed attitudes toward farm animals profoundly. Inevitably, farm animals became statistics rather than individuals, which took into account their marketability, the level of meat production, and the density of customer populations. By the end of the eighteenth century, farm animals were mathematized. The bodies of animals gradually became entities translated into abstract numbers, prices, and pounds per acre grazed. One can hardly blame those who raised farm animals. They faced an insatiable demand for meat from exploding urban populations. Six hundred fifty thousand people lived in London's inner precincts in 1750. At least 74,000 cattle and 570,000 sheep passed through the city's Smithfield meat market alone that year.[7] A century later, the population was about 2.6 million, 2.3 million in Inner London. Two hundred twenty thousand head of cattle and 1.5 million sheep now perished at Smithfield annually. To give some perspective, the population of the *entire* Roman Empire was between 4 and 5 million people in the first century CE. Similar population growth affected European cities: Paris, 556,000 in 1750, 1.3 million in 1850; Berlin, 90,000 in 1750, 419,000 a century later. (In 2014, London's population is 8.2 million, Birmingham's 1 million.) The skyrocketing demand for meat in growing cities large and small helped turn animals into packaged commodities, measured in pounds raised per hectare. This was, in a sense, both a calculating form of Cartesianism and a reflection of an inconspicuous but desperate need for society to feed more mouths than ever before. Even as recently as 1914, millions of poor Europeans almost never ate meat, subsisting on a predominantly carbohydrate diet based heavily on bread.

The population-growth curve accelerated throughout the late eighteenth and the nineteenth centuries. Market economies replaced subsistence agriculture as industrial societies became more urbanized, less close to the land. In the past, animals had played a major role in determining how people lived. Now the reverse became true, at some still-undetermined moment when human society achieved a critical mass where animals had to become a commodity if industrial civilization were to thrive. At the individual level, one could always find people who enjoyed deep personal relationships with a specific animal—for example, a sheepdog, or two or three dairy cows. By no means were all animals thought of as commodities, but many were depersonalized in ways that marked a profound change in our relationship with beasts.

Figure 15.2 *Smithfield Market in 1855. Superstock.*

The Plight of Working Animals

As THE INDUSTRIAL REVOLUTION took hold, horse-powered agricultural machinery such as plows and threshers gradually improved agricultural productivity. Some horse-drawn plows were said to decrease plowing time by as much as a third. Most farm and city horses toiled for long hours and were often worked to death. The market for working horseflesh was enormous. Horse fairs flourished throughout Britain, coinciding with a growing demand for driving horses to haul traps and heavier conveyances, and for large animals for heavy agriculture. In time, breeders crossed heavy farm horses with lighter mares, producing fast, agile animals that had both strength and stamina. As early as 1669, the combination of the two forms produced the animals that pulled fast horse-drawn coaches. By the end of Charles II's reign, in 1685, three express coaches a week ran from London to all major towns, capable of covering eighty kilometers (fifty miles) a day, when conditions were favorable. When the mail coach service began toward the end of the eighteenth century, the network relied on regularly spaced coaching inns, which kept large numbers of horses for coaches that carried both goods and passengers.

Working horses suffered from often-brutal treatment. Overburdened draft animals died in harness, cast into ditches to serve as dog meat when they collapsed from exhaustion. Drivers carried enormous whips to lash their beasts. Even horses used by the aristocracy often suffered harsh treatment. Worn-out animals were slaughtered indiscriminately, their hides worth more than their flesh. A life of overwork awaited almost all horses, except those that contributed to their owner's self-esteem or social prestige. The courage and nobility of such animals were much praised, especially when more humane training methods came into common use during the seventeenth century. But everywhere, horses died by the thousand each year. They might have been grand beasts with graceful motions, but no one was in any doubt that they were subservient to humans, for as eighteenth-century zoologist Thomas Pennant put it, the horse "was endowed with every quality that can make it subservient to the uses of mankind."[8]

Dogs were ubiquitous, used for protecting private property. Often-fierce mastiffs, muzzled during the day, roamed as guard dogs at night. They attacked people, killed sheep, and ran freely in the streets, chasing passersby. Christ's and Trinity Colleges in Cambridge even employed a servant to keep dogs out of their chapels. Dogs pulled carts and sleds, and occasionally plows. Sheepdogs and other working animals were admired for their skills, often even loved. Even so, many were hanged or drowned when no longer useful, and even cooked down for their grease. Many families kept watchdogs, especially farmers and shopkeepers. Until as late as the sixteenth century, beasts owned by the poor and stray dogs had been regarded as filthy vermin, their behavior the subject of common sayings such as "as surly as a butcher's dog." Dogs became a symbol of gluttony, of lust and disorder. The distinction tended to reflect social classes among people.

Most dogs lived with working households and often fended for themselves. Stray canines became pests, so much so that theater owners employed men to chase them out of auditoriums. Dogs were so numerous that a canine tax was proposed without success again and again; there were perhaps a million of them in Britain during the late eighteenth century. (There were about 9.16 million people in

England and Wales in 1801.) Finally, in 1796, concern over rabies epidemics led to a tax aimed at eliminating the dogs of the poor, which were considered less controlled than those of the aristocracy. Draconian measures combated rabies. Thousands of unlicensed dogs perished after the passing of the 1796 law. Roaming animals were considered unsanitary, also violent, when let out by their owners to forage for food. All this was a manifestation of a growing gulf between animals and humans. But some breeds were much respected by aristocratic and working-class owners for their ferocity and stamina, notably the bulldog, "excelling in fight, victorious over their enemies, undaunted in death."⁹

Racing Horseflesh

Fox hunting and flat racing (a race over a level course of fixed distance), the lure of speed in the saddle, were irresistible to both country gentlemen and the nobility. As we shall see, there were close emotional and practical links between these field sports and the seemingly glamorous life of an aristocratic cavalry officer. There was something about the close-packed cavalry charge that was thought to bring out the best in both horse and rider. But this prolonged love affair—it was often nothing less—began on the hunting field and racecourse.

Both fox hunting and flat racing had long histories in Europe. The Romans brought new breeds of foxhounds to Britain in 43 CE. By 1340, medieval lords regularly hunted foxes. King Edward I is said to have founded the first royal foxhound pack in that year. Fox hunting became more popular with the passing of the Enclosure Acts that fenced off commonly held land, which was when jumping became a regular part of the sport. With the advent of railroads in the 1830s, the sport became increasingly popular with the aristocracy, many of whom "rode to hounds" from an early age. This created a demand for fast horses, and to a popular misconception that riding fast after foxes prepared one to lead cavalry into battle. Thoroughbred horses were especially suitable for fox hunting, bred as they were for speed and endurance, so the two sports grew hand in hand.

Flat racing flourished in England as early as 1174, when 6.4-kilometer (4-mile) races became popular near Smithfield, just outside London.[10] Horse racing flourished at markets and fairs, receiving royal support from the animal-loving King Charles II and later seventeenth- and eighteenth-century monarchs, who patronized what had become a popular sport. The breeding of thoroughbred racehorses began in earnest when wealthy owners imported three stallions from the Near East: the Byerley Turk during the 1680s, the Darley Arabian in 1704, and the Godolphin Arabian in 1729. About 160 Eastern stallions ultimately contributed to the creation of thoroughbreds, horses bred for the racecourse. In 1791, the *General Stud Book* became the official register of British horses, and remains so today. Selective breeding for speed and racing ability led to races being shortened progressively and to some extraordinary racehorses. Perhaps the most famous was Eclipse, an undefeated stallion bred in 1764 by Prince William Augustus, Duke of Cumberland, which won eighteen races, and walked 2,250 kilometers (1,400 miles) to get to the race meetings into the bargain. He retired to stud after a career

Figure 15.3 *The racehorse Eclipse as painted by George Stubbs, 1770. Superstock.*

of seventeen months, having no competition. He then sired between three hundred fifty and four hundred winners. Eclipse is said to be ancestral to 95 percent of contemporary English thoroughbreds.

Beloved Pets

AN EMERGING AND PASSIONATE interest in hunting and racehorses coincided with a significant change in human behavior toward highly prized animals. Triggered by the philosophies and scientific discoveries of the Enlightenment during the second half of the eighteenth century, this coincided with a rising enthusiasm for dogs and cats as companions, friends, and even confidants. Devoted owners created miniature cenotaphs for them; portraits of aristocratic owners often included their favorite pets as symbols of power. Equestrian portraits of monarchs and other important figures depicted them with their horses or on horseback—their faithful steeds. The eighteenth century saw a fashion for animal portraits. English artist George Stubbs (1724–1806) painted highly realistic portraits of magnificent racehorses that depicted the powerful anatomy of the beast, posed with its owner, trainer, or even a groom. Pride of ownership, of achievement on the racecourse or while fox hunting at a gallop, created an entire genre of eighteenth-century art. Dogs and cats, painted with or without their owners, sometimes displayed their characters to the artist by a pose, even by an expression in the eyes.[11]

Dogs and cats on the streets were one thing, cherished pets another. For centuries, wealthy aristocrats prized their greyhounds and foxhounds for their fidelity. Effigies of medieval knights lie in cathedrals with a faithful hound at their feet. Gentlewomen cosseted small lap dogs such as spaniels and pugs as companions. Pets became a fashion with royalty as early as Elizabethan times. King James I was obsessed with hounds. He was said to love his dogs more than his subjects. Half a century later, Charles II was famous for his spaniels; he played with them at the Privy Council table while conducting government business. In some aristocratic households addicted to hunting, the foxhounds were better treated than the servants, and enjoyed a much better diet than local villagers. Large country houses teemed with animals of all kinds, even with litters of cats in chairs. Dog droppings and marrow bones littered the hall. A cacophony of barking and howling kept guests awake at night.

Feline fortunes changed gradually after medieval times, especially in crowded cities, where humans and cats lived in close juxtaposition.[12] Many wealthier households apparently kept them as pets, both as mousers and as companions. The earliest-known cat show, using the term loosely, was held at the St. Giles Fair at Winchester, England, in 1598. We know almost nothing about the event, but it was the remote ancestor of the cat shows of today. The seventeenth-century Archbishop of Canterbury, Archbishop Laud, is said to have imported one of the first tabby cats into England, at a time when they cost the huge sum of five pounds (about eight dollars) each. His contemporary the French statesman Cardinal Richelieu cherished large numbers of pet cats, constructing special quarters for them and even providing for their upkeep in his will. Cats crossed to what became the United States as early as the seventeenth century.

"Tirrany or Crueltie Towards Any Bruite Creature"

BY 1700, PET KEEPING was commonplace among affluent families. This obsession with pet keeping burgeoned during the nineteenth century with the population explosion in cities and the emergence of an urban middle class. With this development came notions that animals had characters and individual personalities, which entitled at least some of them to moral treatment. This, and a concern with the evils of live vivisection, generated laws protecting animals against mistreatment. A law passed in Ireland in 1635 prohibited the plucking of wool from sheep instead of clipping or shearing them. The Colony of Massachusetts passed the Body of Liberties Laws in 1641, which stated that "No man shall exercise any tirrany or Crueltie towards any bruite Creature which are usuallie kep for man's use."[13] During the early nineteenth century, repeated efforts to pass legislation to protect working animals died in the House of Commons. One journalist wrote that "England is the hell of dumb animals."[14] None other than Queen Victoria remarked to the home secretary as late as 1868 that "the English are inclined to be more cruel to animals than some other civilized nations."[15] In the case of pit ponies (used underground in coal mines) and other urban working animals, she was right.

The greatest suffering of all befell animals destined to labor in the streets or to be slaughtered in butchers' stalls. There was a grim, mercenary callousness to the way in which horses were worked to death, pigs fattened for the butcher, and donkeys and ponies worked in coal mines, mills, and later railroad yards. As the historian Jason Hribal wrote in 2003, "The farms, factories, roads, forest, and mines have been their sites of production. Here they have manufactured hair, milk, flesh, and power for the farm, the factory, and mine owners. And they are unwaged."[16] The comparison with the sufferings of working people in factories, slums, and the countryside was irresistible.

Even greater cruelties awaited horses drafted into battle as cavalry steeds and pack animals. In times when virtually everything depended on animal power, this included warfare. Images of prancing warhorses and cavalry charging into battle evoked powerful emotions of nationalism and military triumph, but as we shall see, when medieval ways of going to war confronted firepower generated by the Industrial Revolution, reality was gruesomely different from image.

CHAPTER 16

Victims of Military Insanity

THUNDERING HOOVES, CLOSELY PACKED steeds, drawn lances and sabers, brilliantly caparisoned riders sweeping in an irresistible attack—the dream of a mass cavalry charge intoxicated aristocratic leaders raised on field sports. Born to a life of power and display, they rode to hounds at a gallop and bred thoroughbreds on their country estates. Combat and the exultation of victory resembled the rush of a successful hunt. Trumpets, plumes, and all the pomp of the military life turned war on horseback into what has been called an "aristocratic trade." Dazzling uniforms, beautifully turned out horses, and the precision of cavalry maneuvers stirred powerful yearnings for command, for military glory.

Soldiers had ridden into battle for well over three thousand years, long before anyone invented cannons or muskets.[1] Cavalrymen served as scouts, pursued fleeing infantry, and protected the flanks of Roman legions. Generals such as Alexander the Great and Julius Caesar made effective use of lightly armed cavalry units, which were a far cry from heavily armed medieval knights, who engaged, for the most part, in individual combat. These latter may have been symbols of medieval chivalry, but they were lumbering figures, the medieval equivalent of tanks. (The word *chivalry*, derived from eleventh-century Old French for *chevalier*, or "knight," originally meant horsemanship, and the medieval, and earlier, Latin word *caballarius*, "horseman.") Heavy armor and rigid saddles locked knights into positions where they could withstand the shock of a lance blow. But armored riders had much less control of their horses. These large stallions weighed up to about 454 kilograms (1,000 pounds). Considered to be natural fighters and controlled with severe curb bits, they learned to bite, kick, and stamp on their opponents. Mounted knights were dangerous to infantry, but they were no match for lightly armed Mongolian horsemen, who enjoyed a subtle, tactile relationship with their mounts. They paid careful attention to the overall balance of their beasts, and ensured that they had an easy gait and a long stride. They also paid careful attention to a horse's head, its ears, and its alertness and personality—to their relationship with their charge. At the Battle of Mohi in Hungary in 1241, fast-moving Mongol archers played havoc with Hungarian knights, the heavy cavalry unable to respond to the rapidly changing invader's tactics.

Mongol riders learned while infants the use of natural tools for riding—voice, legs, hands, and body. Horses are so sensitive to any touch that they can feel a fly land on their flanks. Thus, they learn to feel the distinctive movements of a rider's body and limbs and can distinguish among subtle changes. They also have excellent memories, which make them readily trainable. Leg squeezes of different intensity move the animal forward; right- or left- leg pressure steers the animal right or left; both legs applied in separate places can cause the beast to turn around. The rider's body when shifted forward or backward tells the horse to speed up or slow down. As the heavily armored knight gave way to cannons, the old horse-handling skills came to the fore once again. By the late eighteenth century, many aristocratic foxhunters and racecourse owners had developed close understandings of their most cherished horseflesh. They assumed that such expertise qualified them to become cavalry officers. In this they were only partially correct. Among other things, a brilliant ability at handling a horse and commanding a charge did not necessarily translate into a concern over the ultimate fate of the steed in the cut and thrust of battle. The story of cavalry during the nineteenth and early twentieth centuries is a tragic commentary on the fine line between being at one with an animal and exposing it to extreme danger without concern for its safety. It's also a story of increasingly impersonal warfare, where horses literally became cannon fodder.

"Grass Before the Mower's Scythe"

BY THE TIME OF the Napoleonic Wars at the very end of the eighteenth century, cavalry were a well-established weapon on the battlefield, their field movements subject to greater discipline. Generals learned that well-planned cavalry charges could have devastating effects. On January 8, 1807, Napoléon Bonaparte was in the midst of a violent but inconclusive battle with the Russians at Eylau, in East Prussia.[2] A Russian attack in the midst of a snowstorm threw his infantry into confusion. Napoléon had but one option: a massive charge by his eleven-thousand-strong cavalry reserve under General Joachim Murat. In one of the great charges of history, Murat's squadrons surged through the Russian infantry around the village of Eylau and divided them in two. The cavalry put hundreds of infantrymen to the sword and rode through the Russian guns. Their large horses trampled down a battalion that attempted to resist. Never had cavalry played such a central role in a major battle, partly because these were mounted on fine-quality horses just requisitioned after the French conquest of Prussia.

Eylau was a textbook example of intelligent cavalry deployment under very severe conditions. But the cost in equine and human lives was enormous. Murat lost a thousand to fourteen hundred well-trained cavalrymen, and numerous horses, but his attack relieved the pressure on the French infantry and allowed them to redeploy. The surgeon general of Napoléon's Grand Army served soup and stew made from the flesh of slain horses to the wounded, apparently with good results, so much so that he promoted the consumption of horsemeat back in France.

By contrast, the Battle of Waterloo, eight years later, provided a dramatic illustration of just how ineffective, even suicidal, such charges could be. Well-disciplined squares of foot guards repelled a French cavalry charge of at least five thousand closely packed trotting horses. The infantry stood their ground and felled horsemen by the dozen with controlled musket volleys. In another engagement in the same battle, a British artillery commander, Cavalié Mercer, faced French cuirassiers. He wrote, "On they came in compact squadrons, one behind the other. . . . Their pace was a slow but steady trot. None of your furious

Figure 16.1 *The fury of the charge. The Royal Scots Greys attack at the Battle of Waterloo, 1815. Pantheon/Superstock.*

galloping charges was this, but a deliberate advance, at a deliberate pace. . . . They moved in profound silence, and the only sound that could be heard from them amidst the incessant roar of battle was the low thunder-like reverberation of the ground beneath the simultaneous tread of so many horses." Then the artillery opened up at close range: "Nearly the whole leading rank fell at once. . . . The discharge of every gun was followed by a fall of men and horses like that of grass before the mower's scythe."[3]

Regiments of Display

FEW CAVALRY OFFICERS DIGESTED the lessons of Waterloo. One expert who did was British cavalryman Capt. Louis Edward Nolan (1818–1854). An accomplished horse master and expert on horse-based military tactics, he wrote *Cavalry: Its History and Tactics*, in 1853, on the eve of the Crimean War. This articulate, well-reasoned manual was to become a definitive source on the subject. During his entire career, much of which he spent studying cavalry in other armies, Nolan placed a great emphasis on the relationship between soldiers and their horses, and on proper leadership, by officers who could judge distance and skillfully mask their intentions in the face of the enemy. Everyone, whether officer or enlisted man, had to keep his eyes and wits about him—judging distances between his mount and neighboring horses; in the case of leaders, riding straight at the enemy; and taking advantage of reconnoitered ground.

A meticulous horse master, Nolan trained individual soldiers to ride well before introducing them to formation riding, which, ultimately, was what cavalry warfare involved. Above all, "a cavalryman should be complete master over [his horse], so as to control and direct him at the slowest or fastest pace with equal ease; he should know how to quiet and subdue the hot-tempered, and put life and action into the sluggish horse."[4] Predictably, this passionate advocate of cavalry warfare adopted the ancient teachings of Xenophon: "Horses are taught not by harshness but by gentleness."

Decisiveness was the mantra of cavalry command, said Nolan, but beware the danger of approaching the enemy at full speed. The shock of contact would probably dismount the rider and break most of his bones. He added: "Men and officers should . . . understand that to gallop forward because the enemy are in that direction is by no means a proof of valour."[5] In other words, mass cavalry charges were an inappropriate use of cavalry in an era of increasingly effective firearms. Nolan wrote of the importance of careful planning, of maintaining reserves, of the strategic advantages of attacking infantry on their flanks, and of the need to reconnoiter and make use of the natural topography. His view of mounted soldiery was forthright: "Cavalry ought to be at once the eye, the feeler, and the feeder of an army. . . . It reaps the fruits of victory, covers a retreat, and retrieves a disaster."[6]

Unfortunately, few senior officers took any notice of Nolan's teachings. Almost to a man, they were wealthy aristocrats, many of them with experience dating back to the Napoleonic Wars of now-outmoded realities of warfare. In an era of sharp class distinctions and inherited wealth, officers purchased high ranks for large sums, even when they had virtually no military experience. It was hardly surprising, then, that cavalry regiments were preoccupied by display. They dazzled an admiring public with beautifully choreographed and executed drills. They wore brilliant uniforms, often subsidized by their wealthy commanders from their own pockets. Lord Cardigan's Eleventh Hussars were a notorious example of arrogant extravagance. Officers and troopers wore cherry-colored overalls (trousers), royal blue jackets edged with gold, and furred pelisses (short, richly adorned cloaks). Their high fur hats defied logic with their bright feathers. Everyone's trousers were absurdly tight, the overall effect utterly gorgeous—and totally impractical. Cavalry officers had a reputation for dashing horsemanship and a passion for horses, but knew nothing about the realities of war. The London *Times* cynically described the Eleventh Hussars' uniforms "as utterly unfit for war service as the garb of the female hussars in the ballet."[7] When the Crimean War broke out in October 1853, allying the British and French against the Russians on the shores of the Black Sea, Queen Victoria's cavalry was ready for glory, her regiments commanded by aristocratic officers, most of whom had never been under fire. They embarked for the Black Sea as if starting a foxhunt. Wisely, the French sent out almost no cavalry.

Crimean Disaster

THE BRITISH ARMY'S PERFORMANCE in the Crimean War was a disaster, despite the bravery of the troops. Quite apart from battlefield casualties, grossly inadequate logistics and water shortages led to the deaths of hundreds of cavalrymen and their suffering, emaciated mounts. The cavalry hovered on the margins until the Battle of Balaclava, in October 1854, where two major charges marked what was ultimately an inconclusive battle on the margins of the Sebastopol fortress. But the charges of the Heavy and Light Brigades brought immortality to Balaclava. (Heavy cavalry were armored riders on heavier horses, used as shock troops. The French called them cuirassiers. A mounted cuirassier wearing his customary breastplate armor, and his horse, could weigh a ton. Light cavalry were generally faster units, using light arms, employed for scouting and patrolling, often protecting vulnerable flanks and pursuing fleeing infantry.)[8]

Between three thousand and four thousand Russian cavalry bore down on the Heavy Brigade under Brigadier General James Scarlett from higher ground. Without hesitation, Scarlett deployed his five hundred horsemen as the Russians trotted downhill toward them. Inexplicably, the enemy halted to redeploy. Three squadrons of the British charged, and crashed headlong into the Russians. Furious hand-to-hand combat ensued. Two other squadrons now charged to the left and right. The great mass of horsemen heaved back and forth, the bodies of the dead and wounded falling across their saddles. The outnumbered Heavy Brigade routed its foes, but that is where it ended. No one pursued the fleeing Russians, who escaped annihilation.

Then came a fateful pause, followed by the infamous Charge of the Light Brigade. Inexplicably, a resplendently attired Lord Cardigan led the brigade in a headlong charge up a narrow valley against batteries of Russian guns both ahead and on the flanks. The cavalry overran the guns, but was forced to retreat in disorder. The entire engagement lasted but twenty minutes. A French general, Pierre Bosquet, famously remarked, "It is magnificent, but it is not war: it is madness."[9] And military insanity it was (see sidebar "Cavalry Folly: Into the Valley of Death").

Cavalry Folly: Into the Valley of Death

The Charge of the Light Brigade ranks among the most futile in history. Dithering commanders and tragic misunderstandings launched about 650 officers and men armed with only lances and sabers and mounted on fast, unarmored horses, on a headlong charge against serried Russian batteries at the end of what poet Alfred Lord Tennyson called "The Valley of Death."[10]

Led by a fearless and foolhardy Lord Cardigan, the Light Brigade advanced at a trot, then a canter and a gallop. Gunfire poured down on the horsemen from the higher ground on either side. The batteries of cannon ahead opened fire. Round shot bounded along the valley floor, hitting horses and men. A corporal fell; his mount continued galloping with the formation. Metal shrapnel fragments tore off arms and legs. Riderless steeds tried to rejoin the formation, behaving like the herd animals they were. Deprived of the reassuring hands of their riders and crazed with fear, they sought the company of other beasts, crowding against officers and men, covering them with blood. The Russian infantry opened fire. "The very air hissed as the shower of bullets passed through us; many men were killed or wounded."[11] The survivors had to avoid horses and men lying dead or flailing on the ground. Dust and smoke masked the charging troops. Now at a gallop and only forty-six meters (fifty yards) from the batteries, the Light Brigade leveled lances and sabers. The gun crews tried to withdraw, but the cavalry were on them. Vicious hand-to-hand fights ensued as the troopers tried to spike the guns, but retreat was inevitable.

The valley floor was a scatter of dead and dying horses and men. Mangled steeds struggled to get up; walking wounded staggered toward safety. Survivors managed to corral riderless beasts, only to have them shot from under them. Troopers led wounded horses laden with suffering men. Three hundred eighty-one beasts were killed or put down. Only 195 officers and men returned to camp. Lord Cardigan was unharmed.

The Charge of the Light Brigade was but the prelude for the horses. During the ensuing winter, the chargers, in mud to their knees, stood exposed to bitter winds and drifting snow. Sometimes they received no more than a handful of barley a day, so they gnawed at saddle blankets and one another's tails. Nearly all the Light Brigade mounts died in a tragic footnote to one of the last occasions when outmoded notions of aristocratic cavalry élan and medieval tactics confronted modern firepower.

To quote Lord Tennyson:

Storm'd at with shot and shell,
While horse and hero fell,
They that had fought so well
Came thro' the jaws of Death
Back from the mouth of Hell
All that was left of them,
Left of six hundred.[12]

The Crimean War was the first of several small conflicts that introduced new military technologies to the battlefield. These included the rifled gun barrel, which improved the range and accuracy of infantry weapons.[13] Despite the impact of industrial technologies, especially during the American Civil War of the 1860s and the Franco-Prussian War of 1870, cavalry tactics changed little, despite the devastating effects of rapid firing, breech-loaded weapons in the hands of both infantry and artillery. The lessons of the American Civil War, which highlighted the flexibility of cavalry that could fight when mounted and on foot at short notice, were largely ignored in Europe. Unlike American cavalry, which relied heavily on pistols and carbines, European cavalry maintained lances as serious weapons in the hands of dragoons and lancers right up to World War I.

Nor did cavalry tactics change, despite the publicity generated by the Charge of the Light Brigade in the Crimea. Take, for example, the celebrated "Death Ride" charge in the Franco-Prussian War, by Major General Friedrich Wilhelm von Bredow's Twelfth Cavalry Brigade at Mars-la-Tour in August 1870. He used the smoke of the battlefield and the rolling terrain to emerge a few hundred yards in front of French infantry and artillery. Bursting out of the smoke at a gallop, the horsemen swept into the guns, but were driven back by French cuirassiers. Von Bredow lost 397 men and 403 horses, about 45 percent of his force. A later skirmish in the Vosges Mountains saw two well-aimed rifle volleys take down two-thirds of a French formation's horses. Seven elite cavalry regiments virtually ceased to exist in one day. An observer remarked that rapid-firing infantry reduced each splendid unit in turn to a line of kicking, bloodstained heaps. Surviving horses galloped wildly over the battlefield until rounded up or hunted back to their own lines by German horsemen, in what one observer called "so thorough a destruction by what may be called a single volley."[14] The deliberate sacrifice of horses and their riders was still, apparently, a valid practice. Yet hard-won experience from elsewhere stared cavalry officers in the face.

Plains Indians and Boers

MASS CHARGES TOOK NO account of the flexibility and mobility of small groups of mounted horsemen, which paid rich dividends in the

American West and later in South Africa. Plains Indians had acquired horses during the sixteenth century soon after the Spanish *entrada*. They pursued buffalo on horseback and also acquired an expertise at raiding, which became intricately mingled with notions of acquiring prestige and honor. Inevitably, violent encounters with newcomers and settlers followed. Between 1866 and 1890, the U.S. Army fought a series of small-scale wars against Plains Indian bands scattered over an enormous area. Indian horsemen attacked with lances and bows, the latter highly effective when shot rapidly at close range—just as they had been with the Mongols on the other side of the world. Eventually, they acquired repeating rifles and other sophisticated weaponry, but tended to fight individually, a strategy deeply embedded in their raiding culture. Some bands selected their horses carefully and bred them for speed, surefootedness, and color.

The military power of Plains Indians was more a product of their skill with breeding and riding horses than it was of discipline and long-term strategy. Plains Indian boys learned to ride when they were as young as five years old, advancing to become skilled riders by the time they were seven or so. U.S. troops, with their superior weaponry, could defeat Indians in close-quarter engagements, but they had difficulty finding them across the enormous, often featureless Plains. So the army employed Indian scouts, said by one general to be worth more than six companies of mounted soldiers.

The cavalry had to cover enormous distances without wearing out their horses, a well-managed unit covering about forty kilometers (twenty-five miles) a day with regular stops and great care taken to minister to horses, loads, and riders. Under such a system, which alternated walking, trotting, and occasional gallops to stretch the horses' legs, a unit could cover as much as over 966 kilometers (600 miles) in a month in perfect order. The cavalry also gained significant advantages by campaigning with good winter clothing during the coldest months when the Indians settled in permanent camps, thereby negating their superior mobility. An English observer described army beasts as 'stout, hard, active and wiry,' and accustomed to hardship. The troopers were, at best, working horsemen, with none of the polish of European cavalrymen, but they knew well to look carefully after their horses. In the end their superior long-term strategy in the field prevailed.

Another defining moment in cavalry history came with the Boer War of 1899–1902. Boer horsemanship and mobility was vastly superior to that of the British, whose mounted forces numbered some eighty thousand at war's end. Many units from Australia and Canada adopted the marauding tactics so successfully employed by the Boers, such as using rifles with longer range like their enemies. The best British units engaged in thorough reconnaissance with carefully gathered intelligence; surprise with speed was acquired with good riding and overwhelming firepower. But the wastage of horses was enormous. The American Civil War saw equine casualty rates in the 50 percent range. No fewer than three hundred and fifty thousand British horses out of half a million perished in the Boer War, a casualty rate in the region of 70 percent. The demands for horseflesh were enormous, but an efficient remount system that called on sources all over the world and a well-organized shipping system kept the cavalry supplied. At one point, the British were shipping six thousand horses a month out of New Orleans, from a base near Kansas City. In South Africa itself, logistics and veterinary care were appalling. Inadequate fodder led to many beasts starving to death. The severe losses were not so much due to the rider, but to inadequate supply lines for mounted units that required elaborate backup, everything from farriers to horse masters.

"We Had to Shoot Quite a Number"

WORLD WAR I WITH its trench warfare, barbed wire, and carefully sited machine guns was a rude and belated wake-up call for conventional cavalry. Mounted units did play somewhat of a role in the early months of the war in the west. Fixed, heavily wired front lines and trench warfare eventually changed the rules, despite the efforts of elderly generals whose ideas were firmly stuck in the colonial battles of Victorian times. They insisted that mounted regiments be kept in reserve, but the massed charge was finally recognized as the anachronism it had been since the Crimean War. Quite apart from the firepower of artillery and machine guns, a few strands of barbed wire were sufficient to stop a galloping regiment in its tracks. In 1917, a British infantry officer watched two brigades of cavalry charge a village during the Battle of Arras. The Germans opened up with massive firepower. "It was a wicked waste of men and horses. . . . The horses seem to have suffered most, and for a while we put bullets into poor brutes that were aimlessly limping about on three legs or else careering around madly in their agony; like one I saw that had the whole of its muzzle blown away."[15] The psychological effects of a thundering charge had dissipated in the face of infantrymen armed with the military technology of an industrial age. Dismounting became an important cavalry tactic as the war unfolded. Occasionally, however, mounted units fought alongside tanks or cut down fleeing troops.

Horse regiments played a more significant role on the much longer Eastern Front. French war correspondent Dick de Lonlay had campaigned with the Russian army in 1877. He described the steppe-bred Don warhorse used by Cossacks as an ideal mount: "frugal to amazing degree, he lives contented with a handful of oats or barley." A Don would munch the thatch of a peasant's hut, was impervious to cold and heat, and responded "to each caress and falls in with the mood of his owner," to which he was devoted. "In combat he takes part with unrestrained rage: mane flowing, with bloodshot nostrils. He kicks and bites the enemy's horses with the greatest furor."[16] De Lonely commented on the deep attachment of the Cossacks to their mounts, a tradition with roots in history. They enjoyed some notable successes during World War I, especially when pursuing small groups. In the open country of the Middle East, British general Edmund Allenby used cavalry so successfully that the Turks withdrew from the war, but Allenby never attempted suicidal mass charges.

More than six million horses saw service during the war, most of them used for hauling artillery and supplies. They were better than motor vehicles at traveling through deep mud and over rough terrain. Six to twelve horses pulled heavier guns, even in deep mud, and towed captured weapons from no-man's-land. A Canadian soldier at the Battle of Vimy Ridge, in 1917, remembered how "the horses were up to their bellies in mud. . . . We had to shoot quite a number."[17] Thousands of beasts died in artillery barrages, and suffered from poison gas and skin diseases. On the German side, fodder shortages led to widespread equine starvation. Abandoned horse carcasses, manure, and poor sanitary conditions contributed to disease in camps along both sides of the front. Chronic horse shortages developed. At the Battle of Passchendaele, also in 1917, infantrymen were told that the loss of a horse was of greater tactical concern than that of a soldier, who was, after all, replaceable. Horsemen whose mounts died were required to cut off one of the hooves and take it to their commanding officer, to prove that the animal had in fact perished. Very few horses on any front returned home. Like ammunition and stores of all kinds, they had become merely a commodity in the first modern industrial war, just like the long-suffering animals that pulled omnibuses and plowed fields back home.

The Great War showed even the most conservative strategist just how helpless horses were against modern weaponry. It was not until the 1930s that trucks, tanks, and other vehicles developed cross-country abilities and levels of reliability that made them essential. The U.S. Army led the changeover, which culminated in the development of the jeep. Only the Germans and Russians employed large cavalry units during World War II, despite the Nazis' emphasis on mechanizing their armies. The Russians deployed as many as two hundred thousand mounted troops, notably Cossacks, whose very name and habitual use of sabers put fear into the hearts of Hitler's fleeing troops. They deliberately called many of their units "Cossacks" even if they weren't, because of the terror this produced in their foes.

Enormous numbers of horses served in German artillery and supply trains. They suffered alongside men in the appalling conditions along the Eastern Front, where animals and humans alike starved to death, the former because they were unable to forage the countryside. Russian horses were much better adapted to winter conditions on the steppe. Among them, six million small horses given by the Mongolians and perfectly adapted to savage weather, being especially mobile during the winter months, gave the Soviets major strategic advantages. The last Russian cavalry units vanished in the 1950s. Except for actions against guerrillas and in very rugged terrain such as that in Afghanistan, mounted troops have little value in today's conflicts. They appear on ceremonial occasions—Britain's Household Brigade is a famous example—and horse patrols help police forces in crowd control.

Mounted soldiers, often of great ability, participated in many great moments in history, but the same events, and many lesser violent conflicts, exposed horses to all the horror and suffering of warfare at its most violent. We should never forget that millions of them suffered, were wounded grievously, or were killed or starved to death in service to their masters, a role thrust on them whether they desired it or not. The artillery officer Cavalié Mercer spent several days on the Waterloo battlefield and was appalled by the suffering of wounded and dying horses. Some struggled, still living, with their entrails exposed, trying vainly to stand. Others lay quietly, lifting their heads, gazing wistfully until they convulsed in death. One beast had lost both its hind legs; Mercer saw it looking about and "sending forth, from time to time, long and protracted melancholy neighing." He couldn't bring himself to put it out of its misery after so much bloodshed. His epitaph for the grievously wounded mounts echoes over two centuries in three words that say it all: "Mild, patient, enduring,"[18]

CHAPTER 17

Cruelty to the Indispensable

GRIM, MERCENARY CALLOUSNESS—SUCH behavior toward farm animals and the beasts that powered a rapidly industrializing world was commonplace long before James Watt developed the steam engine and the cotton gin revolutionized the cotton industry. One only had to visit the Smithfield Market, once outside the city walls but now nestled inside London, to experience the savagery addressed at farm beasts destined for the stockyard. Most people avoided the place, but witnessed cruelty to working animals almost daily.

"The ground was covered, nearly ankle-deep, with filth and mire; and a thick steam, perpetually rising from the reeking bodies of the cattle, and mingling with the fog, which seemed to rest upon the chimney-tops, hung heavily above. All the pens . . . were filled with sheep; tied up to posts by the gutter side were long lines of beasts and oxen, two or three deep."[1] Novelist Charles Dickens gives a graphic description of London's Smithfield meat market in *Oliver Twist* in 1838, with its jostling, disorderly, and drunken crowds of butchers, drovers, thieves, and destitute vagabonds. The suffering the Smithfield beasts endured beggars description, a purgatory their predecessors had endured since medieval times. Not that anyone seemed to care, there being virtually universal apathy toward the hell for animals that was Smithfield. It took a well-publicized cholera scare in 1855 and concern over tainted meat and offal to close the live-animal meat market and move it farther from the city.

The British had a reputation throughout Europe for harsh cruelty toward animals and an indifference toward animal suffering, this in a country where Christian eloquence about morality and religion was in full flow. Biblical doctrines that placed humans at the pinnacle of living things provided a convenient rationale. But ambivalence about animals haunted religious teachings. How did one account for the affection between humans and their pets? Pampered animals thrived in medieval religious houses, much to the dismay of the authorities. Franciscan policy, laid down at the General Chapter of Narbonne in 1260, stated that "No animal be kept, for any brother or any convent . . . except cats or certain birds for the removal of unclean things."[2]

Nevertheless, as we've seen, pet keeping became commonplace among the elite, as religious superstitions faded. Affection toward cherished animals became more commonplace during the seventeenth century. John Locke, the founder of modern educational theory, emphasized the importance of teaching children "to be tender to all sensible creatures."[3] An early children's book *Goody Two-Shoes*, published in 1765, featured a heroine, Margaret Meanwell, who cared for mistreated animals. Anthropomorphic and affectionate animals have been heroes and heroines in books for the very young ever since. It's no coincidence that teaching pet care and responsibility in school is a foundation both of animal welfare movements and of the ethical, kind treatment of animals today. By the time *Goody Two-Shoes* appeared, there was at least some emerging awareness of animal rights, as from the philosopher Jeremy Bentham (1748–1832), one of the founding thinkers on animal rights. He loved "everything which has four legs," including both cats and mice.[4] Bentham's thinking, and that of others, led to the first efforts to mitigate cruelty to animals.

Protecting Animals

BENTHAM AND OTHERS MIGHT have loved their cherished beasts, but early-nineteenth-century working animals in Britain, elsewhere in Europe, and in North America, suffered from all manner of cruelty, including being worked to exhaustion and subjected to the fierce indignities of popular sports such as bull baiting and dog fighting, and to elite passions such as fox hunting. The English of the day almost took pride in their tough attitudes toward animals, as if these reflected a courageous national character. The House of Commons first considered an animal protection bill aimed at bull baiting in 1800, but few members attended the debate; the bill died. The *Times* remarked that the issue was beneath the dignity of Parliament. After all, it was a sport that fostered "courage." Like the poor and enslaved, domesticated animals endured vicious treatment—in the animals' case, live vivisection, torture, and ruthless exploitation.

A genuine concern for animal welfare took generations to manifest itself, almost two centuries after Ireland proscribed pulling wool off sheep. The first concrete steps came at the behest of Colonel Richard Martin, an Irish Member of Parliament with a penchant for dueling (and winning). He campaigned against bear baiting and dog fighting, a struggle that culminated in the Ill Treatment of Cattle Bill of 1822.[5] Amended legislation covered all domesticated, four-footed beasts. Two years later, the Society for the Prevention of Cruelty to Animals came into being.[6] (In 1840, it became the Royal Society for the Prevention of Cruelty to Animals, or RSPCA.) In 1835, an amendment to the 1822 act forbade animal baiting and animal fighting contests. The 1835 legislation aimed firmly at lower-class blood sports with all the social disorder they seemed to propagate. Gentlemen's field sports, such as fishing, fox hunting, and shooting, continued to flourish, being outside the law.

The SPCA came into being to enforce the Martin law, but it was not until 1832 that it had enough members to begin publishing its ever-more-elaborate annual reports, which documented its lobbying efforts and court cases in which the society's enforcement officers had intervened and prosecuted offenders successfully. The reports pulled no punches, but were aimed almost entirely at the "lower classes," especially people working with horses, donkeys, and dogs. One report told a heartbreaking story of a horse "covered with sweat, and in the greatest possible agony, and although [the beast was] wholly unable to move, the prisoner continued beating it on the sides with the sharp edge of a steel stay busk, having broken a thick stick over it, a part of which he still carried."[7] The RSPCA was one of the great philanthropic successes of the nineteenth century. By 1900 it had achieved a level of respectability where it was "one of the standard charities remembered by British maiden ladies and others when making their wills."[8]

The society faced a task of mindboggling scale when animal power was a staple of urban life, mining, and agriculture. The RSPCA's main focus was on working animals and the often-illiterate people who handled them. Many draft and packhorses wilted under heavy loads, and collapsed, to be cast into a ditch. As early as 1581, Sir Thomas Wroth counted twenty-one hundred horses traveling between Shoreditch and Enfield, near London. Another observer remarked that two thousand of them would be dead in a ditch within seven years. The casualties were much higher by the eighteenth century, with many more beasts on the road.

For a long time, scientists pondered a fundamental question. How much power would a horse supply, not only when hauling, but also when engaged in other tasks? In 1699, for example, a group of scientists associated with the French Academy compared the horizontal pushing force of a horse and a man.[9] They concluded that a horse provided the equivalent of six or seven men. In this way of thinking, equines and human workers were a form of interchangeable machinery.

This was no mere academic argument in a Europe heavily dependent on animal power, where the doctrines of René Descartes held powerful sway. Horses and oxen turned grain mills and operated factory machinery. They powered water pumps that emptied mine shafts, sawed wood, and provided power for everything from ferries to construction equipment and cranes. Descartes had proclaimed animals to be like machines, an attractive proposition for owners, who valued their beasts for their profit potential. By the late eighteenth century, the notion of machinelike animals in the service of people held powerful sway. As noted earlier, Robert Bakewell spent his career trying to find out which animal was best for turning food into money. There was a different calculation for those who operated working horses. The best animals were those that produced the most work for the least food.

The machine arguments gained even more authority with the patenting of the steam engine by James Watt in 1775. In a stroke of genius, Watt created a measure he called "horsepower," which he defined as 4,562 kilogram meters (33,000 foot pounds) a minute.[10] His engines often replaced dray horses in factories, so he developed his method of estimating power by experimenting with strong dray animals as a way of calculating how many horses a steam engine would replace. One of Watt's customers, a Nottingham cotton manufacturer, used a steam engine to replace the eight to ten horses that powered his mill. London brewery operators were also early users of steam engines instead of horses. Watt's "horsepower" measurement may have been a crude approximation, but the term is still in use today in the automobile industry. When a French engineer, Baron Prony, invented the dynamometer in 1821 as a way of measuring force overcoming resistance in motion, generations of research enabled comparisons among different animals. Even in the face of steam engines, working horses remained profit-making machines for farmers and transportation companies, but also for mines.

Underground Ponies

FROM THE MID-EIGHTEENTH CENTURY, thousands of ponies labored deep underground in coal mines, especially in Britain and Australia, but also, to a limited extent, in the United States.[11] As mines expanded and distances from the mineshaft to the working face became longer, animals replaced women and child laborers. Pit ponies were small and compact, rarely more than twelve hands high, invariably geldings or stallions. They were low set and thick bodied, their bones heavy set and strong. Many British pit ponies were Shetlands, and animals were imported from as far away as Iceland and Russia. They were often stabled deep underground and worked for as long as twenty years, but usually for much shorter lifetimes, seemingly adapting to the dark and working up to eight hours a day. The best animals were those of equable temperament, aged between about four and five years. Their retirement aboveground tended to be short, as they had trouble adjusting to herd behavior and the open air. Some were born underground and never saw the light of day. Mine owners tended to feed them well, on chopped hay and maize, and provide ample freshwater and good ventilation, bringing them to the surface only when the mine closed during colliery holidays. They also made sure that one hauler was responsible for a specific beast, so that a bond was created between them.

The use of pit ponies continued throughout the nineteenth century, against a background of steadily rising public concern about their treatment. Such ponies became a catalyst for animal welfare movements, but

Figure 17.1 *Pit ponies in a Welsh colliery, 1931. Science & Society/
Superstock.*

little changed for decades. The Coal Mines Regulation Act of 1887 provided the first legislation to protect pit ponies, but was limited to providing
inspectors and regulating the height of haulage-way roofs. Protest groups
such as the National Equine Defence League and the Scottish Society to
Promote Kindness to Pit Ponies put so much pressure on the government
that a royal commission was formed. In 1911, new legislation required daily
logs, a competent horse trainer for every fifteen ponies, and a minimum
working age of four years. At the height of pony hauling in 1913, there were
as many as seventy thousand ponies underground in Britain, but they were
gradually replaced by mechanical hauling, being used mainly on shorter
runs in later times. By the late 1930s, their number had dropped to thirty-
two thousand. As recently as 1985, there were still 561 ponies underground
in Britain. The last beast retired in 1999. There are now finally moves to ban
the use of pit ponies, but in fact technology has effectively replaced them.

The Urban Beast

PIT PONIES LABORED FAR from daylight; many more equines worked
in growing urban settings. The factories and cities of an increasingly

industrialized Britain and Europe may have hailed the advantages of steam, but they still relied heavily on animal power, not only in mines, but to haul loads, plow the soil, and operate grain mills— to mention only a few tasks. Steam locomotives carried food and freight to city terminals, but there remained the problems of onward transport, local delivery, and public transportation (see the sidebar "Horse Buses"). Urban horse populations skyrocketed, rising faster than human ones by the 1870s. Cities with more than a hundred thousand people averaged about one horse per fifteen people, but the ratio varied widely from city to city. In 1900, 130,000 horses worked in Manhattan, while Chicago had 74,000, and Philadelphia 51,000.[12] These figures refer to animals housed in the city, not to those stabled on cheaper suburban land or farm animals that hauled produce to urban consumers. Every late nineteenth-century city depended heavily on workhorses for both stationary tasks and hauling. They even moved entire houses using capstans. For all its technological prowess, the early Industrial Revolution depended just as heavily on beasts. As late as 1850, animal energy provided 52.4 percent of total work output—probably an underestimate.[13] As railroads came into being, fewer and fewer people rode horses except for farmers, jockeys on racetracks, the military, and the police. The number of leisure riders was tiny.

Horse Buses

The double-decker buses and motor coaches of today are the descendants of a long tradition of horse-drawn transport in urban settings that began nearly two centuries ago. It's safe to say that horses shaped public transport in nineteenth-century cities, for they made it possible for passengers to travel longer distances, from one neighborhood to another, to stores, or from a railroad station to home. Horses hauled omnibuses as early as the 1820s, the first service being in Nantes, France, beginning in 1823. The owner, Stanislaus Baudry, named his new vehicle *voiture omnibus*, "vehicle for all." The idea caught on; Baudry expanded to Bordeaux, and then into Paris. On the other side of the Channel, tollgate keeper John Greenwood founded the first British bus line, with two horses and carts equipped with longitudinal wooden benches. Unlike with stagecoaches, no reservations were necessary. Greenwood and others developed a network of bus services, many of them feeders to railway stations. An enterprising coachbuilder, George Shillibeer, started London's first formal bus service in 1829, developing a "new vehicle . . . capable of accommodating 16 or 18 persons, all inside."[14] The bus looked like a horse-drawn van, but with windows on the sides. Three nicely matched bay horses hauled the omnibus. The service was an immediate success, contributing to a boom in horse-drawn omnibuses. In 1851, horse buses carried thousands of people to the Great Exhibition at Crystal Palace in fine style, but business slumped thereafter, as demand plummeted. By this time, horse-drawn omnibus services were commonplace in European cities. Horse buses had appeared in New York City in the late 1820s.

Figure 17.2 *A New Zealand stamp depicting a horse omnibus. Such vehicles became widespread in the mid- to late-nineteenth century. Shutterstock.*

Around 1860, mass-produced, affordable steel made it possible to run horse buses on rails, which ensured a much smoother ride than on unpaved streets. The horses could now cover longer distances and haul three to ten times the people. The number of London horse buses peaked at 3,736 vehicles in 1900, most drawn by two beasts. There were also express suburban services that ran into the City of London, drawn by four carefully matched horses. But progress caught up with equine transportation during the 1890s. Electric propulsion and tram lines now offered a viable alternative, without the logistical problems of disposing of manure, transporting fodder, and so on. Within two decades, horse buses vanished from London's streets, the last one in August 1914, although outlying rural bus lines remained in service until as late as 1931. They survived in Berlin until 1923.

Horse buses were pretty basic transportation, with little more than wooden benches for passengers to sit on. Double-deckers were commonplace. The upper passengers sat on longitudinal wooden benches open to the elements. From the beginning, horse-drawn omnibuses were middle-class urban transportation. The poor continued to walk to work until cheaper tram and train fares appeared in the 1890s.

Looking after working horses challenged even experts. A well-known American engineer, Robert Thurston, remarked in 1895 that the oat-fueled horse was not only intelligent and willing, but "a self-contained prime mover." Many factors came into play: diet, the amount of food consumed, and fatigue levels after eight-hour shifts. There were studies of gaits and of average speeds of draft and coach horses—the optimum speed, according to Thurston, being about 4 kilometers (2.5 miles) an hour. Eventually, controlled experiments with dynamometers showed that streetcar horses used seven times the energy to start the vehicle they were towing than to keep it moving. The Chicago Street Railway produced figures that showed that horses cost $0.0372 per car mile to operate, compared with electric cars, at $0.02371.[15] The study may have been a powerful factor in the disappearance of the horse from city streets. But for generations, working horses were profitable, which made the RSPCA's task even harder.

Equipment became increasingly important, including horse blankets, and blinders (blinkers), which calmed horses in heavy traffic. After trial-and-error testing, many companies limited their horses to five hours' work daily. Longer working days, with their constant stopping and starting, increased the incidence of injuries to the leg, always the weak spot. Street railways depreciated their horses over five years, then sold them even if they were healthy, knowing that lameness increased thereafter. These preventive strategies were so successful that attempts to replace horse-drawn vehicles with steam-powered ones failed.

By the mid-nineteenth century, horse breeding for all manner of tasks had become a highly profitable business. In the United States, the demand for large, powerful horses led to a boom in the importation of large European breeds such as Belgians and Percherons—as many as ten thousand annually during the 1860s. Improved breeding using European stallions increased the size of draft animals by 50 to 75 percent between 1840 and 1900.[16] Savvy breeders took advantage of railroads to raise larger horses on the calcium-rich grasses of the Midwest. Breeders, feeding lots that raised and broke in animals, central markets in cities like Chicago—an efficient marketplace brought lower horse prices as the nineteenth century wore on. Standards in the marketplace were such that street railway companies could demand ten-day, no-questions-asked returns for the animals they purchased. Police departments paid for thirty-day warranties, given the difficulties of training their steeds. There were secondary markets for used horses, for black animals sought by funeral directors. Mining companies purchased animals with visual impairments at much cheaper prices, since animals that worked underground often went blind anyway.

Then there were the by-products—stable manure, even street sweepings sold for fertilizer. Before chemical fertilizers came into use, greenhouse farmers prized manure because of the heat it gave off. (By the 1890s, chemicals were so successful for this purpose that stables had to pay for dung to be removed from their premises.) Even in death, a horse was valuable for its hide, for hair as furniture stuffing, for pet food, and for many other uses. Veterinarians or the agents of humane societies shot hundreds of sick, aged, or disabled beasts a year. Others were worked to death, especially when prices were low or business was slack. A carcass might be worth more than a living animal. Rendering companies developed special lifts for removing deceased animals from the streets.

Smarter owners, many of them responsible for large herds, were well aware of the importance of the bond between driver and beast. City streetcar companies required their drivers to groom their charges before going home in the evening. Bonding was important, but the traditional bit and whip were still the predominant ways of controlling animals. This, inevitably, led to some brutal treatment and neglect, which caused owners to worry about their drivers' behavior when away from the stables. "Know every horse as a mother knows her child," adjured one company. "Animals always remember the people who treat them right," wrote one Baltimore driver. His African-American employer even hired a "hoodoo man" to care for his horses.[17] Owners encouraged their drivers to name their horses and even went so far as to match African-American drivers with black beasts. Individual names were important in heavy traffic, where a horse would recognize a driver's call among dozens of others on a noisy street. Not that it prevented use of the whip. One stable management manual even recommended lighting a fire under draft horses to get them moving a heavy load.

Training urban horses required patience and care. Drivers kept a sharp lookout for objects as trivial as a blowing piece of paper that might frighten their charges and cause it to break into a gallop, a natural reflex in the wild. Accidents were commonplace, especially in heavy traffic, and often caused by frightened horses stampeding en masse in crowded streets. In reality, equines were inefficient in strictly business terms. They produced manure and urine and were noisy. They also had the inconvenient habit of dying unexpectedly while on the job and were susceptible to injuries. An epidemic of a particular horse disease could, and did, bring entire cities to a standstill. By the end of the nineteenth century—the century of the horse if ever there was one—the limits of urban horsepower had been reached. There were no further improvements to be achieved by breeding. Inevitably, horse-drawn transportation withered in the face of electric streetcars and the internal combustion engine.

Vivisection and Rabies

THE RSPCA ENJOYED SOME success, but cruelty remained, although the invention of the internal combustion engine reduced the number of suffering cab, omnibus, and packhorses dramatically. By the end of the nineteenth century, Britain's reputation for kindness to animals was almost second to none, and in fact many writers compared the records of Britain favorably with those of southern Catholic countries. Delve more deeply, however, and one confronts a profound ambivalence in the animal-human relationship. Nowhere is this more striking than in the debates over vivisection, which reached a crescendo during the late nineteenth century.[18] The RSPCA faced a quandary. On the one hand, it presented comprehensive, closely argued reasons for a total ban on animal vivisection as a form of animal abuse, whether for research or teaching and demonstration purposes, this during debates over the Cruelty to Animals Act of 1876. On the other, respected scientists insisted that medical research was of such importance that prohibiting vivisection was out of the question. The RSPCA's primary concern had been with the seemingly irrational behavior of uneducated members of society toward working animals. Ardent antivivisectionists were often sentimentalists, animal fanciers, especially concerned with the suffering of animals normally kept as pets. Impersonal modern science was the villain to such people; whereas to scientists, it represented one of the great achievements of contemporary society. The latter's organized lobbying efforts argued for a continuation of carefully regulated vivisection in the name of that Victorian ideal, human progress.

There were other ambivalences, notably the hysterical response to rabies, which was one of the passionate debates that emerged in Victorian society. The chances of contracting rabies, a disease associated in the popular mind with contamination and that most Victorian of evils, Sin with a capital *S*, were infinitesimal. Only seventy-nine

Britons died of rabies in 1877, by far the worst year for fatalities during the entire century. Controversy swirled around the causes of the disease, with some people believing that spontaneous generation led to infection; others, that it was contagion from dog bites. To many people, especially numerous cynophobes, dogs were the villains. This distrust of dogs sometimes reached epidemic proportions, prompting the *Kennel Review* to remark that hydrophobia was "a peculiar madness that seizes men and impels them to destroy dogs."[19] Much of the contagion hypothesis revolved around accusations of guilt, and dogs were the villains, which made them a police matter.

Controlling disease meant watching those canines that deviated from conventional moral and physical norms. Inevitably, the character of both dog and owner became intermingled. For instance, the aggressive poaching and hunting dogs kept by the "lower classes" were suspect. So were smaller pet dogs kept by the poor under squalid conditions. The logical solution seemed to be to kill the suspects. Tens of thousands of dogs perished in the face of perceived rabies threats. According to historian Harriet Ritvo, only 5 percent of the dogs slaughtered during the nineteenth century were mad; three quarters of them were epileptic or strange looking. Ironically, rabies was in decline in Europe owing to the overhunting of wolves on the Continent. Alternatives were muzzling, confinement, and quarantine, despite the development of an rabies vaccine by Louis Pasteur during the 1880s—developed after lengthy experimentation on live animals. The long-term solution for the British Isles was quarantine, first introduced in 1902 and now regulated by European Union and U.K. rules.

"The Lower Class of Persons"

BY THE END OF the nineteenth century, treating animals well had become part of what has been called "Englishness." By midcentury, prevention of cruelty to animals—and this meant cruelty to working animals and animals owned by the lower classes—had become a major concern of middle-class reformers. Bear baiting and other such sports became symbols not only of animal suffering but of moral depravity. A flood of middle-class Victorian children's literature preached self-control and masking passions, the argument being that those who treated their fellow creatures badly would end up being evil in later life. Thus arose a pervasive association of cruelty to animals with bad behavior, one that had strong undertones of social discipline and religious morality. The RSPCA's literature of the day contained heartrending descriptions of struggling, lame horses; of dogs hauling carts while "beaten with a heavy chain."[20] Much of this was absolutely sincere, but most of it was aimed at the "lower class of persons," said to possess less sense than many of the horses and other animals they tended.

Aristocratic pastimes such as fox hunting were occasionally criticized, but for the most part, they came under the category of "innocent amusements." Alongside the anticruelty movement, a new phenomenon illustrated an enduring dichotomy in our relationship with animals: the dramatic explosion of pet ownership, which became a passion, not only of monarchs and nobility, but of the burgeoning middle class.

CHAPTER 18

To Kill, to Display, and to Love

THE VICTORIANS EXPERIENCED A profound dichotomy over animals. There was common, and widespread, indifference to suffering beasts that labored on every side. Cruelty and ruthless exploitation of working animals in peace and in war persisted, despite the best efforts of the RSPCA and a growing number of other animal rights organizations to improve their working conditions. (Some such groups used the harsh treatment of animals as part of a broader moral crusade directed at the working classes.) Animals labored in cities without automobiles or internal combustion engines, even with the advent of railroads and steam power. As we have seen, to many people they were ubiquitous, just part of the scenery of urban life. Many poor urbanites had never visited the countryside or a farm and had never seen cattle or sheep in their natural habitats.

Exotic Beasts

INDIFFERENCE TO THE PLIGHT of working animals flourished alongside a popular fascination with exotic wild animals. Perhaps this is hardly surprising, since much of the world was still little explored. Enterprising showmen titillated the public with displays of rare beasts. A bison, an elephant, even a llama from Peru, exhibited in the Haymarket off Piccadilly in 1805, attracted large crowds.[1] Menageries became fashionable attractions. By 1825, London's Bartholomew Fair hosted at least three of them. One collection of the large cats even allowed visitors free admission if they brought a dog or cat: they could watch it being fed to the lions.[2] The Exeter 'Change Menagerie, in Central London,

Figure 18.1 *The Exeter 'Change Menagerie, c. 1820. The exhibits included an elephant in a cage so small it could barely turn around. Aquatint after George Rowlandson (1757–1827). Superstock.*

became a major attraction—two upstairs rooms in a commercial building crammed with animals caged so tightly that they could barely turn around. In 1812, the larger of the two rooms housed two tigers, a lion, a hyena, a leopard, a panther, and even a camel. There were traveling shows as well, including one in 1816, at which a lioness escaped from her wagon and attacked one of the horses. All the caged beasts sent a powerful message of domination over distant lands, not only of their animals but of their inhabitants as well.

Curiosity seekers visited commercial menageries such as the Exeter 'Change or George Wombell's shows. The Zoological Society of London opened its gardens in a corner of Regent's Park in 1828 with serious scientific goals. No fewer than 112,226 people visited what the society called "a general Zoological Collection." The animals, and their carcasses when they died, were available for serious research; access to the gardens was for members only or by invitation, but not for the poor or the populace as a whole. This policy didn't endure, for financial reasons, however fashionable the London Zoo became among the elite.

Such menageries rapidly became a symbol of progress and enlightenment, of emerging empire. The zoo became, as one commentator in the *Quarterly Review* observed, a way of rescuing the poor from "the fascinations of the public house."[3] Humble visitors were thought to find "improvement" and, indirectly, to participate in conquests of remote, recently explored places.

The Zoological Society used its gardens to make sense of the animal kingdom, to highlight for the general public the links between different species. The Zoo encouraged interaction with the animals, especially feeding the bears, which became so popular that the humor magazine *Punch* showed a group of them suffering from dyspepsia caused by "31,457 buns."[4] Camel and elephant rides and petting small animals were grist for the popular mill, despite the danger of losing one's hat to a monkey or baboon, or being spat upon by a camel or llama. The greatest attraction was always the big cats, especially when viewed at feeding time as they growled and roared and tossed about meat and bones with wild abandon. Some animals, like Obaysch, the first live hippopotamus to visit Europe since Roman times, became celebrities, as did numerous gifted chimpanzees. To achieve such status they had to be either large or possessed of unusual intelligence. Stocking the Zoo became a quasi-official duty for consuls and colonial officials, just as collecting Ancient Egyptian antiquities had been a charge for British and French diplomats in Cairo after the Napoleonic Wars.

Maintaining exotic animals in captivity meant successful breeding, and even attempts to domesticate some of them for human use. A small number of wealthy landowners maintained breeding menageries on their estates. Most preferred animals that could be eaten. At his death in 1851, Edward Smith Stanley, Earl of Derby, maintained a park with 345 mammals and 1,272 birds from 94 species. Most were antelope and deer, also llamas, zebras, and other animals gathered not for display but for breeding experiments. Many groups devoted to what was called "acclimatizing" enjoyed feasts of dishes created from exotic beasts. The Acclimatization Society hosted a dinner in 1863 that included bird's nest soup, kangaroo ham, Syrian pig, leporine, and Chinese sheep.

Kill! Kill! Kill!

MENAGERIES OFFICIAL AND UNOFFICIAL displayed exotic beasts of all kinds as spoils of a growing empire. But they also symbolized the high-risk, adventurous lives of the bold individuals who collected and hunted such creatures. The living trophies of empire went up for sale in London's wild animal shops, large and small. Most of the animals they sold were smaller species, for to obtain a beast such as a lion meant killing the mother and capturing her cubs, a dangerous undertaking under the best of circumstances.

The frontiers of empire moved away from coasts and into remoter parts of Africa and Asia during the mid-nineteenth century. Many officials collected young animals, especially the most desirable beasts such as lions, tigers, elephants, or zebras.[5] Acquiring, caring for, and shipping them was both expensive and time consuming, so the emphasis shifted to spectacular hunting trophies. Now hunters sought magnificent beasts, killed deep in the bush and then sent home to be stuffed and displayed against suitable backgrounds. The symbolism was obvious: victory in the field over animals just as it was over rebellious tribesmen on India's Northwest Frontier or Zulu warriors in southern Africa. Trophy displays of dangerous animals appeared in museums and attracted large crowds. The Great Exhibition of 1851 included all manner of game animals, from rare British birds to Indian tigers. Exhibits of suitably mounted hunting trophies graced the Paris Exposition of 1867. A collection of hunting trophies "'ecured in the wildest parts of North America by the prowess of British sportsmen" graced the American Exhibition of 1887 in London.

Big-game hunting seemed romantic and dangerous, adventure that unfolded in remote lands and deep in the bush. Elephants and rhinoceroses charged, bears stood on their hind legs to challenge repeater rifles, expert stalkers tracked wary antelope through thick brush. Magnificent, slaughtered antelope or hippopotami in carefully arranged rows graced photographs published in books and displayed, alongside the stuffed heads of the prey, in palatial country houses. Some big-game hunters such as Roualeyn George Gordon-Cumming (1820–1866) and Frederick

Courteney Selous (1851–1917) traveled deep into the African interior. Gordon-Cumming became an elephant ivory hunter for five years. In 1849, he returned home with thirty tons of trophies and a safari wagon—also a Bushman. In 1850, he published a popular book about his adventures and opened an exhibit that thrived for eight years and appeared at the Great Exhibition in 1851. For an extra charge, the visitor could hear Gordon-Cumming, the "lion hunter," lecture with a musical accompaniment. He became a popular celebrity, widely admired as "the greatest hunter of modern times."[6]

While Gordon-Cumming exuded a love of sport and trophy hunting, Frederick Courtney Selous had a long career in colonial service and as a soldier. By 1895, he had spent more than twenty years as an ivory hunter and specimen collector in southern Africa. Eschewing lantern slides, then a hot attraction, he lectured while surrounded by "certain of the most remarkable lions and other animals which had fallen to the lecturer's gun."[7] He told captivating stories of encounters with lions and hostile warriors that held his audiences spellbound for well over an hour. In 1919, his widow presented no fewer than 524 stuffed mammals from his collection to the Natural History Museum in London, including 19 lions.

By the outbreak of World War I, dead wild animal heads by the hundreds adorned country houses and museums. (Our values have changed. Now many of the same trophies reside in junk stores in an era with far more austere views on big-game hunting.) The mounted bestiary testified to the bloody triumphs of government officials and sportsmen intent on bagging fine specimens, then skinning and drying them in the field before shipping them home, where expert taxidermists attempted to reproduce the animal as it had appeared in the wild. Selous wrote of an eland, a large antelope by any standards, that he hoped to see "set up in such a manner that would recall to my mind, to some degree, the splendid creature he looked when alive."[8]

During the nineteenth century, the big-game hunter emerged not only as a popular hero and a "sportsman," but as an empire builder striking out into virgin imperial territory. His hunts were a symbol of advancing civilization, the subject of patriotic fervor. Colonial

administrators, military officers, even missionaries, and just plain leisure travelers with a "proclivity" for shooting descended on Africa
and Asia, repeater rifles in hand. A tidal wave of big-game narratives weighed down Victorian bookshelves, a genre remarkable for
its monotonous and enthusiastic recounting of slaughter, whether of
African elephants, Bengal tigers, or North American buffalo. Such
hunting raised violent passions in its practitioners, an overwhelming
sense of power. They wrote of "whole hecatombs of slaughter," of big-
game hunting as "one of the most powerful affections of the human
mind." They also talked of the salutary effects of life in the open, in
the wilderness, where one's qualities of resourcefulness and enterprise
came to the fore. Invariably, the hero was cool in manner, restrained,
and of course, had a sense of humor. The published accounts stressed
riskier hunts, described the death throes of the quarry in dispassion-
ate prose, everything coming down to an insatiable lust to kill some
animal or other. Killing game became a passion for those who served
in the colonies.

As firearms became more accurate and shooting large animals
became easier, the emphasis shifted from wholesale slaughter to the
bagging of superlative heads and horns. Game became scarcer, which is
hardly surprising given the tallies of victims in many hunting narratives.
A good day's hunting in India's Mysore State could include twenty-nine
buffalo, about a hundred fifty hippopotami, and ninety-one elephants
in "a most splendid hunt." By the time a reaction set in against indiscriminate hunting, large tracts of the world had been denuded of their
larger animals, this apart from the depredations of the fur trade in
North America and elsewhere.

Meanwhile, the focus of empire changed from conquest and force to
administration. As part of that much more prosaic task, a need to con-
serve, manage, and protect wild animals slowly replaced the most violent confrontation between animals and humans in history. Big-game
hunting represented part of the dilemma about animals that confronted
the Victorians—and that, to a considerable extent, still confronts us
today. Nowhere was this ambivalence more evident than in the emerging
middle-class passion for domestic pets.

Purebreds and Mongrels

WHEN THE POET LORD Byron buried his Newfoundland dog Boatswain in 1808, he interred it on sacred ground with an epitaph that spoke of "all the Virtues of Man without his vices."[9] By Byron's time, pet keeping was becoming commonplace among more ordinary folk, in a period when displaying public affection toward animals became more acceptable.

During the mid-nineteenth century, a positive cult of pet keeping arose in Victorian society, generating a huge trade in live animals, with twenty thousand such street traders in London alone.[10] Thieves even stole animals and returned them for a ransom, this apart from a booming trade in everything from dog collars to animal brushes, and in books aimed at pet fanciers, hitherto written mainly for owners of hounds and gun dogs. Pet fancying became a virtual obsession for many people, with fanciers becoming the backbone of the RSCPA and other anticruelty groups.

Nowhere does one witness Victorian ambivalence more clearly than among dog fanciers. From the beginning, a hierarchy developed between the dogs of well-heeled masters and mistresses at one end of the spectrum and working canines and their owners at the other. Dog fanciers cherished elite patronage as a way of identifying with their social superiors. For example, terriers and pugs enjoyed high popularity; bulldogs, originally an animal associated with fighting and lower-class sporting activities, achieved great popularity as pets during the late nineteenth century. By then, the lines had been drawn firmly between sporting dogs of the countryside and the pets of urban fanciers. Canines occupied a whole range of social ranks, with a strong preference among the aristocracy for breeds with little association with lower-class pet lovers. As the nineteenth century unfolded, so the chasm between purebred dogs—the breeds were usually artificial formulations—and mongrels widened. Mixed-breed animals were thought to cause much of the mischief and dog-biting incidents in city streets, and were shunned. Experts solemnly advised pet fanciers to steer clear of mongrels and to embrace purebred animals.

Part of the ever-closer attention paid to breeds came from the growing popularity of dog shows.[11] The first truly formal event, sponsored by a sporting gun maker named Pape, was in Newcastle-on-Tyne, in northeastern England, on June 28, 1859. There were sixty entries in the show, with classes for pointers and setters only. The idea soon achieved remarkable popularity. A large show with more than a thousand entries, at Chelsea, on the west side of London, opened to wide acclaim in 1863. Not that these were the first such functions, for highly informal shows were commonplace in London public houses well before 1859. The audience served as exhibitors and judges, reaching what Harriet Ritvo calls a "convivial consensus." These events often took place in rooms used on other days for rat-killing contests. For all their humble, and probably often disorderly, ancestry, dog shows caught on like wildfire, many of them purely local events that prepared exhibitors for the major shows of the national circuit. In 1899, almost fifteen hundred dogs competed in the national Kennel Club show. Wrote an expert in 1900, "Taking out Saturdays and Sundays, there is a Dog Show being held somewhere or other on every ordinary day of the year."[12]

"LOVE ME, LOVE MY DOG!"

Old Lady. "MARY, DEAR, WOULD YOU MIND CHANGING SEATS WITH POOR FLUFF? HE LIKES HAVING THE AIR IN HIS FACE!"

Figure 18.2 *This cartoon by George Bowers speaks volumes about the Victorian passion for pets. Cartoonstock.*

All this activity revolved around dog breeding. The shows themselves were usually models of decorum, but the conditions behind the scenes were appalling. Cages were inadequate, and water and food were in short supply; chains were too short, so the animals were let out frequently. Under such circumstances the risks of infection, especially from distemper, were very high, so much so that entrants were in as much danger of losing their lives from disease as they were from inquisitive spectators. No railroad provided adequate accommodation for show dogs. They huddled in filthy vans, often dying from cold and hunger. The atmosphere, even at big shows, was conducive to cheating and misrepresentation. The Kennel Club, formed in 1873, came into being as a way of establishing the pedigrees of different breeds. The club's untiring efforts paid off when showing dogs became a well-regulated and respectable pastime. This was largely the work of middle-class dog fanciers, who were determined to carve out a place in the strongly hierarchical British society of the day.

Felines, Fowls, and Lagomorphs

AT THE TIME WHEN dog shows became all the rage, cats were not regarded as fancy or prestigious animals. Classifying them into distinct breeds was virtually impossible, but the first cat show, held at London's Crystal Palace in July 1871, was a smash hit, and was said to be a process of discovery, a chance to compare different felines.[13] The show was so successful that, within a decade, annual events became commonplace throughout Britain. Originally, coat colors distinguished what appeared to be classes of cats, but efforts to establish divisions almost invariably came back to color, except for imported breeds such as the Siamese. Longhairs, shorthairs, tabbies—all were grist for the classificatory mill as a plethora of specialized cat societies came into being during the late nineteenth century. What was at issue was a search for a hierarchy of cats, just like that attributed to dogs. The search was, of course, illusory, often clothed in the doting rhetoric of obsessed cat owners.

Dogs and cats became big business, but we often forget that the Victorians kept all manner of pets—everything from exotic African and Asian beasts in the private zoos of the aristocracy to tropical birds, snakes, and fish in the heart of cities. Selective breeding of rabbits began as early as medieval times, when they were treated as domesticated farm animals. Several breeds had emerged by the sixteenth century, but the real boom in house rabbits came in the nineteenth century, in the hands of lagomorph owners, as dedicated to rabbits as their fellow enthusiasts were to dogs and cats. New breeds were selected out for their color, size, or other display characteristics as rabbit shows gained popularity. The enthusiasm for exotic breeds reached its height with the so-called Belgian hare craze, which saw thousands of them imported into Britain and the United States after 1888. Unfortunately, at the same time, rabbits came into widespread use for medical laboratory experiments and for studies of the human reproductive system, among other things. Chickens had been familiar farm animals for thousands of years, but a fashion for display birds developed in the late nineteenth century, with the importation of exotic, finely feathered birds from Asia, including the long-feather-footed Silkie from China (see sidebar "Taming the Fowl").

Taming the Fowl

Chickens were everywhere in Victorian England: crowded into urban tenements, wandering in farmyards, always available for the pot. Today they are a food staple throughout the world.[14]

Domesticated chickens have a still-little-understood genealogy, which extends back at least seven thousand years, probably longer. The earliest-known possible domesticated fowls are said to have come from archaeological sites dating to about 5400 BCE, in arid northeastern China, their putative bones far north of the ancestral homeland of the bird. None other than Charles Darwin of *On the Origin of Species* fame declared that the ancestor of the chicken was the red jungle fowl *Gallus gallus*, a theory recently confirmed by DNA research. Jungle fowls thrive from northeastern India to the

Philippines, but they are probably not the only ancestors of domestic fowls. Other ancestors may include the gray jungle fowl of southern India, but the DNA trail is inconclusive. People probably domesticated chickens in several tropical locations.

Once domesticated, chickens spread widely down trade routes and traveled with armies, perhaps also on ships. Their westward spread may have started in the Indus Valley, whose cities traded with Mesopotamia more than four thousand years ago. Chicken bones come from the port of Lothal, on the Indus Valley's west coast, a flourishing port for Indus cities of the day. Cuneiform tablets from Mesopotamia dating to 2000 BCE refer to "birds of Meluha" and, somewhat later, to "royal birds of Meluha" (Meluha being the Indus Valley), perhaps a reference to chickens. Chickens arrived along the Nile slightly later, as fighting birds or exotics, but did not become popular among ordinary Egyptians for another millennium. The Egyptians appear to have developed artificial incubation, which allowed chickens to lay more eggs.

Roosters can behave quite fiercely, armed as they are with a bony leg spur. As people discovered thousands of years ago, these birds can be bred and trained to fight with small knives and spurs attached to their legs. Cockfighting became popular throughout the ancient Mediterranean world and, later, in European and American cities. Westerners consider it inhumane; Louisiana was the last U.S. state to ban it, in 2008.

Eggs were a delicacy for the Romans, who developed the omelet and stuffed roasted birds. In 161 BCE, a law, triggered by concerns about gluttony, limited the consumption of chickens to one per meal. Fowls accompanied armies, their behavior observed before battle, an impending victory being forecast by a bird's good appetite. The popularity of chickens declined after the collapse of the Roman Empire, perhaps because the large, organized farms and production systems that protected the birds from predators went out of use. Powerful symbolism has surrounded, and still surrounds, the chicken in many societies. For example, in the Gospels, Peter denies Jesus "before the cock crows." During the ninth century, Pope Nicholas I ordered that a figure of a rooster be placed atop every church in Christendom. Many churches still have cockerel weather vanes.

Today's mass raised fowls are a far cry from the chickens of the past, valued for their fighting prowess and their powerful spiritual associations. They were said to make wonderful pets, and even to be excellent mousers.

Whether the focus was cats, dogs, prize horses, or rabbits, pet fancying thrived on the sentimentality of owners, often lampooned by *Punch*. Those who raised animals for food and other purposes often ridiculed pet fanciers, on the grounds that the latter's animals were useless except for emotional or rhetorical purposes. True, but it was the efforts of such animal lovers that gradually transformed public attitudes toward animals.

The kinship between humans and animals has never been static, having been at the mercy of changing social norms and fleeting trends. But an ambivalence about beasts endured in nineteenth-century societies, with their huge chasms between rich and poor. Many people in nineteenth-century Britain felt strongly that economics and the demands of a job were far higher priorities than the humane treatment of animals. At the other extreme was the deep, almost sexual pleasure that many wealthier members of society took in hunting, especially the aristocracy, the so-called huntin', shootin', and fishin' crowd. In 1860, the poet and literary critic Matthew Arnold memorably described the upper classes as "barbarians" with a "passion for field sports." Oscar Wilde went even further when he described fox hunting as "the unspeakable in pursuit of the uneatable."[15]

We in a seemingly more enlightened age—and that is questionable—deplore the indiscriminate nineteenth-century slaughter of animals large and small in the name of "sport" as vicious exploitation of helpless creatures. Can we condemn the Victorians? Of course we can, but to do so is to miss the point. So many diverse strands shaped the relationship between animals and humans during the nineteenth century that it's impossible to detect a single unfolding narrative: rhetoric and symbolism were influential, as were interactions between individuals, between members of different social classes, and between people as varied as antivivisectionists, big-game hunters, humanists, pet fanciers, social agitators, and scientists. Nineteenth-century British society—to take only one example—had many, greatly entangled threads, as does the Britain of today. The often tragic history of Victorian animals is a reflection of the differences between the people and groups who interacted with them.

In her Golden Jubilee address of 1887, Queen Victoria noted "with real pleasure, the growth of more human feeling towards the lower animals."[16] She was correct, for profound changes were under way that continued into the twentieth century, only to be dampened by the currents of two world wars and severe economic depression. Decades were to pass before enthusiasm for animal welfare resurfaced vigorously, during the 1960s and 1970s; it continues to this day. Queen Victoria would have been pleased; Britain is now regarded as a world leader in animal protection.

Selective Benevolence

OVER THE CENTURIES AND millennia, we've learned a great deal about animals. We know that their behavior and physical attributes play a powerful role in how we perceive them. Cats, dogs, horses, and rabbits fare better than sharks or snakes in the popular imagination, still affected by stereotypes of them, developed during the nineteenth century, as savage and dangerous beasts. We have also learned that human economic, cultural, and demographic factors play a major role in how we perceive of, and treat, animals. So do age, education, ethnicity, occupation, religion, and sex.

Bioethicist Peter Singer points out that contemporary attitudes toward animals are "sufficiently benevolent—on a selective basis."[17] However, this benevolence is in constant danger of erosion unless we make a radical break with more than two thousand years of Western thought that place humans above animals. Singer argues that children have conflicting attitudes toward animals. Their parents encourage them to eat meat to make them strong. At the same time, the children are read stories with animal characters that invariably end happily, and are surrounded with cuddly pets such as cats and dogs, or stuffed animals. In the increasingly urbanized societies of today, fewer and fewer children experience the realities of a farm: the pens, the stalls, animals trucked to the marketplace to become meat. If they see a farm, it is often from an automobile, with buildings but few animals in sight. We are isolated from the animals we eat. Indeed, it is often a surprise for a young child to learn that he or she is eating animal flesh. Numerous wildlife programs appear on television, to the point that many viewers know more about leopards and great white sharks than they do about chickens or calves raised in cages where they can barely move. Nor is the public as a whole aware of the enormous body of research involving animals that goes on behind closed doors. Massive ignorance walls us off from animals raised for food or recruited into laboratory science. There's a widespread assumption, too, that the situation cannot be so bad, for surely the government or some animal welfare organization would have stepped in. The fact is that we do not want to know the truth about the victims of such treatment, partly because we don't want it to weigh on our consciences. The victims are, after all, nonhumans.

It is perfectly true that there are large, influential animal welfare groups in many countries, among them the Humane Society of the United States and the RSPCA, whose early activities we describe in chapter 17. Over the past century, these admirable organizations have become more concerned with pets and wild beasts than with farm animals. In recent years, however, numerous, more radical animal liberation and animal rights groups have come into being that have raised public consciousness about the cruelties of intensive animal production. In response, the more prominent well-established organizations have now become more aggressive about the plight of farm and laboratory animals.

Ultimately, in confronting this issue, we confront a fundamental assumption enshrined deeply in Western thought: that humans come first. Thus, animal problems have no force as a serious moral or political issue in society. To assume this means to believe that animals simply don't matter, that their suffering is less important than that of people. Much of this distress is pain—and we know that animals suffer pain as much as we do. Think, for a moment, of the suffering we impose on animals. Peter Singer estimates that more than a hundred million cattle, pigs, and sheep, also billions of chickens, go through the industrial food mill a year. In addition, some twenty-five million animals become victims of experiments. We like to think that we are less savage than other beasts, but this is a delusion. We kill other animals for food, for sport, for products to adorn our bodies. For thousands of years we've also tortured animals, as well as humans, before putting them to death. We may talk of bears or lions as savage predators, but we are the super killers.

We also ignore the extent to which nonhuman animals have complex social lives and relationships with other individual beasts. Chimpanzees and wolves have intricate social lives, as do many other species. Witness the discomfort sheep feel when separated from their flock. Yet we persist in talking of such behaviors as "instinct." As the Cro-Magnons of twenty thousand years ago fully realized, animals are not inanimate creatures that one can mold for one's own purposes. And as Singer points out, "having given up the role of tyrant, we should not try to play God either."[18]

Singer and others have argued that it's indefensible to discriminate against living things purely on the basis of the species to which they belong. It's just like discrimination on the basis of race. Animals have interests, and these interests are not necessarily ones that are beneficial to people. The practice of raising and killing animals for food is deeply ingrained in today's industrial societies and involves very powerful and affluent vested interests. Nevertheless, animal liberation groups have made significant gains in recent years. Veal crates (containers that severely restrict the movement of calves through their short lifetimes) are now illegal in the United Kingdom. Battery cages (cages that prevent free movement) for chickens are outlawed in the Netherlands and Switzerland; Sweden has proposals for a complete ban on any devices that prevent animals from moving around freely. Unfortunately, there have been relatively few gains in the United States.

In the final analysis, we humans have the power to oppress other species, to exploit the domesticated animals that helped shape our history. Animals cannot, of course, protest their treatment or vote, as people can. This leaves us humans with the responsibility, with a wrenching dilemma that pits morality and altruism against ruthless exploitation and self-interest. Will we continue on a course that is morally indefensible? Herein lies the question of questions for the future of the enduring, ever-changing relationship between people and animals. At present, most animals are our servants, to be exploited, eaten, and handled in ways that suit our needs and not those of the eight varied beasts that were once our equal partners on earth and that changed history.

Acknowledgments

I LIVE SURROUNDED BY a menagerie of beasts—cats, a horse, mosquito fish, turtles, and rabbits—for my wife and daughter are serious animal people. Indeed, I'm known in local rabbit circles as the "Bunny Husband." This book began amid the ever-changing crosscurrents of our animals. They have taught me just how complex our relationships with them can be. The book also stems from the passionate urgings of Susan Rabiner, my much-esteemed agent, who first encouraged me to look at history from the perspective of animals as much as people. Two years later, I emerged from a morass of diverse sources and numerous conversations with a complex, fascinating, and surprisingly little-known story, very different from the simpler tale I originally had in mind. From the beginning, I decided to attempt a global book with an international compass, even if most of the emphasis is on the Old World, not the Americas—for obvious reasons. When planning the book, I decided from the outset that I would write a purely historical account, which would not be distracted by the passionate debates about animal rights of today. These controversies receive daily airing in the media and are much covered by authors with very diverse viewpoints. The roots of today's activism and concern often lie in little-remembered events that unfolded in the past, especially over the past two centuries. My objective has been to write a straightforward and, I hope, entertaining historical story that provides a context for our ambivalence over animals in the twenty-first century.

I've attempted to write history that draws on a broad range of disciplines, ranging from archaeology and molecular biology to history, cuneiform studies, animal behavior, and medieval manuscripts—to mention only a few. Herein lies the fascination of what turned into a complex historical jigsaw puzzle. This is a history peopled with agreement and disagreement, with remarkable characters, and above all, with the eight animals that transformed our history. I am of course responsible for the accuracy and conclusions of this book, and, doubtless, I will hear in short order from those kind, often anonymous individuals who enjoy pointing out errors large and small. Let me thank them in advance.

The research for this book involved threads of mental inquiry collected over a lifetime as an archaeologist. I found my African experience especially valuable, for I was lucky to live among subsistence farmers and to spend time among game herds a half century ago, experiences that profoundly colored my perspectives on the past. To drink beer with an Ila chief in central Zambia, who grazed dozens of cattle on the nearby Kafue River Flats, was an unforgettable lesson in the realities of subsistence herding. To walk among lechwe antelope and impala in the wild, to have elephants walk through my camp at dawn, were experiences that gave me a sense of the intimacy between hunter and hunted. I realize now that this story was maturing in my mind long before Susan suggested that I write it.

The book draws on an enormous academic literature, much of it obscure in the extreme, often contradictory, occasionally brilliantly insightful. As is inevitable, it involves the research of dozens of scholars. Years of discussions with colleagues in many disciplines have also contributed to the story, but they extend back so far that I cannot possibly remember them all. Please forgive me if I offer only a collective thank-you. I'm deeply grateful for your insights, criticism, and encouragement. Special thanks are due to Mitch Allen, Gojko Barjamovic, Nadia Durrani, Barbara Fillion, Charles Higham, Danielle Kurin, David Mattingly, Susan Keech McIntosh, Fiona Marshall, George Michaels, Richard Nelson, James Ngato, Thijs Porck, Harriet Ritvo, Stuart Smith, Alex Wilson, the late professors Desmond Clark and Grahame Clark (no relation), among many others.

Susan Rabiner helped develop the idea and is always there for me. The debt that I owe my former editor, Peter Ginna, is enormous. He has breathed on drafts and offered encouragement and deep reservoirs of timely advice. I've learned a huge amount about writing from him. This book is as much his as mine. Rob Galloway of Bloomsbury Press edited the manuscript skillfully. My friend Shelly Lowenkopf, himself an author and editor of vast experience, has been at my side since the beginning. We've shared moments of triumph and literary despair for many years, and drunk innumerable gallons of coffee in the process. Steve Brown, again an old friend, drew the maps with his usual perception and skill. Last, my gratitude to Lesley and Ana, who have introduced me to the realm of animals at a very special level. Without them or, indeed, our various beasts, this book would never have come into being. And perhaps I should in particular acknowledge the cats, which, as usual, always sit on my keyboard at the wrong moments.

Notes

The academic and popular literature surrounding the history of animals, and especially their domestication and behavior, proliferates daily. The specialized literature is a maze of brilliant ideas, controversies, repetition, and downright speculation, enlivened with occasional insightful syntheses. The notes that follow attempt to guide the reader through the morass. Most articles and books cited here have comprehensive bibliographies for those who wish to navigate further through what is often a fascinating, if often obscure, literature.

Chapter 1: Partnership

1. Paul Bahn, *Cave Art: A Guide to the Decorated Ice Age Caves of Europe* (London: Francis Lincoln, 2007), pp. 96–101. A general account of Late Ice Age hunters and their sites appears in my *Cro-Magnon: How the Ice Age Gave Birth to the First Modern Humans* (New York: Bloomsbury Press, 2010).

2. My discussion is based on Adrian Tanner, *Bringing Home Animals: Religious Ideology and Mode of Production of the Mistassini Cree Hunters* (London: C. Hurst, 1979), chapters 6–8. For another compelling example, see Dorothy K. Burnham, *To Please the Caribou: Painted Caribou-Skin Coats Worn by the Naskapi, Montagnais, and Cree Hunters of the Quebec-Labrador Peninsula* (Seattle: University of Washington Press, 1992). I'm grateful to Dr. Barbara Filion for making perceptive comments on this chapter.

3. Genesis 1:28.

4. Tim Ingold, "From Trust to Domination: An Alternative History of Human-Animal Relations," in Aubrey Manning and James Serpell, eds., *Animals and Human Society* (London: Routledge, 1994), p. 5. The paragraphs that follow draw heavily on this important paper.

5. The Koyukon description relies on Richard Nelson, *Make Prayers to the Raven: A Koyukon View of the Northern Forest* (Chicago: University of Chicago Press, 1983), quote from p. 240. Nelson's ideas are central to much of this chapter.

6. This section is based on David Lewis-Williams, *Seeing and Believing: Symbolic Meanings in Southern San Rock Paintings* (New York: Academic Press, 1981). See also David-Lewis Williams and Sam Challis, *Deciphering Ancient Minds: The Mystery of San Bushman Rock Art* (London: Thames and Hudson, 2011). For a description of the figures referred to here, see Harald Pager, *Rock Paintings of the Upper Brandberg* (Köln: Heinrich Barth Institute, 1989).

7. Nelson, *Make Prayers to the Raven*, p. 17.

8. Ibid., p. 83.

9. Ibid., p. 31.

10. This section is based on Tim Ingold, *Hunters, Pastoralists, and Ranchers* (Cambridge, UK: Cambridge University Press, 1980), chapters 1 and 2.

11. Samuel Hearne, *A Journey from the Prince of Wales's Fort in Hudson's Bay to the Northern Ocean* (Toronto: The Champlain Society, 1911), p. 214. Samuel Hearne (1745–1792) was an explorer, naturalist, and fur trader who, while an employee of the Hudson's Bay Company, was the first European to travel north overland to the Arctic Ocean.

12. Discussed by Tim Ingold, *Hunters*, pp. 144ff.

13. Hussein A. Isack, "The Role of Culture, Traditions and Local Knowledge in Co-Operative Honey-Hunting between Man and Honeyguide: A Case Study of Boran Community of Northern Kenya," in N. J. Adams and R. H. Slotow, eds., *Proceedings of the 22nd International Ornithological Congress, Durban* (1999), pp. 1351–57. See also H. A. Isack and H-U. Reyer, "Honeyguides and Honey Gatherers: Interspecific Communication in a Symbiotic Relationship," *Science* 243, no. 4896 (1989): 1343–46. For honeyguides generally, see Herbert Friedmann, *The Honeyguides: U.S. National Museum Bulletin* (Washington, D. C.: Smithsonian Institution, 1955). The image of a honeyguide even appeared on a Kenyan postage stamp in 1993.

Chapter 2: Curious Neighbors and Wolf-dogs

1. The literature is huge. This chapter draws heavily on two sources: Darcy F. Morey, *Dogs: Domestication and the Development of a Social Bond* (Cambridge, UK: Cambridge University Press, 2010); and James Serpell, *The Domestic Dog in Evolution: Behavior and Interaction* (Cambridge, UK: Cambridge University Press, 1996). Both are critical syntheses of archaeological and biological research on dogs, and of earlier literature on the subject.

2. K. Dobney and G. Larson, "Genetics and Animal Domestication: New Windows on an Elusive Process," *Journal of Zoology* 269, no. 2 (2006): 261–71. The quote is from p. 267.

3. Fagan, *Cro-Magnon*, p. 3.

4. A nice summary of Big Bad Wolf in popular culture appears at http://en.wikipedia.org/wiki/Big_Bad_Wolf, where the *Sesame Street* reference occurs. Other wolf tales include "Little Red Riding Hood," which appears in Brothers Grimm. See Edgar Taylor and Marian Edwards, *Grimm's Fairy Tales* (Amazon: Create Space Independent Publishing Program, 2012). There are, of course, many other versions of evil wolf stories, among them Aesop's fables and the immortal Russian tale "Peter and the Wolf."

5. Account based on David Mech, *The Wolf: The Ecology and Behavior of an Endangered Species* (New York: Random House, 2012).

6. Morey, *Dogs*, p. 75. These paragraphs are based on chapter 4 of this work.

7. See also discussion in ibid., pp. 27–29.

8. There is a rapidly proliferating literature on early dog domestication in Europe and on "dog-wolves." Among the latest papers is Pat Shipman, "How Do You Kill 86 Mammoths? Taphonomic Investigations of Mammoth Megasites," *Quaternary International* 30 (2014): 1–9. See also Mietje Germonpré et al., "Palaeolithic Dogs and the Early Domestication of the Wolf," *Journal of Archaeological Science* 40 (2013): 786–92.

9. Raymond and Laura Coppinger, *Dogs: A Startling New Understanding of Canine Origin, Behavior, and Evolution* (Chicago: University of Chicago Press, 2002).

10. Morey, *Dogs*, p. 80.

11. The literature is growing rapidly. Two useful papers (among many): G. Larson et al., "Rethinking Dog Domestication by Integrating Genetics, Archeology, and Biogeography," *Proceedings of the National Academy of Sciences USA* 109 (2012): 8878–83, doi: 10.1073. Also C. Vila et al., "Multiple and Ancient Origins of the Domestic Dog," *Science* 276 (1997): 1687–89, doi: 10.1126/science.276.5319.1687.

Chapter 3: Cherished Companions

1. Description and discussion in Morey, *Dogs*, p. 24ff.

2. Norbert Benecke, "Studies on Early Dog Remains from Northern Europe," *Journal of Archaeological Science* 14, no. 1 (1987): 31–49.

3. E. P. Murchison et al., "Transmissible Dog Cancer Genome Reveals the Origin and History of an Ancient Cell Lineage," *Science* 343, no. 6169 (2014): 437, doi: 10.1126/science.1247167.

4. Summary in Fagan, *Cro-Magnon*, chapter 12.

5. S. P. Day, "Dogs, Deer, and Diet at Star Carr," *Journal of Archaeological Science* 23, no. 5 (1996): 783–87.

6. Morey, *Dogs*, pp. 80ff, summarizes the evidence.

Chapter 4: Down on the First Farms

1. This passage draws on M. Rosenburg et al., "Hallan Çemi, Pig Husbandry, and Post-Pleistocene Adaptations along the Taurus-Zagros Arc (Turkey)," *Paléorient* 24, no. 1 (1998): 25–41.

2. A charming general account of pigs is Lyall Watson, *The Whole Hog* (Washington, D.C.: Smithsonian Books, 2004).

3. Peter D. Dwyer, "Boars, Barrows, and Breeders: The Reproductive Status of Domestic Pig Populations in Mainland New Guinea," *Journal of Anthropological Research* 52 (1996): 481–500.

4. A general survey: Keith Dobney et al., "The Origins and Spread of Stock-Keeping," in Sue Colledge et al., eds., *The Origins and Spread of Domestic Animals in Southwest Asia and Europe* (Walnut Creek, CA: Left Coast Press, 2013), pp. 17–26. See also Benjamin S. Arbuckle et al., "The Evolution of Sheep and Goat Husbandry in Central Anatolia," *Anthropozoologica* 44, no. 1 (2009): 129–57. Comprehensive bibliographies appear in both these papers.

5. John Mionczynski, *The Pack Goat* (Portland, OR: Westwinds Press, 1992).

6. Juliet Clutton-Brock, *Animals as Domesticates* (East Lansing, MI: Michigan State University Press, 2012), provides an excellent regional summary of domestication, used for this chapter. For genetics, see Susana Pedrosa et al., "Evidence of Three Maternal Lineages in Near Eastern Sheep Supporting Multiple Domestication Events," *Proceedings of the Royal Society, Biological Sciences* 272, no. 1577 (2005): 2211–17. See also M. A. Zeder, "Central Questions in the Domestication of Plants and Animals," *Evolutionary Anthropology* 15, no. 3 (2006): 105–17.

7. A. J. Legge and P. A. Rowley-Conwy, "Gazelle Killing in Stone Age Syria," *Scientific American* 255, no. 8 (1987): 88–95. Also Guy Bar-Oz et al., "Role of Mass-Kill Hunting Strategies in the Extirpation of the Persian Gazelle (*Gazella subgutturosa*) in the Northern Levant," *Proceedings of the National Academy of Sciences* 108, no. 18 (2011): 7345–50.

8. Sir Richard Burton, *The Lands of Midian (Revisited)*, Vol. 1 (London: Routledge, 1879), p. 293.

9. This section is based on Benjamin S. Arbuckle et al., "The Evolution of Sheep and Goat Husbandry," *Anthropozoologica* 44, no. 1 (2009): 129–57.

10. M. A. Zeder, "Animal Domestication in the Zagros: An Update and Directions for Future Research," in E. Vila et al., eds., *Archaeozoology of the Near East VIII* (Lyon: Maison de l'Orient et de la Méditerranée, 2008), pp. 243–78.

Chapter 5: Working Landscapes

1. Francis Pryor, *Farmers in Prehistoric Britain*, 2nd ed. (Stroud, UK: The History Press, 2006), combines both Pryor's lifetime of archaeological fieldwork with his sheep farming experience.

2. A summary appears in Francis Pryor, *Fengate* (Botley, UK: Shire Publications, 1982). A series of technical reports published subsequently describe the excavations. The references can be accessed online. Christopher Evans et al., *Fengate Revisited* (Oxford, UK: Oxbow Books, 2009), is a reappraisal.

3. Ibid.

4. Francis Pryor, *Flag Fen: Life and Death of a Prehistoric Landscape* (Stroud, UK: Tempus, 2005).

5. J-D. Vigne et al., "Early Taming of the Cat in Cyprus," *Science* 304, no. 9 (2004): 259. The earliest-known Egyptian cats are burials of two adults and four kittens from at least two litters deposited in a cemetery at Hierakonpolis (Nekhen), which served as the capital of Upper Egypt before unification in about 3100 BCE. The burials date to between 3800 and 3600 BCE. Wim Van Neer et al., "More Evidence for Cat Taming at the Predynastic Elite Cemetery at Hierakonpolis (Upper Eygpt)," *Journal of Archaeological Science* 45, no. 1 (2014): 103–11.

6. Jaromir Malek, *The Cat in Ancient Egypt*, rev ed. (London: British Museum Press, 2006).

7. Diodorus Siculus, *Library of History*, volume 1, trans. C. H. Oldfather (Cambridge, MA: Harvard University Press, 1933), 1:83, 1:5.

8. Roy Rappaport, *Pigs for the Ancestors*, 2nd ed. (Prospect Heights, IL: Waveland Press, 2000).

Chapter 6: Corralling the Aurochs

1. Julius Caesar, *The Conquest of Gaul*, trans. Jane Gardner (Baltimore, MD: Penguin, 1982), p. 47.

2. Temple Grandin, *Humane Livestock Handling* (North Adams, MA: Storey Publishing, 2008).

3. A prolific literature surrounds cattle domestication: P. Ajmone-Marsan et al., "On the Origin of Cattle: How Aurochs Became Cattle and Colonized the World," *Evolutionary Anthropology* 19, no. 4 (2010): 148–57; M. D. Teasdale and D. G. Bradley, "The Origins of Cattle," *Bovine Genomics* 5 (2012): 1–10. See also Ruth Bullongino et al., "Modern Taurine Cattle Descended from Small Number of Near-Eastern Founders," *Molecular Biology and Evolution* 29, no. 9 (2012):

2101–4. Most recently, Jared E. Decker et al., "Worldwide Patterns of Ancestry, Divergence, and Admixture in Domesticated Cattle," *PLOS Genetics* 10.1371/journal.pgen.1004254 (2014).

4. James Mellaart, *Çatalhöyük* (London: Thames and Hudson, 1967), describes the original excavations. A large international research team has been working at the site in recent years. Ian Hodder, *The Leopard's Tale: Revealing the Mysteries of Çatalhöyük* (London: Thames and Hudson, 2011), updates the story for a general audience. See also Benjamin S. Arbuckle et al., "Evolution of Sheep and Goat Husbandry," pp. 139–41. On history houses, see Ian Hodder, ed., *Religion in the Emergence of Civilization: Çatalhöyük as a Case Study* (Cambridge, UK: Cambridge University Press, 2010).

5. Jacques Cauvin, *The Birth of the Gods and the Origins of Agriculture* (Cambridge, UK: Cambridge University Press, 2007).

6. Klaus Schmidt, *Göbekli Tepe* (Istanbul: Arkeoloji Sanat Yayýnlarý, 2013).

7. Surveyed in Brian Fagan, *The Long Summer* (New York: Basic Books, 2004), chapter 7.

8. Edmund Spenser, *A View of the State of Ireland* (annoted by H. J. Todd) (Charleston, NC: Nabu Press, 2012), pp. 496–97.

9. Muhammed ibn Khaldun, *The Muqaddimah*, trans. Franz Rosenthal, (Princeton, NJ: Princeton University Press, 2004) 2, 2. See http://asadullahali.files.wordpress.com/2012/10/ibn_khaldun-al_muqaddimah.pdf.

10. E. E. Evans-Pritchard, *The Nuer* (Oxford: Clarendon Press, 1940). Quote from p. 16.

11. Ibid., p. 26.

12. Studies of more recent Nuer happenings: Sharon E. Hutchinson, *Nuer Dilemmas: Coping with Money, War, and the State* (Berkeley: University of California Press, 1996); and Raymond C. Kelly, *The Nuer Conquest: The Structure and Development of an Expansionist System* (Ann Arbor: University of Michigan Press, 1985).

Chapter 7: "Wild Bull on the Rampage"

1. Quotes in this paragraph are from *The Epic of Gilgamesh*, trans. Maureen Gallery Kovacs (Stanford, CA: Stanford University Press, 1989). See http://www.ancienttexts.org/library/mesopotamian/gilgamesh/tab1.htm. Quotes from Tablet 1.

2. A summary of the Apis cult: http://en.wikipedia.org/wiki/Apis_(god).

3. Serapeum of Saqqara: http://en.wikipedia.org/wiki/Serapeum_of_Saqqara; R. T. Ridley, "Auguste Mariette: One Hundred Years After," *Abr-*

Nahrain 22 (1983–1984): 118–58, offers an excellent appraisal of this remarkable man.

4. Ana Tavares, "Village, Town, and Barracks: A Fourth Dynasty Settlement at Heit el-Ghurab, Giza," in Nigel and Helen Strudwick, eds., *Old Kingdom: New Perspectives* (Oxford: Oxbow Books, 2013), pp. 270–77.

5. Jeremy McInerney, *The Cattle of the Sun* (Princeton, NJ: Princeton University Press, 2010), pp. 49–54.

6. Discussion in Ibid., pp. 54–59.

7. Homer, *Odyssey*, book 3, lines 6–7.

8. This section is based on McInerney, *Cattle of the Sun*, a definitive study of Greek cattle sacrifice. For ancient sacrifice in the Mediterranean world generally, see Anne M. Porter and Glenn M. Schwartz, eds., *Sacred Killing: The Archaeology of Sacrifice in the Ancient Near East* (Warsaw, IN: Eisenbrauns, 2012).

9. Plutarch's famous remark is quoted by McInerney, *Cattle of the Sun*, p. 36. A description of the sacrificial procedure appears on p. 37.

10. McInerney, *Cattle of the Sun*, pp. 4–5.

11. Discussed by ibid., pp. 173–84.

12. Aristotle, *The Nichomachean Ethics*, trans. H. Rackham (Cambridge, MA: Harvard University Press, 1982), 7:1–2.

13. Strabo, *Geography*, trans. H. C. Hamilton and W. Falconer (London: George Bell, 1903), 5, 2, 7. See http://www.perseus.tufts.edu/hopper/text?doc=Perseus:text:1999.01.0239&redirect=true.

14. Marcus Terentius Varro, *De Res Rustica*, trans. W. D. Hooper and Harrison Boyd Ash (Cambridge, MA: Harvard University Press, Loeb Classical Library, 1934), 2:2, 2:11.

15. Ibid., 1:3.

16. This passage is based on K. D. White, *Roman Farming* (Ithaca, NY: Cornell University Press, 1970). Also Geoffrey Kron, "Food Production," in Walter Scheidel, ed., *The Roman Economy* (Cambridge, UK: Cambridge University Press, 2012), pp. 156–74.

17. Adam Dickson, *A Treatise of Agriculture* (London: A. Donaldson and J. Reid, 1762).

18. Quotes in this paragraph from Cato the Elder, *De Agricultura* (160 BCE), trans. W. D. Hooper and Harrison Boyd Ash (Cambridge, MA: Harvard University Press, Loeb Classical Library, 1934), 54:4; on dogs, see Cato, *De Agricultura* 1:4.

19. Columella, *On Agriculture*, vol. 2, books 5–9, trans E. S. Forster and Edward H. Heffner (Cambridge, MA: Harvard University Press, 1954), 6:2.

Chapter 8: "Average Joes"

1. Apuleius, *The Golden Ass,* trans. Sara Ruden (New Haven, CT: Yale University Press, 2011), 4:69. Lucius Apuleius (c. 125–180 CE) was a Numidian Berber who traveled widely. He was a prolific writer, but his most famous work is *The Metamorphoses,* commonly known as *The Golden Ass.* Apuleius was active in several cults, which may account for the protagonist's joining the cult of Isis.

2. Apuleius, *The Golden Ass,* 11:257.

3. B. Kimura et al., "Donkey Domestication," *African Archaeological Review* 30, no. 1 (2013): 83–95. On genetics, see B. Kimura et al., "Ancient DNA from Nubian and Somali Wild Ass Provides Insights into Donkey Ancestry and Domestication," *Proceedings of the Royal Society B: Biological Sciences* 278, no. 1702 (2011): 50–57.

4. Stine Rossel et al., "Domestication of the Donkey: Timing, Processes, and Indicators," *Proceedings of the National Academy of Sciences* 105, no. 10 (2008): 3715–20.

5. Frank Förster, "Beyond Dakhla: The Abu Ballas Trail in the Libyan Desert (SW Egypt)," in Frank Förster and Heiko Riemer, *Desert Road Archaeology in Ancient Egypt and Beyond* (Köln: Heinrich-Barth-Institut 2013), pp. 297–338. Also Stan Hendrickx, Frank Förster, and Meryl Eyckerman, "The Pharaonic Pottery of the Abu Ballas Trail: 'Filling Stations' along a Desert Highway in Southwestern Egypt," in Förster and Riemer, *Desert Road Archaeology,* pp. 339–80. This book is an admirable series of papers on the Saharan donkey trade.

6. Hans Geodicke, "Harkhuf's Travels," *Journal of Near Eastern Studies* 40, no. 1 (1981): 1–20.

7. Two monographs on the ongoing Theban Desert Road Survey: John Coleman Darnell and Deborah Darnell, *Theban Road Survey in the Egyptian Western Desert. Vol 1: Gebel Tjauti Rock Inscriptions* (Chicago: Oriental Institute Publications, 2002) and John Coleman Darnell, *Theban Desert Road Survey II: The Rock Shrine of Pahu, Gebel Akhenaton, and Other Rock Inscriptions from the Western Hinterland of Naqada* (New Haven, CT: Yale Egyptological Seminar, 2013). See also http://www.yale.edu/egyptology/ae_theban.htm.

8. On Deir el-Medina's donkey trade, see A. G. McDowell, *Village Life in Ancient Egypt: Laundry Lists and Love Songs* (Oxford: Oxford University Press, 1999). Quotes from pp. 86, 90.

Chapter 9: The Pickup Trucks of History

1. H. B. Tristram. *The Natural History of the Bible* (London: Society for Promoting Christian Knowledge, 1883), p. 39.

2. G. Bar-Oz et al., "Symbolic Metal Bit and Saddlebag Fastenings in a Middle Bronze Age Donkey Burial," *PLOS One* 8, no. 3 (2013): e58648 doi. 20. 1371/journal.pone. 0058648.

3. *Wisdom of Sirach*, Sir.33, 33:24 (see http://quod.lib.umich.edu/cgi/r/rsv/rsv-idx?type=DIV1&byte=3977004 *The Wisdom of Sirach*), a work of ethical teachings, was written by the Jewish scribe Shimon ben Yeshua ben Eliezer ben Sira of Jerusalem during the early second century BCE.

4. Zachariah 9:9.

5. Judges 5:10.

6. This passage is based on J. G. Dercksen et al., *Ups and Downs at Kanesh: Chronology, History and Society in the Old Assyrian Period* (Leiden: Nederlands Instituut voor het Nabije Oosten, 2012); Mogens Trølle Larsen, *The Old Assyrian City-State and Its Colonies* (Copenhagen: Akademisk Forlag, 1976); and K. R. Veenhof, *Aspects of Old Assyrian Trade and Its Terminology* (Leiden: E. J. Brill, 1972).

7. Cécile Michel, "The *Perdum*-Mule, a Mount for Distinguished Persons in Mesopotamia during the First Half of the Second Millennium B.C.," in Barbro Santillo Frizell, ed., *PECUS: Man and Animal in Antiquity*, Proceedings of the Conference at the Swedish Institute in Rome, September 9–12, 2002 (Rome: Swedish Institute in Rome, 2004), pp. 1–20.

8. E-mail to the author dated March 18, 2013. I am grateful to Dr. Barjamovic for his advice on Assyrian caravans.

9. This passage benefits from Mark Griffith, "Horsepower and Donkeywork: Equids and the Ancient Greek Imagination: Part One," *Classical Philology* 101, no. 3 (2006): 110–27; and Griffith, "Horsepower and Donkeywork: Equids and the Ancient Greek Imagination: Part Two," *Classical Philology* 101, no. 4 (2006): 307–58.

10. Notably Aesop's writings. Aesop (c. 620–564 BCE) was a fabulist whose fables have achieved lasting immortality. He is said to have been a slave who was later freed, but he may have been a legendary figure. Many of his fables have animal protagonists. A good example is "The Driver and the Donkey on the Cliff": http://mythfolklore.net/aesopica/oxford/486.htm. See Aesop, *Aesop's Fables*, a new translation by Laura Gibbs (Oxford: Oxford University Press [World's Classics]), 2002.

11. Varro, *De Res Rustica*, p. 70.

12. Columella, *De Agricultura*, p. 67.

13. T. E. Berger et al., "Life History of a Mule (c. 160 A.D.) from the Roman Fort Biriciana/Weißenburg (Upper Bavaria) as Revealed by Serial Stable Isotope Analysis of Dental Tissues," *International Journal of Osteoarchaeology* 20, no. 1 (2010): 158–71.

14. Bartholomeus Anglicus (c. 1203–1272) was a Franciscan encyclopedist and scholar based in Paris. Quote from his *De Proprietatibus Rerum* (1240), 1:24.

15. Robert Graves, *The Golden Ass: The Transformations of Lucius* (reprint; London: Macmillan, 2009), p. xv.

16. Anonymous, *Special Forces Use of Pack Animals*, U.S. Army Special Forces Manual FM3–05.213 (FM 31–27), Washington, D.C. 2004. Quotes from pp. ivff. See www.fas.org/irp/doddir/army/fm3–053–05–213.pdf

Chapter 10: *Taming* Equus

1. This section draws on Pita Kelekna, *The Horse in Human History* (Cambridge, UK: Cambridge University Press, 2009), chapters 1 and 2.

2. Przewalski's horse. A convenient summary: http://en.wikipedia.org/wiki/ Przewalski's_horse; Tarpans: http://en.wikipedia.org/wiki/Tarpan. See also Dixie West, "Horse Hunting in Central Europe at the End of the Pleistocene," in Sandra L. Olsen et al., eds., *Horses and Humans: The Evolution of Human-Equine Relationships* (Oxford: BAR International Series 1560, 2006), pp. 25–47.

3. For a summary of Solutré, see Fagan, *Cro-Magnon*, pp. 215–23.

4. Kelekna, *The Horse in Human History*, pp. 22–38.

5. Sandra L. Olsen, "Early Horse Domestication: Weighing the Evidence," in Olsen et al., eds., *Horses and Humans*, pp. 81–113. See also David Anthony, "Bridling Horsepower: The Domestication of the Horse," in Sandra L. Olsen, ed., *Horses through Time* (Boulder, CO: Roberts Rinehart, 1996), pp. 57–82.

6. D. V. Telegin, *Dereivka: A Settlement and Cemetery of Copper Age Horse Keepers on the Middle Dnieper* (Oxford: British Archaeological Reports, International Series 287, 1986). See also Kelekna, *The Horse in Human History*, pp. 32ff.

7. Bits have generated a huge literature. One summary is David Anthony et al., "Early Horseback Riding and Warfare: The Importance of the Magpie around the Neck," in Olsen et al., eds., *Horses and Humans*, pp. 137–56. Also Gail Brownrigg, "Horse Control and the Bit," in Olsen et al., *Horses and Humans*, pp. 165–77.

8. Elena E. Kuzmina, "Mythological Treatment of the Horse in Indo-European Culture," in Olsen et al., eds., *Horses and Humans*, pp. 263–70. Discussion in Kelekne, *The Horse in Human History*, pp. 34ff.

9. Sandra L. Olsen, "The Exploitation of Horses at Botai, Kazakhstan," in Marsha Levine et al., *Prehistoric Steppe Adaptation and the Horse* (Cambridge, UK: McDonald Institute for Archaeological Research, 2003), pp. 83–103.

10. Stuart Piggott, *Wagon, Chariot, and Carriage* (London: Thames and Hudson, 1992), chapters 1 and 4, surveys the data.

11. Ibid., p. 31.

Chapter 11: The Horse Masters' Legacies

1. Edward Shaughnessy, "Historical Perspectives on the Introduction of the Chariot into China," *Harvard Journal of Asiatic Studies* 48 (1988): 211.

2. Kelekna, *The Horse in Human History*, chapter 5, was a critical source for this chapter.

3. Ibid., chapter 4, provided material for this section; also Piggott, *Wagon, Chariot and Carriage*, pp. 42ff.

4. On Kikkuli, see www.flickr.com/photos/exit120/5020830577/.

5. Peter Raulwing, "The Kikkuli Text: Hittite Training Instructions for Chariot Horses in the Second Half of the 2nd Millennium B.C. and Their Interdisciplinary Context," http://www.lrgaf.org/Peter_Raulwing_The_Kikkuli_Text_MasterFile_Dec_2009.pdf.

6. Ann Nyland, *The Kikkuli Method of Horse Training* (New York: Smith and Sterling, 2008), quote from p. 8.

7. James Breasted, *Ancient Records of Egypt: Historical Documents* (Chicago: University of Chicago Press, 1906), pp. 147–48.

8. Robert Drews, *Early Riders: The Beginnings of Mounted Warfare in Asia and Europe* (New York: Routledge/Francis and Taylor, 2004), p. 48.

9. T. T. Rice, *The Scythians* (London: Thames and Hudson, 1958), is still an admirable general description. See also Kelekna, *The Horse in Human History*, chapter 3; and David W. Anthony, *The Horse, the Wheel, and Language: How Bronze-Age Riders from the Eurasian Steppes Shaped the Modern World* (Princeton, NJ: Princeton University Press, 2007).

10. Summarized by Piggott, *Wagon, Chariot, and Carriage*, pp. 112–14.

11. Sergei Rudenko, *Frozen Tombs of Siberia: The Pazyryk Burials of Iron-Age Horsemen*, trans. M. W. Thompson (Berkeley: University of California Press, 1970).

12. Quotes in this paragraph from Xenophon, *On Horsemanship*, trans H. G. Dakyns, (Project Gutenberg, 2008), books 9, 10, 11, 12, at http://www.gutenberg.org/files/1176/1176-h/1176-h.htm.

13. Ibid., p. 75.

14. Piggott, *Wagon, Chariot, and Carriage*, chapter 3, explores this issue.

15. Ibid., pp. 74–80.

16. Marcus Terentius Varro, *De Res Rustica*, p. 391.

Chapter 12: Deposing Sons of Heaven

1. Robert Bagley, "Shang Archaeology," in Michael Loewe and Edward L. Shaughnessy, eds., *The Cambridge History of Ancient China* (Cambridge, UK: Cambridge University Press, 1999), pp. 124–231.

2. This chapter relies heavily on H. G. Creel, "The Role of the Horse in Chinese History," *American Historical Review* 70, no. 3 (1965): 647–72. See also Kelekna, *The Horse in Human History*, chapter 5, where numerous references will be found.

3. Liancheng Lu, "Chariot and Horse Burials in Ancient China," *Antiquity* 67 (1999): 824–38.

4. Ying-shih Yu, "The Hsiung-Nu," in Denis Sinor, ed., *The Cambridge History of Early Inner Asia* (Cambridge, UK: Cambridge University Press, 1990), pp. 118–19.

5. For a lavishly illustrated account of Shihuangdi and his terra-cotta regiment, see Roberto Ciarla, ed., *The Eternal Army: The Terracotta Soldiers of the First Emperor* (Vercelli, Italy: White Star Publishers, 2012).

6. Kelekna, *The Horse in Human History*, pp. 142ff.

7. Creel, "The Role of the Horse," p. 658.

8. René Grousset, *The Empire of the Steppes: A History of Central Asia*, trans. Naomi Walford (New Brunswick, NJ: Rutgers University Press, 1970), provides an account of these expeditions. See also Kelekna, *The Horse in Human History*, pp. 146ff.

9. Creel, "The Role of the Horse," p. 659.

10. Kelekna, *The Horse in Human History*, pp. 148–50.

11. A huge literature surrounds Genghis Khan: George Lane, *Genghis Khan and Mongol Rule* (Westport, CT: Greenwood Press, 2004), is a useful starting point. Quote: J. A. Boyle, trans., *Tarikh-i Jahan Gusha*, in *The History of the World Conqueror* (Manchester, UK: Manchester University Press, 1967), p. 105.

12. For a summary account of Kublai Khan, see Ann Paludan, *Chronicle of the Chinese Emperors* (London: Thames and Hudson, 1998), pp. 148–53.

13. Creel, "The Role of the Horse," pp. 669–71.

Chapter 13: "Animals Designed by God"

1. Richard Bulliet, *The Camel and the Wheel* (New York: Columbia University Press, 1990), offers a comprehensive account of camel domestication and the controversies associated therewith. This passage is based on his chapters 2 and 3.

2. A. S. Saber, "The Camel in Ancient Egypt, *Proceedings of the Third Annual Meeting for Animal Production under Arid Conditions* 1 (1998): 208–15.

3. Bulliet, *The Camel*, chapters 3 and 4, covers camel saddles, but there are references to different types throughout his book.

4. Ibid., chapter 4.

5. Quoted from ibid., p. 95.

6. For a brief summary of Petra, see Andrew Lawler, "Reconstructing Petra," *Smithsonian* 38, no. 3 (2007): 42–49.

7. Discussion in Bulliet, *The Camel*, chapter 5.

8. Andrew Wilson, "Saharan Trade in the Roman Period: Short, Medium- and Long-Distance Trade Networks," *Azania* 47, no. 4 (2012): 409–49.

9. This section is based on E. W. Bovill and Robin Hallet, *The Golden Trade of the Moors* (London: Marcus Weiner, 1995).

10. N. Levetzion and J. F. P. Hopkins, eds., *Corpus of Early African Sources for West African History* (Cambridge, UK: Cambridge University Press, 1981), p. 118.

11. Ghislaine Lydon, *On Trans-Saharan Trails* (Cambridge, UK: Cambridge University Press, 2009), chapter 5.

12. Mardochée Aby Serour (1826–1886) was a rabbi from Akka, Morocco, who did much to open up Saharan trade routes to non-Muslims during the nineteenth century. He was an enthusiastic botanist and plant collector. Quote from Lydon, *On Trans-Saharan Trails*, p. 221.

13. Ibn Battuta (1304–1377) was a Moroccan explorer of Berber descent. Quote from Lydon, *On Trans-Saharan Trails*, p. 226.

14. Michael Benanov, *Men of Salt* (Guilford, CT: Lyons Press, 2008). See also http://news.nationalgeographic.com/news/2003/05/0528_030528_saltcaravan.html.

15. Analysis in Bulliet, *The Camel*, chapter 7.

16. Owen Lattimore, *Mongol Journeys* (London: Jonathon Cape, 1941). This passage draws on this fascinating book. See also Daniel Miller and Dennis Sheehy, "The Relevance of Owen Lattimore's Writings for Nomadic Pastoralism Research and Development in Inner Asia," *Nomadic Peoples* 12, no. 2 (2008): 103–15.

17. Mildred Cable and Francesca French were British Protestant missionaries who traveled widely in Central Asia during the 1920s and early 1930s. Strong, independent-minded, and bold, they left China in 1936 when all foreigners were expelled by a local Kansu warlord. Mildred Cable and Francesca French, *The Gobi Desert: The Adventures of Three Women Travelling across the Gobi Desert in the 1920s*, 2nd ed. (Coventry, UK: Trotamundas Press, 2008), p. 115.

18. Quotes in this paragraph are from Lattimore, *Mongol Journeys*, pp. 77 and 116.

19. Ibid., p. 139.

Chapter 14: Dominion over Beasts?

1. This section draws on Peter Edwards, *Horse and Man in Early Modern England* (London: Continuum Books, 2007).

2. Quoted in ibid., p. 5.

3. Ibid., p. 189.

4. Ibid., p. 197.

5. Ibid., p. 28.

6. Lloyd Charles Sanders, *Old Kew, Chiswick, and Kensington* (London: Methuen, 1910), p. 104.

7. John Evelyn, William Bray, and John Forster, eds., *The Diary and Correspondence of John Evelyn, F.R.S.*, vol. 2 (London: Bell and Daidy, 1910), p. 211. Diary entry for December 7, 1684.

8. John Flavel, *Husbandry Spiritualized*, 6th ed. (London: T. Parkhurst), p. 206.

9. Jeremiah Burroughes (1600–1646) was a well-known Puritan preacher who served as a pastor in England, the Netherlands, and finally London, where he became known as "the morning star of Stepney" for his eloquent sermons. Quote from *An Exposition of the Prophesie of Hosea* (London: R. Dawlman, 1643), p. 576.

10. John Florio (trans.), *Shakespeare's Montaigne: The Florio Translation of the Essays. A Selection* (New York: New York Review of Books Classics, 2014, [1580]). Quote from the essay "An Apologie de Raymond Sebond," Book 12, section 2.

11. For a discussion of Descartes and Cartesianism, see Linda Kalof, *Looking at Animals* (New York: Reaktion Books, 2007), chapter 5.

12. Oliver Goldsmith (1730–1774) is famous for his novel *The Vicar of Wakefield* (1766) and for the play *She Stoops to Conquer* (1773). Quote from Keith Thomas, *Man and the Natural World* (Oxford: Oxford University Press, 1966), p. 35.

13. This passage draws on Thomas, *Man and the Natural World*, pp. 92ff.

14. Kalof, *Looking at Animals*, pp. 59–64. Esther Cohen, "Animals in Medieval Perceptions: The Image of the Ubiquitous Other," in Manning and Serpell, eds., *Animals and Human Society*, pp. 59–80; Andreas-Holger Maehle, "Cruelty and Kindness to the 'Brute Creation': Stability and Change in the Ethics of the Man-Animal Relationship, 1600–1850," in Manning and Serpell, eds., *Animals and Human Society*, pp. 81–105.

15. T. Porck and H. J. Porck, "Eight Guidelines on Book Preservation from 1527: How One Should Preserve All Books to Last Eternally," *Journal of Paper Conservation*, 13(2) (2012): p.20.

16. The illustration and quote appear in a copy of Augustine of Hippo's *De Civitate Dei contra Paganos*, completed by him in 426 CE and made by Hildebert and another artist Everwin. The manuscript is in Prague's Capitular Library (codex A21/1, folio 153r).

17. Pangur Bán, which means "white Pangur," is the cat's name. The Old Irish poem was written by an anonymous monk, probably at the Benedictine abbey on Reichenau Island, in Lake Constance. It's possible that the author was Sedulious Scottus, as the poem is stylistically somewhat similar to his work. See Whitley Stokes and John Strachan, eds., *Thesaurus Palaeohibernicus: A Collection of Old Irish Glosses, Prose, and Verse* (Cambridge, UK: Cambridge University Press, 1904), pp. 293–94.

18. Sir Kenelm Digby (1603–1665), courtier, natural philosopher, and diplomat, was, among his other achievements, the father of the modern wine bottle. Quote from his *A Late Discourse ... Touching the Cure of Wounds by the Powder of Sympathy* (London: R. Lowdes, 1658), p. 117. The "Powder of Sympathy" was a form of sympathetic magic.

19. Jane Ingelow (1820–1897) was a prolific novelist and poet. She was widely popular in Victorian times, her works being popular domestic entertainment. She is largely forgotten today. Quote from her *High Tide on the Coast of Lincolnshire, 1571* (London: Roberts Brothers, 1883), lines 40–42.

Chapter 15: "The Hell for Dumb Animals"

1. P. K. O'Brien, "Agriculture and the Industrial Revolution," *Economic History Review*, 2nd ser., 1 (1977): 169.

2. Henry Peacham, *The Worth of a Peny: Or a Caution to Keep Money* (London: S. Giffin, 1664), p. 31. Peacham (1578–c.1644) was a writer and poet, and is best known today for a work entitled *The Compleat Gentleman* (1622).

3. Pehr Kalm (1716–1779) was an explorer, botanist, agricultural economist, and also a student of Carl Linnaeus. He wrote the first scientific description of Niagara Falls. Quote from Keith Thomas, *Man and the Natural World*, p. 26.

4. Thomas, *Man and the Natural World*, pp. 94ff, covers this material.

5. Harriet Ritvo, *Animal Estate: The English and Other Creatures in the Victorian Age* (Cambridge, MA: Harvard University Press, 1987), chapter 1, covers beef breeding admirably. For Robert Bakewell, see pp. 66ff.

6. William Fitzstephen (died c. 1190) was a cleric and administrator who worked for Archbishop Thomas Becket and witnessed his murder in Canterbury Cathedral in 1170. Fitzstephen's account of London forms part of Becket's biography. Quoted from Matthew Senior, *Enlightenment*, p. 105.

7. Thomas Maslen, *Suggestions for the Improvement of Our Towns and Houses* (London: Smith, Elder, 1843), p. 16.

8. Thomas Pennant, *British Zoology: A New Edition*, vol. 1 (London: Wilkie and Robinson, 1812), p. 11.

9. Ritvo, *Animal Estate*, pp. 107–13.

10. Janet Clutton-Brock, *Horse Power* (Cambridge, MA: Harvard University Press, 1992), pp. 170–77, summarizes the history of horse racing and the importation of Arabians.

11. Madeleine Pinault Sorensen, "Portraits of Animals, 1600–1800," in Matthew Senior, ed., *A Cultural History of Animals in the Age of Enlightenment* (New York: Berg, 2007), pp. 157–98.

12. Adam Alasdair, *The Cat: A Short History* (Seattle, WA: Amazon Digital Services, 2012), summarizes feline fortunes through history.

13. Kolof, *Looking at Animals*, p. 125.

14. Ritvo, *Animal Estate*, p. 126.

15. Christopher Hibbert, ed., *Queen Victoria in Her Letters and Journals* (London: John Murray, 1984), p. 205.

16. Jason Hribal, "Animals Are Part of the Working Class," *Labor History* 44, no. 3 (2003): 112–37.

Chapter 16: Victims of Military Insanity

1. This passage is based on Louis A. Di Marco, *War Horse: A History of the Military Horse and Rider* (Yardley, PA: Westholme Publishing, 2008).

2. A summary of the Battle of Eylau appears at http://en.wikipedia.org/wiki/Battle_of_Eylau.

3. Cavalié Mercer (1783–1868), who later became a general, was a British artillery officer at the Battle of Waterloo. His six-gun artillery troop fought off French heavy cavalry, refusing to withdraw into an infantry square. Cavalié Mercer, *Journal of the Waterloo Campaign Kept throughout the Campaign of 1815* (London: William Blackwood, 1870). Quotes from volume 1, pp. 319–21. The book was edited for publication by his son Cavalié A. Mercer.

4. Capt. Louis Edward Nolan (1818–1854) was an accomplished horse master and expert on cavalry tactics, best known for his controversial role in the Charge of the Light Brigade, at which he was killed. See the biography David

Buttery, *Messenger of Death: Captain Nolan and the Charge of the Light Brigade* (Barnsley, UK: Pen and Sword, 2008). Nolan's *Cavalry: Its History and Tactics*, first published in 1853, is a classic analysis of the subject. Originally published by Thomas Bosworth in London, the book was reprinted with an introduction by Jon Coulston (Yardley, PA: Westholme Publishing, 2007). Quote from p. 37. The quote from Xenophon, later in the paragraph, appears on p. 105.

5. Nolan, *Cavalry*, p. 125.

6. Ibid., p. 97.

7. Cecil Woodham-Smith's *The Reason Why* (London: Penguin Reprint, 1991) is a classic, detailed, and beautifully written account of the Charge and its complex prelude. Quote from p. 138.

8. This passage and the sidebar "Cavalry Folly: Into the Valley of Death" are based on Woodham-Smith, *The Reason Why*. To appreciate the full nuances of the Crimean disaster, I recommend reading the entire volume.

9. Quoted by Woodham-Smith, *The Reason Why*, p. 242.

10. Alfred, Lord Tennyson's poem "The Charge of the Light Brigade" was written in 1854 to memorialize the event.

11. Buttery, *Messenger of Death*, p. 114.

12. Alfred, Lord Tennyson, "The Charge of the Light Brigade" (Seattle: Amazon Digital Services, 2012), p. 3.

13. This passage is based on John Ellis, *Cavalry: The History of Mounted Warfare* (New York: Putnam, 1978), chapter 7; and Di Marco, *War Horse*, chapter 8.

14. Quotes by John Ellis, *Cavalry*, p. 148.

15. Ibid., p. 176.

16. Quotes in Di Marco, *War Horse*, pp. 319–21.

17. G. J. Meyer, *A World Undone: The Story of the Great War 1914 to 1918* (New York: Bantam Dell, 2006), p. 321.

18. Mercer, *Journal*, vol. 1, p. 335.

Chapter 17: Cruelty to the Indispensable

1. Charles Dickens, *Oliver Twist* (London: Penguin, 2002, [1838]), p. 171.

2. James Serpell and Elizabeth Paul, "Pets and the Development of Positive Attitudes to Animals," in Manning and Serpell, eds., *Animals and Human Society*, p. 133. The Romans also kept pets: Michael MacKinnon, "'Sick as a Dog': Zooarchaeological Evidence for Pet Dog Health and Welfare in the Roman World," *World Archaeology* 42, no. 2 (2010): 290–309.

3. Serpell and Paul, "Pets," p. 137. *Goody Two Shoes* is still in print, or available as an e-book through Amazon.com.

4. Serpell and Paul, "Pets," p. 135.

5. These paragraphs rely heavily on Ritvo, *The Animal Estate*, pp. 144ff. Col. Richard Martin (1754–1834) was Member of Parliament for Galway and an advocate of Catholic Emancipation and animal welfare. He was famous in Parliament for his humorous speeches. His colorful campaigning for animals made him the butt of cartoonists' work. King George IV nicknamed him "Humanity Dick."

6. Ritvo, *Animal Estate*, pp. 130ff, covers the early history of the SPCA.

7. Ibid., pp. 138–39.

8. Ibid., p. 108.

9. This passage draws on Clay McShane and Joel A. Tarr, "The Horse as Technology: The City Animal as Cyborg," in Sandra Olsen et al., eds. *Horses and Humans*, pp. 365–75. See also Clay McShane and Joel A. Tarr, *The Horse in the City: Living Machines in the Nineteenth Century* (Baltimore, MA: Johns Hopkins University Press, 2011), pp. 3–4.

10. A. Briggs, *The Power of Steam: An Illustrated History of the World's Steam Age* (Chicago: University of Chicago Press, 1982).

11. The literature on pit ponies is surprisingly thin. John Bright's *Pit Ponies* (London: Batsford, 1986) is a very general account. For an overall view, I relied on http://en.wikipedia.org/wiki/Pit_pony.

12. U.S. Bureau of the Census figures for 1901 and 1913 quoted by McShane and Tarr, "The Horse," p. 365.

13. Ibid.

14. David Voice, *The Age of the Horse Tram: A History of Horse-Drawn Passenger Tramways in the British Isles* (Strathpeffer, Scotland: AHG Books, 2009). The quote is from the *Morning Post*, July 7, 1829.

15. Robert Thurston, "The Animal as a Machine and Prime Mover," *Science* 1, no. 14 (1895): 365–71.

16. A. H. Sanders, *A History of the Percheron Horse* (Chicago: Breeder's Gazette Print, 1917).

17. R. L. Freeman, *The Arabbers of Baltimore* (Tidewater, MD: Tidewater Publications, 1987), p. 19.

18. Ritvo, *Animal Estate*, chapter 4, has an admirable summary.

19. Harriet Ritvo, "Animals in Nineteenth-Century Britain: Complicated Attitudes and Competing Categories," in Manning and Serpell, eds., *Animals and Human Society*, p. 110.

20. Ritvo, *Animal Estate*, p. 139. Dog cart hauling was finally outlawed in Britain in 1854.

Chapter 18: To Kill, to Display, and to Love

1. Ritvo, *Animal Estate*, chapter 5, provides an admirable survey and is my primary source for this section.

2. Ritvo, *Animal Estate*, p. 207.

3. Ibid., p. 215.

4. *Punch* 60 (1871): 240.

5. Ritvo, *Animal Estate*, chapter 6, provides a comprehensive summary of the developments described in this section.

6. Quote from Ritvo, *Animal Estate*, p. 250. See also Roualeyn Gordon Cumming, *Five Years of a Hunter's Life in the Far Interior of South Africa* (London: John Murray, 1850).

7. Ritvo, *Animal Estate*, p. 253. Selous wrote several books, among them *Travel and Adventure in South-East Africa* (London: R. Ward, 1903).

8. Quoted by Ritvo, *Animal Estate*, p. 253.

9. Lord Byron, "Epitaph to a Dog" (1808), http://www.poetryloverspage.com/poets/byron/epitaph_to_dog.html

10. Surveyed in Ritvo, *Animal Estate*, chapter 2.

11. Ibid., p. 98.

12. Ibid.

13. Described by ibid., pp. 115–21.

14. Andrew Lawler, *Why Did the Chicken Cross the World? The Epic Saga of the Bird that Powers Civilization* (New York: Atria Books, 2014).

15. Matthew Arnold, *Culture and Anarchy: An Essay in Political and Social Criticism* (New York: Macmillan, 1883 [UK edition, 1869]), pp. 77–78. Oscar Wilde's reference to "the unspeakable" is a remark made by Lord Illingworth in act 1 of Wilde's play *A Woman of No Importance*, performed in London in 1893 (Seattle: Amazon Digital Services, 2011).

16. Serpell and Paul, "Pets," p. 127.

17. This section is based on Peter Singer's classic book-length essay *Animal Liberation*, rev. ed. (New York: Harper Perennial, 2009). Quote from p. 213. This book is essential reading for anyone interested in the issues surrounding animal liberation, as is another classic: Steven M. Wise, *Drawing the Line: Science and the Case of Animal Rights* (Cambridge, MA: Perseus Books, 2002).

18. Singer, *Animal Liberation*, p. 226.

Index

Ur (Sumerian city), 80
Use of Pack Animals (military manual),
    128–30

Van Dyck, Anthony, 204
Varro, Marcus Terentius, 95, 96, 98,
    161–62
veal crates, 267
Vedbaek hunting site, 38
Victoria, Queen, 224, 230, 265
Victorian era, xvii, 250–52, 253,
    258–61, 264–65
vivisection, 207, 223, 241, 250
von Bredow, Friedrich Wilhelm, 233

waterfowl, hunting of, 32, 36, 37–38
Watt, James, 239, 242–43
Wen (Zhou Dynasty ruler), 164, 167
West Africa, xvi, 187, 189
wheat, 96
wheel technology, 145–47, 164
wild ass. *See* African wild ass (*Equus
    africanus*)
wild boar (*Sus scrofa*), 43, 45, 46, 47, 78
wild camels, 182
wildcat (*Felis sylvestris lybica*), 67
Wilde, Oscar, 264, 291n15
wild horse (*Equus ferus*), 133–35, 139,
    141
wild oxen. *See* aurochs (*Bos
    primigenius*)
William Augustus, Prince, 221
Winckler, Hugo, 150
Wisdom of Sirach, 117
wolf-dogs (dog-wolves), 27–28, 32, 34
Wolsey, Cardinal, 126
wolves, xiii, 21–40
    Big Bad Wolf stereotype, 22–23,
        275n4(Ch2)

cooperative hunting by, 24–25
dogs evolved from, 21–22, 26–28,
    30–31
domestication into dogs, 28–30, 31
dominance hierarchy, 23
as neighbors of humans, 25–26
religious doctrine and, 23
as scavengers, 14, 21, 24, 26
slaughter of, 23
Woodham-Smith, Cecil, 289n7
wool, English, 201, 216
working animals, xiii–xiv, xvi–xvii,
    205–6, 218–20, 223–24, 241–42.
    See also draft animals; pack
    animals
World War I, 235–37
Wroth, Sir Thomas, 242
Wudi, Emperor, 169–70
Wu Ding, 163
Wu-ling of Zhao, 166

Xenophon, 129, 157–59, 229
Xerxes, King, 157
Xiongnu nomads, 168–69, 170, 171

Yam kingdom, 111, 112
Y chromosome studies, 31
Yenisei River, 146
Younger Dryas, 44–45. *See also* drought
Yuezhi people, 168, 170

Zachariah (prophet), 117
Zeus, 91
Zhang Qian, 170
Zhao Zu, 168
Zhou Dynasty, 164–65
Zimri-Lim, King, 152–53
Zoological Society of London,
    254–55

A Note on the Author

Brian Fagan is emeritus professor of anthropology at the University of California–Santa Barbara. Born in England, he did fieldwork in Africa and has written about North American and world archaeology and many other topics. His books on the interaction of climate and human society have established him as the leading authority on the subject; he lectures frequently around the world. He is the editor of *The Oxford Companion to Archaeology* and the author of *The Attacking Ocean*, *Beyond the Blue Horizon*, *Elixir*, *Cro-Magnon*, *The Great Warming*, *Fish on Friday*, *The Little Ice Age*, and *The Long Summer*, among many other titles.